Women in Ancient Greece

Women in Ancient Greece

A Sourcebook

Bonnie MacLachlan

continuum

Continuum International Publishing Group

The Tower Building
11 York Road
London SE1 7NX

80 Maiden Lane
Suite 704
New York, NY 10038

www.continuumbooks.com

First published 2012

British Library Cataloguing-in-Publication Data
A catalogue record for this book is available from the British Library.

ISBN: HB: 978-1-4411-3286-4
PB: 978-1-4411-7963-0

Library of Congress Cataloging-in-Publication Data
A catalog record for this book is available from the Library of Congress.

Typeset by Fakenham Prepress Solutions, Fakenham, Norfolk NR21 8NN

Contents

Introduction

In the study of the ancient world, we have all benefited in recent years from the focus on women and gender interaction in the Mediterranean. This shift in attention was launched by the publication of Sarah Pomeroy's *Goddesses, Whores, Wives and Slaves: Women in Classical Antiquity* in 1975. Suddenly we were invited to interrogate the texts, inscriptions and material culture surviving from the Classical world in new ways. And asking fresh questions invigorated our readings of the evidence. It breathed on the embers of a fire that had been preserved for millennia but was losing vigour under the weight of traditional assumptions about the lives of the people behind the words and artifacts.

Greece and Rome were, to a large degree, patriarchal cultures, and our investigation into the lives of their women has not been without its challenges as we seek to listen for the female voice, to get access to what mattered to girls and women. Those responsible for most of those texts and artifacts were men, and the attitudes toward women that they convey, whether idealizing or dismissive, originate with individuals who for the most part controlled the narrative.

This has not been a deterrent to fruitful searches, however, inquiries motivated by a determination to find the authentic voice of women in those male-authored (and in the few remaining female-authored) texts, and in those inscriptions, sculptures and vase paintings that have survived from the Classical world. Many of the important publications that resulted from these investigations into the lives of Greek women can be found in the sources listed in this text.

This book is intended to supply a survey of ancient textual sources (which I have translated into English) – literary, historical, philosophical and inscriptional – to be used in the study of women in ancient Greece. It is by no means a complete compilation, but offers several lenses through which to look at the lived experiences of our female forebears in Greece. The earliest surviving texts that can help in the quest date from the Archaic period (*c.* 800–480 BCE), and material relating to this era is contained in the first four chapters. After 480 BCE and the ending of the Persian Wars, political changes that included the rise of the Athenian city-state introduced a new era, the Classical period. Considerable textual documentation survives from this chapter of Greek history – literary, historical and philosophical, together with forensic speeches and inscriptions that support the inquiry into the lives of women. A selection from this considerable body of material is found in Chapters 5 to 14. With the defeat of Athens by Sparta at the end of the 5th century BCE another political transition occurred that altered the social configuration of Greek life. The post-Classical era, the Hellenistic period, is conventionally dated from the death of Alexander the Great in 323 BCE until *c.* 100 BCE. The political and social shift that occurred around the Mediterranean world with the empire established by Alexander had major consequences for the lives of women, and the last chapter contains a wide variety of sources that document a "modernization" of their lived realities.

Throughout the book, I have selected texts that apply to life not only on the Greek mainland but to the Greek diaspora, the communities along the eastern shores of the Mediterranean, in Egypt and in the Greek west (southern Italy and Sicily). I have also looked for material that documents the lives of non-elite women – such as the foreigners in Athens, lower class and slave women, prostitutes.

Much of this evidence is not documentary. There were no comprehensive archives in ancient Greece, no formal registries of births, marriages or divorces, for example. There were no census data to provide evidence for the lifespan or occupation (where this was the case) of women. Literary evidence, whether drawn from poetry or drama, is, of course, largely fictional – then as now. But those fictions were the product of a conceptual framework that we can test for inter-textual consistency, with the aim of getting a glimpse of what mattered most to the ancient Greeks, what stories and images reflected and informed the priorities in their lives. For this reason, I have included a considerable number of excerpts from literary works, from the Homeric epics to Hellenistic epigrams. My hope is that readers who have not yet been drawn to read the whole of the longer works will be tempted to do so.

Some of the important literary texts drew on the rich array of mythical material accessible to the Greeks. These were tales, as I tell my students, that are self-evidently not true, but while untrue in an empirical sense they were carriers of the deepest truths about the complex value systems that governed Greek life, and merit sensitive attention on our part. We assume that the courtroom speeches quoted in this book are closer to documentary evidence about everyday life, but these were partisan by nature, and were delivered with rhetoric that was designed not to tell the whole story. We must be vigilant, therefore, as we read, and aim to become as informed as possible by having recourse to the widest possible array of evidence as we assess the texts in front of us. Even inscriptions tell only part of the story: those on tombs may have been carved to suit the personal agenda of the survivor; laws written on stone in public places were prescriptive, not descriptive. How compliant were the readers? Who had the skills to read them?

In our reconstruction of the lives of girls and women in ancient Greece, we cannot expect to produce a consistent picture. Details will contradict one another, arising from different time periods or locations, or from authors with different standpoints. But often the contradictions are fruitful, leading us to ask further questions that give us a fuller understanding of the situation. Our goal should be to produce a coherent, if not consistent, picture.

For the texts quoted, I have tried to present very brief introductions that set them in context. Much more investigation will bear fruit, and I have supplied brief suggestions for further reading at the end of each chapter, which should both raise and answer some interpretive questions about this material, or signpost the reader to other sources that may do so. These will be up to date, of course, only as of the time of submission of this manuscript to the publisher. The website Diotima (http://www.stoa.org/diotima) is devoted to the study of women and gender in the ancient world, and is an important electronic resource that will continue to supply titles of new publications. For journal articles in classical studies generally the databases found on JSTOR and Project MUSE are extremely helpful. An electronic record, with a brief summary in French, of books as well as book chapters and articles in classics is available online through *L'Année Philologique*.

I have arranged the texts under 15 headings. For the most part, this follows the chronological order just described, but of necessity some of the material is synchronic. Mythical material describing the Amazons, for example, includes narratives that were compiled in the Bronze Age (in the second half of the third millennium BCE) but surface in descriptions of the 5th century BCE historian Herodotus. The authors of some texts claim to have preserved material from several centuries earlier. Athenaeus, for example, a Greek rhetorician and grammarian from the 3rd century CE with a taste for the salacious, quotes Hermippus, a biographer and near contemporary of Aristotle, who provided Athenaeus with the information that the great philosopher kept up a relationship with a courtesan until his death and produced a son with her.

The series of texts that follows begins with the cosmic tales of Hesiod (7th century BCE), which recount the birth of the gods and explain the creation of the first woman and the female sex. Pandora was as dangerous as she was beautiful, the product of male anxiety on the part of Zeus, who wanted to punish a would-be younger successor. Two of the Olympian goddesses are the subject of Chapter 2, which quotes from hymns originating early in the Archaic period. These hymns provided a narrative of foundational moments in the divine biographies of Aphrodite and Demeter, goddesses important to women. Mortal as well as divine women inform much of the action and most of the emotional energy that drives the dramatic plots of the Homeric epics, and are the focus of the material quoted in Chapter 3.

Excerpts from other poetry of the Archaic period, songs of a more personal nature than epic, are found in Chapter 4. They range from the homoerotic lyrics of Sappho to the misogynistic lampoons of Hipponax and Semonides. In Chapter 5, we turn to the Classical period. This extensive chapter covers texts that describe events in the female lifecycle, primarily referring to women in Athens, for which we have the most evidence. This is followed by a chapter with quotations largely drawn from litigation speeches that provide information about women and property. How much property could women own? Did they have the right to dispose of it? With property largely under the control of men, what kind of pressure was there on a daughter who was an only child, and stood to inherit her father's property? Chapters 7 and 8 include quotations from documents describing the lives of foreign women and prostitutes.

Since religious rituals provided definition and meaning for the principal stages in a Greek woman's life, and offered almost the only occasions where women could perform in public (Chapter 9, on women's religious life), contains a broad array of texts and inscriptions. This is followed by a chapter documenting the variety of ways in which women were depicted on the Athenian dramatic stage, in both tragedy and comedy. How do we explain viragos like Clytemnestra or Medea in a culture dominated by men? Was the agency of Lysistrata a male fantasy or a plausible reality in the Greek male imaginary?

In Chapter 11, the texts address the lives of Dorian women in Sparta or Crete, who could exercise in the nude with men or inherit property in their own right, contrasting strongly with the experience of Athenian women. This is followed in the next chapter by discussions of Plato and Aristotle about the role of women in the ideal state, and their attitudes about Dorian social arrangements inform their reflections. Warrior women, mythical and real, are the subject of texts found in Chapter 13.

What about the physical makeup of the female body and how the Greeks understood it? The records left by Hippocratic medical practitioners, who were mystified by the reproductive apparatus inside women (because dissection was not permitted) provide us with a fascinating glimpse at the ways in which ideology can inform analysis.

The last chapter documents the major transition in the expectations and experiences of Greek women found in the Hellenistic period. Suddenly, it appears, women could sign marriage contracts, exert agency in erotic relationships, belong to philosophical movements, compose poetry that was included with male-authored verses, walk unaccompanied in public. One text (fictional) describes two women comparing notes on dildoes.

Working with these ancient texts takes us on a fascinating journey, and a thoughtful interrogation of them obliges us to think about the lived reality of contemporary women interacting with each other and men. This selection of writings is just that, a selection. It is well supplemented by the ample collection assembled in 1982 (updated in 1992) by Mary Lefkowitz and Maureen Fant, *Women's Life in Greece and Rome. A Source Book in Translation*, published by Johns Hopkins University Press/Duckworth. (I am grateful to them for identifying many of the texts included here.) For interpretation of the available evidence, textual and material, I recommend two very useful handbooks: Sue Blundell's *Women in Ancient Greece* (Harvard University Press 1995) and *Women in the Classical World. Image and Text*, a collective production by Elaine Fantham, Helene Foley, Natalie Kampen, Sarah Pomeroy and H.A. Shapiro (Oxford University Press 1994). A variety of other investigations of particular subjects relevant to the study of women in ancient Greece can be found in the bibliography.

The translations are my own, with Latinized forms for words except where convention suggests otherwise. I am extremely grateful to Ashley Skinner for verifying translations and references, to Judith Fletcher whom I consulted on a number of points and to Carol Agocs for help with proof-reading. I extend my deepest gratitude also to Michael Greenwood of Continuum Press and Kim Storry of Fakenham Prepress Solutions, for their professionalism in seeing the project launched and brought to conclusion.

Bonnie MacLachlan
University of Western Ontario
London, Ontario, Canada

Abbreviations for works cited

ABSA *Annual of the British School at Athens* (2001). "'Working Women': Female Professionals on Classical Attic Gravestones," vol. 96, 218–319

AP *The Greek Anthology*. W.R. Paton (ed. and transl.) (1916). Cambridge, MA

BGU Ägyptische Urkunden aus den Königlichen Museen zu Berlin 1895. Bd I Griechische Urkunden. Berlin

CEG *Carmina Epigraphica Graeca. Saeculorum VIII-V A.Chr.N.* P.A. Hansen ed. (1983). Berlin

DK H. Diels & W. Kranz (eds) 1951. *Die Fragmente der VorSokratiker*. Berlin

DT *Defixionum Tabellae. Quotquot innotuerunt tam in Graecis orientis quam in totius occidentis partibus praeter Atticas in corpore inscriptionum Atticarum* A. Audollent ed. (1904). Paris

DTA *Defixionum Tabellae Atticae*. R. Wünsch ed. (1897). Berlin

FGE *Further Greek Epigrams: Epigrams Before A.D. 50 from the Greek Anthology and Other Sources, Not Included in "Hellenistic Epigrams" or "The Garland of Philip."* D.L. Page ed. (1981). [Revised and prepared for publication by R.D. Dawe and J. Diggle.] Cambridge/New York

Hercher R. Hercher ed. (1965). *Epistolographoi Hellenikoi*. Amsterdam

HSCP *Harvard Studies in Classical Philology*

IC *Inscriptiones Creticae* IV. M. Guarducci ed. (1950). Rome

IG II² *Inscriptiones Atticae Euclidis Anno Posteriores*. J. Kirchner ed. (1974). [Vol. 2 repr. from original 1931, vol. 3 from original 1935, vol. 4 from original 1940.] Chicago

IMagn *Die Inschriften von Magnesia am Maeander*. O. Kerlin ed. (1900). Berlin

IvO *Inschriften von Olympia*. W. Dittenberger, K. Purgold, E. Curtius, & F. Adler (eds) (1896). Berlin

Kaibel G. Kaibel (1878). *Epigrammata Graeca ex lapidibus conlecta*. Berlin

Kenyon F.G. Kenyon ed. (1954). *Hyperidis Orationes et Fragmenta*. Oxford

Kern   O. Kern ed. (1922). *Orphicorum Fragmenta*. Berlin
Littré   E. Littré ed. (1961). *Hippocrates. Oevres Complètes*, vols 1–10.
                Amsterdam
LSAM   *Lois sacrées de l'Asie Mineur*. F. Sokolowski ed. (1955). Paris
LSCG   *Lois sacrées des cités grecques*. F. Sokolowski ed. (1969). Paris
LSCG Suppl.   *Lois sacrées des cités grecques suppl.* F. Sokolowski ed. (1962).
                Paris
PCG   *Poetae Comici Graeci*. R. Kassel & C. Austin (eds) (1983–2001).
                Berlin
P. Eleph.   *Elephantine-Papyri*. O. Rubensohn ed. (1907). Berlin
P. Tebt.   *Tebtunis Papyri*, vol. 1. B.P. Grenfell, A.S. Hunt, & J.G. Smyly
                (eds) (1902). London
Peek   W. Peek ed. (1955). *Griechische Vers-Inschriften*. Berlin
Pleket   H.W. Pleket ed. (1969). *Epigraphica*, vol. 2. Leiden
PMG   *Poetae Melici Graeci*. D. Page ed. (1962). Oxford
Rabe   H. Rabe ed. (1971). *Scholia in Lucianum*. Stuttgart
RO   P.J. Rhodes & R. Osborne (eds) (2003). *Greek Historical
                Inscriptions 404–323 BC*. Oxford
SB   *Sitzungsberichte der Koeniglich Preussischen Akademie der
                Wissenschaften zu Berlin*. 1905. Berlin
SEG 41   *Supplementum Epigraphicum Graecum*. 1994. Amsterdam
SEG 52   *Supplementum Epigraphicum Graecum*. 2002. Leiden/Boston
Select Papyri *Select Papyri with an English Translation*. (A.S. Hunt, C.C. Edgar
                & D.L. Page (eds) (1950–52). London
Sn.-M   H. Maehler ed. (1971–75). *Carmina cum Fragmentis. Pindarus
                (post B. Snell)*. Leipzig
Suda   *Suidae Lexicon*. T. Gaisford ed. (1834). Oxford
Supp. Hell.   *Supplementum Hellenisticum*. H. Lloyd-Jones & P. Parsons (eds)
                (1983). Berlin/New York
TGF   *Tragicorum Graecorum Fragmenta*, vol. 5.1. R. Kanicht ed. (2004).
                Göttingen
V   E. Voigt ed. (1971). *Sappho et Alcaeus*. Amsterdam
Von Staden   H. Von Staden (1989). *Herophilus. The Art of Medicine in Early
                Alexandria*. Cambridge
W   M.L. West ed. (1971). *Iambi et Elegi Graeci*. Oxford
Wehrli   F. Wehrli ed. (1944). *Die Schule des Aristoteles*, vol. 1. Basel
ZPE   *Zeitschrift für Papyrologie und Epigraphik*. Bonn

PART 1

THE ARCHAIC PERIOD

Where it all began: women in Hesiod

We possess two epic poems by Hesiod of Boeotia, dating from *c.* 700 BCE. The *Theogony* is a poetic account of the birth of the cosmos and the gods. Out of undifferentiated matter came the Earth ("Gaia"), who gave birth on her own to the Skygod ("Ouranus"). Mating with him, Gaia eventually produced a generation of formidable children, including the Titans. But Ouranus lay outstretched over Gaia, preventing the birth of the Titans until Gaia provided her son Cronus with a sickle, with which he castrated his father. The genitals of Cronus fell into the sea where the foamy matter took the form of the beautiful goddess Aphrodite, who came out of the water onto the shore of the island of Cyprus.

The beautiful, awe-inspiring goddess stepped out,
and around her tender feet the grass grew. Gods and men call her by name
Aphrodite, because she was nursed on sea-foam (*aphros*). (194–198)

Eros was her companion, and handsome Desire followed her,
and as soon as she was born she went to join the company of the gods.
She holds this prerogative from the beginning,
and has it as her allotment among mortals and the immortal gods:
the intimate conversations of young girls, smiles and wiles
and sweet delight, love-making and tenderness. (201–206)
(Hesiod, *Theogony*)

Freed from the womb of Gaia, Cronus and his wife Rhea became the primary divine couple among the Titans. Cronus, fearful of a son who would replace him, proceeded to swallow his children as they were about to be born. Rhea, on the advice of Gaia and Ouranus, substituted a stone for the last conceived child, Zeus. Cronus swallowed the stone, and Zeus became the firstborn of the next generation of gods and was transported to safety.

Zeus was the chief god of the Olympians, but like his father he feared for the security of his position. Indeed, a challenge to this supremacy was mounted by a child of the Titans, Prometheus, who stole fire from Zeus in order to benefit the race of men. As punishment for this theft, Zeus gave men the "gift" of a race of women. He asked Hephaistus, the god of crafts, to produce the first woman, Pandora, whose body was dazzlingly beautiful to look at. Other gods would give her the special features that would ensure that she and her female successors would be irresistible but also a source of never ending toil and grief for men. Hesiod records the story in both his *Theogony* and *Works and Days*. The following excerpt is taken from the latter, an epic poem in the form of advice/warning to his farmer-brother. The excerpt begins with Zeus addressing Prometheus.

"For (men to come) I will give an evil thing in return for the (stolen) fire,
an evil in which they will all take delight in their hearts, warmly embracing their own downfall."
So he spoke, and the father of gods and men laughed.
He ordered widely-renowned Hephaistus
to mix water with earth right away, to put inside (the creature) the voice
and strength of a mortal, to liken her to the immortal goddesses in her face,
with her body desirable and beautiful, like that of a maiden. He ordered Athena
to teach her tasks, to weave highly intricate fabric.
He ordered golden Aphrodite to pour beauty around her head,
together with painful desire and limb-gnawing sorrows.
And he bade Hermes, messenger-god, slayer of Argos,
to place in her the mind of a bitch and a thievish personality.
So he spoke, and they obeyed Lord Zeus, Son of Cronus.
Straightway the famous Lame One fashioned from earth
the likeness of an innocent maiden, following the counsel of the son of Cronus.
The grey-eyed goddess Athena belted and adorned her;
the divine Graces and the powerful regent Persuasion
placed golden necklaces around her skin;
the fair-tressed Hours garlanded her with spring flowers.
Pallas Athena fitted every sort of adornment on her skin.
In her breast the messenger-god, slayer of Argos,
produced lies and wheedling words and a thievish personality
at the behest of loud-thundering Zeus.
The herald of the gods produced a voice in (her), and he named this woman
Pandora ("All-gifts"), because all those having their home on Olympus
gave her gifts, a disaster for men who earn their livelihood. (56–82)

For beforetime, the race of men lived on the earth
without trials and without hard work
and harsh diseases that give death to men.
But the woman drew a great lid off a jar with her hands

and scattered (the contents). For mortals she was contriving baneful troubles.
Hope alone remained inside the unbroken container,
under the lips of the jar, nor did it fly out the opening.
For before this could happen (Pandora) put in place the lid of the jar,
at the behest of aegis-bearing, cloud-scattering Zeus. (90–99)
(Hesiod, *Works and Days*)

That the "race of women" descended from Pandora should precipitate a life of toil for men is explained by Hesiod in his *Theogony* by analogy with drones in a beehive: the worker bees toil to gather food while the drones remain idle, waiting to fill their bellies with the hard earned food gathered by others. (Later writers like Semonides and Xenophon will also use the analogy of the hive to describe the consequences for men of living with women [see below, pp. 47 and 61].)

From her is descended the race of females,
a great calamity for mortals, females living together with men
and suited not for wretched poverty but for plenty.
Just as when in the covered hives the bees
feed the drones, (creatures) contrivers of works that bring ill –
whereas the bees hasten all day long until sunset,
day after day, and produce the clear beeswax,
while the drones remaining in the sheltered hives
scrape together for themselves the hard-earned work of others into their bellies –
just so did high-thundering Zeus produce women
as a bane for mortal men, accomplices of (men's) harsh labours.
(Hesiod, *Theogony* 590–602)

This provides Hesiod with a template for the relationship between mortal women and men. When the poet in *Works and Days* offers advice to his brother about marriage he suggests that the "devouring" capacity of a wife necessitates careful planning:

Do you be timely in bringing a wife to your house,
when you are not far short of thirty years of age
nor very much older. This is an appropriate time for marriage.
Let your wife have reached puberty four years prior, and let her marry in the fifth.
Marry a virginal girl, so that you can instruct her in respectable habits.
The best girl to marry is one who lives near you, so that you can look her over carefully
and not marry one who would provoke glee in your neighbours.

A man acquires nothing better than a good wife,
nor indeed nothing more horrific than a bad one –
a meal-snatcher who scorches her husband without fire,
however stalwart he might be, and hands him over to premature old age.
(Hesiod, *Works and Days* 695–705)

FURTHER READING

Brown, A.S. 1997. "Aphrodite and the Pandora Complex," *Classical Quarterly* 47.1, 26–47

Kenaan, V.L. 2008. *Pandora's Senses. The Feminine Character of the Ancient Text*. Madison, WI.

Marquardt, P.A. 1982. "Hesiod's Ambiguous View of Woman," *Classical Philology* 77.4, 283–291

Panofsky, D. and I. 1956. *Pandora's Box. The Changing Aspects of a Mythical Symbol*. London

Sussman, L.S. 1978. "Workers and Drones, Labor, Idleness and Gender Definition in Hesiod's Beehive," *Arethusa* 11 27–41

Walcott, P. 1984. "Greek Attitudes Towards Women: the Mythological Evidence," *Greece & Rome* 31, 37–47

Zeitlin, F. 1996. "Signifying Difference: The Case of Hesiod's Pandora," in *Playing the Other. Gender and Society in Classical Greek Literature*, 53–86. Chicago/London

2

Aphrodite and Demeter: goddesses in the Homeric Hymns

The Homeric Hymns were songs honouring the Greek gods and goddesses. They sometimes narrated an episode in their divine biography, and were probably sung at festivals devoted to them. In antiquity they were erroneously believed to have been composed by Homer, hence the name.

Aphrodite's sexual powers and her own passion are the subject of one of these hymns, composed (we think) not long after Hesiod's compositions. The hymn opens with an account of the extent of her powers to generate sexual passion in gods, mortals, birds and all creatures over land and sea. It makes the point, however, that there are three goddesses who are immune to her power – Athena, Artemis and Hestia – all of whom devote themselves to other pursuits. Athena prefers military action and teaching various crafts to men and women. Artemis prefers the untamed life, roaming the mountains and joining in the dance of her followers. Hestia, pursued by both Poseidon and Apollo, swears a great oath touching the head of Zeus, that she will remain a virgin for all time and enjoy the honour she receives at the central hearth fire of each house.

The narrative unfolds at the point where Zeus becomes angry at the extent to which he is at the mercy of Aphrodite's powers, which keeps him coupling with mortal women and ignoring his wife Hera. He retaliates by striking Aphrodite with passion for a mortal man, Anchises, a Trojan cowherd on the mountains of Ida. Aphrodite prepares for this love encounter by going to Paphos and getting bathed by the Graces, then anointed with oil and dressed in fine garments. As the goddess reaches Ida, even the wild animals are subdued and otherwise affected by her power.

She came to Ida with its many springs, mother of wild beasts,
and went directly to the steading across the mountain. After her
darted the grey wolves and the fierce lions,
bears and swift leopards hungry for deer.
She was delighted in her heart when she saw them,
and cast sexual desire in their breasts,

and they all lay down in couples in the shadowy haunts.
(*Homeric Hymn to Aphrodite* 5.68–74)

As she comes across the cowherd she takes upon herself the disguise of a young girl. Anchises still senses something greater than the ordinary, seeing her shining robes and her golden jewellery, and greets her as a goddess or nymph. Aphrodite continues with her deception, and claims that she is from nearby Phrygia, and was dancing with other young girls of marriageable age in honour of Artemis when she was snatched by Hermes and brought to Anchises to be his bride. She asks for the proper arrangements to be made between his family and hers, assuring him that hers would provide many fine dowry gifts. Persuaded by her false talk, Anchises is overcome with desire.

"If you are mortal and a mortal mother bore you
and your father is the famous Otreus as you say
and you have come here at the behest of the immortal messenger
Hermes, and you will be called my wife for all time,
then no one of gods or morals will stop me from making love with you
right now, not even if the far-shooter himself, Apollo,
should shoot deadly weapons from his silver bow;
I would wish, in that case, woman in the likeness of a goddess,
to mount your bed then go down to the House of Hades."
(*Homeric Hymn to Aphrodite* 5.145–154)

Anchises removes the gleaming jewellery from Aphrodite, then her breastband and her golden robes. Next, the hymnist tells us:

By the will of the gods and by fate,
a mortal man lay with an immortal goddess, not knowing clearly (what he was doing).
(*Homeric Hymn to Aphrodite* 5.166–167)

Aphrodite then casts sleep over Anchises. Before waking him up she sheds her disguise and resumes her dazzling stature as a goddess. When he recognizes the truth, he cowers.

When he saw the throat and the lovely eyes of Aphrodite
he was terrified and turned his eyes away in another direction.
He covered his handsome face again in his cloak,
begging her with winged words as he addressed her:
"Straightway when I saw your face with my eyes, goddess,
I recognized that you were a divinity. You did not tell me the truth.

But by Zeus of the aegis I beseech you,
do not allow me to live among mortals deprived of my manhood
but take pity on me, since a man does not live full of vitality
when he has slept with an immortal goddess."
(*Homeric Hymn to Aphrodite* 5.181–189)

Aphrodite assures Anchises that he will suffer no harm at her hands or from the gods, but will enjoy the honour of having a glorious son – the Trojan hero, Aeneas – born of their liaison. She will not continue the love affair, however. Anchises might suffer the fate of Tithonus, a Trojan taken by the Dawn goddess to be her lover. She secured for him immortal life but not eternal youth, and as he withered away she hid him because he was a source of embarrassment and repugnance. Aphrodite, already burning with shame at having succumbed to passion for a mortal, wishes to distance herself as much as possible from the affair.

For me there will be wide-spread reproach among the immortal gods
continually for all time, because of you,
those who formerly would dread my intimate whisperings and wiles
with which I commingled gods and mortal women.
My design would subdue them all.
But now my mouth will no longer be capable of mentioning this
among the immortals, since I was completely infatuated,
terribly, wretchedly – unspeakably. I was struck out of my mind;
I put a child under my breast-band, having had sex with a mortal.
(*Homeric Hymn to Aphrodite* 5.247–255)

Another of the Homeric Hymns, dated to *c.* 600 BCE, honours Demeter, the Graingoddess. The narrative begins with the abduction of her beloved young daughter. Her father Zeus had agreed to give her to his brother Hades, to become his bride in his kingdom of the Underworld. While picking flowers in a meadow with her peers, the daughters of Ocean, the girl reaches for a stunningly beautiful narcissus. (Gaia had sent this forth, being complicit with Zeus in his abduction plan.) As she reaches for the flower the earth opens and Hades snatches her into his chariot. Her screams are heard by Hecate, daughter of a Titan, by the Sungod Helios and, of course, by her mother. Demeter, gripped with pain, races over the earth day and night, chasing after her daughter, neglecting to eat, drink or bathe. Eventually, accompanied by Hecate, she learns from Helios (who sees all) what has happened and realizes that this was a scheme that had been arranged by Zeus. Angered at all the gods, she abandons the immortals and, disguised as an old woman, sits by the "maidens' well" at Eleusis, where young women come to draw water. There she meets the daughters of the Eleusinian king who invite her to become the nurse of their infant brother. The group of women arrive at the palace where they meet the queen Metaneira, Even in her disguise, the goddess is an awe-inspiring presence.

She stepped onto the threshold with her feet, and her head
reached the roof-beam. She filled the doorway with divine brilliance.
Awe, reverence and pallid fear seized (Metaneira).
She gave over her couch to her and bade her sit down.
(*Homeric Hymn to Demeter* 188–191)

But Demeter refuses to sit. She stands in silence, until a servant girl Iambe sets a stool for her. On this she sits, brooding sorrowfully until Iambe breaks her mood with jesting. The goddess is provoked to laughter and her dark mood is lightened. She agrees to become the nurse of the infant Demophoön, offering the assurance that she knows how to keep him impervious to malevolent magical charms. The boy flourished like a god under her care, as she anointed him with divine ambrosia during the day, and by night bathed him in fire. One night, however, Metaneira caught sight of this and shrieked in alarm. Demeter, furious, left the child on the floor and cursed the mother for preventing her from making the child deathless and immortal with her care. She reveals herself as Demeter, and requests of the Eleusinians a temple with an altar and rituals of appeasement. She then sheds her disguise.

So speaking she changed her size and stature,
thrusting off old age, and beauty wafted around her.
An alluring perfume spread out from her fragrant robes,
and a lustre shone afar from the skin of the immortal goddess.
Golden tresses covered her shoulders.
The well-built house was filled with brilliance like that of lightning
as she went through the halls. (Metaneira's) knees immediately went slack.
(*Homeric Hymn to Demeter* 275–281)

The goddess's wrath at her treatment by mortals continues, and as they sow seeds in the earth she prevents them from growing. Humans are threatened with famine, and the gods with loss of sacrificial gifts on their altars. Zeus takes action, sending the messenger goddess Iris to attempt to placate Demeter, but the goddess is resolute. When other gods try to persuade her with gifts she offers the only condition on which reconciliation would be possible – the return of her daughter Persephone. Zeus sends Hermes to Hades, and the Underworld god agrees to return his bride. He tells Persephone she may return to her mother, but reminds her of the honours she would acquire as his queen – to be mistress of everything in his realm and possess the powers to dispense punishment for souls who are unjust or who fail to appease her with appropriate sacrifices and gifts. Covertly, he gives her a pomegranate seed to eat, which will ensure her return for part of each year. Persephone is reunited with her mother, but the mutual joy is tempered by Demeter's recognition that her daughter has eaten of Underworld food, and will therefore need to return. Mother and daughter share their stories in the company of Hecate, who will become the attendant of Persephone. Zeus sends Rhea to Demeter, to persuade her to rejoin the immortals and to renew the earth's bounty. The hymn closes with the ascent of the three generations of women – Rhea, Demeter and Persephone – to Olympus.

FURTHER READING

Bergren, A. 1989. "The Homeric Hymn to Aphrodite. Tradition and Rhetoric, Praise and Blame," *Classical Antiquity* 8, 1–41

Brumfield, A.C. 1981. *The Attic Festivals of Demeter and their Relation to the Agricultural Year.* New York

Foley, H. 1994 ed. *The Homeric Hymn to Demeter. Translation, Commentary and Interpretive Essays.* Princeton

Giacomelli, A. 1980. "Aphrodite and After," *Phoenix* 34.1, 1–19

Passman, T. 1993. "Re(de)fining Woman: Language and Power in the Homeric Hymn to Demeter," in M. De Forest ed., *Woman's Power, Man's Game: Essays on Classical Antiquity in Honor of Joy K. King*, 54–77. Wauconda, IL

3

Women divine and mortal in the Homeric epics

The "Homeric" epics, possibly composed by a single poet roughly contemporary with Hesiod, involve two chapters of the Trojan War saga. The *Iliad* gives us a narrative of events on the battlefield at Troy prior to the final victory of the Greeks, when their hero Achilles refuses to participate in the fighting because of a slight to his honour. Captive women taken after military conquests by the Greeks in skirmishes before the major confrontation were awarded as prizes to the best warriors. As commander-in-chief Agamemnon had been awarded one of these women, Chryseis, whom he refuses to surrender when her father, a prophet-priest of Apollo, comes to retrieve her and offers a ransom for her return. The father's appeal and his ransom are rejected, so the priest turns to the god for help. Apollo punishes the Greeks with a plague until Agamemnon relents. Broader tensions between the commander and his principal warrior are played out in a struggle over the concubine prize of Achilles, whom Agamemnon demands as compensation for his loss. For both Agamemnon and Achilles the loss of their awarded concubines amounts to an intolerable blow to their prestige.

In the first book of the *Iliad*, when the prophet who accompanied the Greeks to Troy reveals the reason why his troops have been stricken, Agamemnon replies to him angrily, making clear the terms on which he would relent, which initiates the quarrel with his best soldier.

[Agamemnon] Now you spout oracles before the Greeks,
proclaiming that it was on account of this that the far-shooter caused us grief –
because I was not willing to accept a splendid ransom for the girl Chryseis,
since I wanted to keep her in my tent.
You see, I prefer her to my lawful wife Clytemnestra,
for she was not inferior
in body or stature, in her mind or her skills.
But even so, I am willing to give her back again, if this is best.
I want the troops to be safe rather than perish.
But make ready a prize for me straightway, so that I won't be the only one
of the Argives without a gift of honour, since that is not appropriate.
All of you – look how my prize is going elsewhere!
(*Iliad* 1.109–120)

[Achilles] Noblest son of Atreus, most covetous of all,
how will the great-hearted Achaeans ever give you a prize?
We don't exactly see a great common stock (of them) lying around.
(*Iliad* 1.122–124)

Despite Achilles' assurance that the troops would recompense their commander when there is another supply of captive women once they have taken Troy, Agamemnon stands firm.

Godlike Achilles, however brave you may be, don't try
to conceal something in your mind, since you won't outwit me nor will you
persuade me. Now is it the case that for yourself you want to hang onto your prize
but you want me to sit here like this without one, while you order me to give mine
back?
Now if the great-hearted Achaeans give me a gift of honour,
furnishing one that suits my taste, well – see that it is a fair trade.
But if they don't give me one, then I'll take one myself –
either yours or I'll go and take the prize belonging to Ajax
or Odysseus. And whoever I come to is going to be furious!
(*Iliad* 1.131–139)

Agamemnon prepares to send Chryseis back to her father on a ship loaded with bulls for sacrifice, to be captained by one of his chief warriors, perhaps Achilles. The hero responds angrily to Agamemnon's demand to take his as the replacement spear-bride, making reference to the fact that the Greeks are fighting the Trojans not for military reasons but for the personal pleasure of Agamemnon and his brother Menelaus, whose wife had been abducted by the Trojan prince Paris.

Oh, voracious you, wrapped in shamelessness,
how is any forward-minded Achaean going to be persuaded by your words
to follow on your course or to fight men by force?
For I didn't come here to fight the spear-bearing Trojans
since, in my view, they are not the ones who have done me wrong.
They never drove off my cattle or horses,
nor laid waste the crops from very fertile Phthia,
the land that nurtures men, since there are right many shadowy mountains
and an expanse of the roaring sea between here and there.
But it was for *you*, shame-faced one, that we came, to please *you*,
to exact satisfaction from the Trojans for Menelaus and for *you*, you dog-faced one.
You don't care a whit about this nor think twice about it.

And now you are threatening to snatch my prize by yourself,
(an honour) for which I worked very hard, and the sons of the Achaeans gave her to me.
I never have a prize equal to yours,
whenever the Achaeans sack a well-inhabited fortress of the Trojans.
(*Iliad* 1.149–164)

Captain Agamemnon and his chief warrior continued their passionate dispute until Achilles, realizing that it was fruitless to protest further, removed himself from the fighting. This leaves the Greeks considerably weakened. The gods take sides in the fighting, some supporting the Trojans and others the Greeks, and some of them take an active role in strengthening and protecting individual heroes on the battlefield. The partisan actions are played out in tensions that erupt on Olympus until Zeus steps in and stops their direct engagement in the war. Zeus' wife Hera, who has taken the side of the Greeks and wishes to protect them from the successful incursions of the Trojans that followed the departure of Achilles, decides that seducing her husband will keep him from interfering with her pro-Greek activities. To ensure that she will be successful in her plan Hera dresses in her finest, anoints her skin with sweet-smelling fragrances and prevails upon Aphrodite to hand over her embroidered breastband, which will ensure that she will be irresistible. Because Aphrodite supports the Trojans Hera lies about the reason for her request.

Give me now (the power of) love-making and desire,
with which you subdue all immortals and mortals.
For I am going to the extremities of the bountiful earth,
to Ocean, the progenitor of the gods, and Mother Tethys,
who nursed me attentively in their house and reared me,
taking me from Rhea, when far-seeing Zeus
had cast Cronus down under the earth and the barren sea.
I will go to see them and resolve the impasse of their quarrel.
For a long time now they have been estranged from one another,
avoiding sex and love-making, since anger weighs upon their spirit.
(*Iliad* 14.198–207)

Aphrodite readily complies, noting that it would not be appropriate to refuse Hera, wife of Zeus:

She spoke, and undid the embroidered sash from her breast,
intricate, on which all charms had been fashioned:

therein was love-making, and desire and seductive intimate talk
that fools the mind even of those who think prudent thoughts.
She placed it in her hands and spoke about it in detail:
"Look here, put around your breast this embroidered band,
on which everything has been figured.
I declare that the purpose you have in mind will not come to nothing."
(*Iliad* 14.214–221)

Determined to ensure that Zeus will be rendered inactive for a while, Hera leaves Olympus and descends to the island of Lemnos, where she persuades Hypnos, god of sleep, to cast on Zeus a deep sleep after their love making. She overcomes Hypnos' reluctance to meddle with the supreme god by the promise of a beautiful wife, one of the Graces. Hera then speeds to Ida, a mountain peak near Troy, where she is spotted by Zeus.

Cloud-gathering Zeus espied her.
When he saw her, it was as when passion blinded his shrewd thinking,
like the time when he first mingled with her in love,
when they climbed into bed together without their own parents knowing it.
(*Iliad* 14.293–296)

Standing close to her, Zeus questions what she is doing in this place. Hera gives him the same deceptive tale she told Aphrodite. Zeus is captivated by her beauty, and asks her to delay her trip to Oceanus and Tethys, so they would waste no time in making love. He is, he proclaims, utterly overwhelmed by desire for her, to a degree he had never experienced in his other sexual encounters, which he proceeds to enumerate. Hera continues to tease him, protesting that it is not appropriate to have sex in the open:

Most awe-inspiring son of Cronus, what a proposal you made!
If you yearn to lie with me in love
on the peaks of Ida, with all of it obvious in broad daylight,
then how would it be if one of the gods who live forever
were to see us sleeping, and went and broadcast it to all the gods?
I at least would not get up from our love-nest
and come back to your house, for it would provoke indignation.
But if you want to, and you are keen on this in your heart,
there is a bedchamber that your own son Hephaistus made for you,
one fitted with strong doors attached to the doorposts.
Let's go and lie there, since love-making is your desire.
(*Iliad* 14.330–340)

Zeus counters with the proposal that he enfold them in a dense golden cloud, to be out of sight of the other gods. He does this, and as they make love the earth bursts forth with lush grass and fresh flowers.

So he spoke, and the son of Cronus enfolded his wife in his arms.
The shining earth beneath them brought forth fresh lush grass,
dewy lotus and crocus, hyacinths
thick-clustered and soft, which kept them up off the ground.
On this they lay together, and they wrapped themselves in a cloud,
golden and beautiful, while glistening dew fell down upon them.
(*Iliad* 14.346–351)

Despite the degree to which the *Iliad* is a tale of war and male heroism, sexual passion is a principal factor behind much of the action. It was, after all, taking revenge for the abduction of Helen by Paris that was the motivation for the Greeks to attack Troy. What about the portrait of Helen herself in Troy? We meet her on several occasions. On the first, she is summoned by the goddess Iris to come to the city walls and observe the Greeks and Trojans awaiting the outcome of a proposed duel between Helen's two "husbands," Menelaus and Paris (also called Alexander), which would not only settle possession of the beautiful woman, but avert a protracted battle. Iris finds Helen in the royal hall, weaving a fabric on which she is embroidering the battles between the Greeks and Trojans that were being waged over her. Helen responds to Iris' summons.

(The goddess) cast sweet desire in her heart
for her former husband and her city and her parents.
Straightway she covered herself with shimmering white linen
and started out of her chamber, shedding soft tears.
(*Iliad* 3.139–142)

The duel is aborted when Aphrodite rescues Paris, shrouding him in mist and whisking him to his chamber. She then goes to find Helen, who is still at the city wall. Helen recognizes Aphrodite despite the disguise the goddess had assumed, and angrily rejects Aphrodite's request that she join Paris in their bed.

Divine power, why would you long to deceive me with this?
Now where among well-settled cities will you lead me instead,
to those of Phrygia or lovely Maeonia,
if there is one of the mortal men dear to you in that place too,
since now Menelaus has defeated noble Alexander
and wants to lead loathsome me home again?

Is this why you are standing here now plotting deception?
You go and sit beside him; withdraw from the way of the gods.
Don't turn around on foot and go back to Olympus,
but ever fuss over him and protect him,
until he makes you his wife or even his slave.
I won't go there – for it would be a source of reproach
if I were to share that man's bed. All the Trojan women will blame me afterwards,
and I have constant sorrows in my heart.
(*Iliad* 3.399–412)

Aphrodite is enraged, and threatens Helen with severe reprisals until she complies out of fear. Helen faces Paris in the bedchamber and berates him, while displaying conflicting feelings:

You have come back from the war; I wish you had died there,
defeated by a man of might who used to be my husband.
Earlier you used to boast that you were a better man than Menelaus dear-to-Ares
in strength – both with your hands and the spear.
But go now, challenge Menelaus dear-to-Ares
to fight again face-to-face. But then again, I bid you stop, and not wage war
in hostility against blond Menelaus or do battle
foolishly, lest you soon be broken by his spear.
(*Iliad* 3.428–436)

Helen felt a particular closeness to Hector, the Trojan champion warrior and brother of Paris. As Paris ponders whether to go back into the war Helen turns to Hector with words of self-condemnation that include a lingering reproach against Paris:

Oh, brother-in-law of mine – me a dog, horrible contriver of evil,
I wish that on that day when first my mother bore me
a dreadful gust of wind had carried me off,
to go to a mountain or into the wave of the loud-roaring sea,
where the wave would have swept me away before these things had come to pass.
But since the gods appointed these evils in this way,
would that I had been the wife of a better husband,
one who recognized their indignation and the extent of his disgrace before men.
(*Iliad* 6.344–351)

The poet has Helen make clear her role in the plot and overall purpose of the epic.

"On us Zeus has brought an evil doom,
so that we will be subjects for song for men to come hereafter."
(*Iliad* 6.357–358)

As Hector is the nobler warrior, so is his marriage a nobler one than that of his brother Paris. Hector had married Andromache, left without a family when Achilles had sacked her city, and together they had a son Astyanax. Perhaps the most touching scene in the *Iliad*, a tale so full of brutality, is the one in which Andromache tries to prevent Hector from returning to battle. The intimacy of their conversation and the interaction with their baby is rendered the more poignant because of the strong sense we have that these are their last moments together.

As he went through the great town
he came to the Scaean gates, the place where he would pass through on his way
to the plain.
There he met his bountiful wife, as she was running to meet him –
Andromache, daughter of great-hearted Eëtion, who had dwelt under wooded
Plakos
in Thebe-under-Plakos, the lord of Cilissian men.
It was his daughter who belonged to bronze-helmeted Hector.
She met him now, and along with her came her handmaid
holding their child at her breast, still a tender-minded baby,
Hector's beloved son, like a shining star,
whom Hector would call Scamandrion, but others
Astyanax ("Lord of the City"), for Hector alone was the city's protector.
Andromache stood near him, shedding tears.
She took his hand in hers and spoke to him, and called him by name.
"Wondrous man, your strength will destroy you, and you have no pity
for your innocent child or for ill-fated me, who soon will be
your widow. For soon the Achaeans will kill you,
all of them rushing at you. For me it would be better,
once I have lost you, to sink down under the earth. For there will be no other
comfort, when you have brought on your destiny,
only grief. I have no father and honoured mother.
For the great Achilles slew my father
and destroyed the well-inhabited city of the Cilicians,
Thebe of the towering gates. He slew Eëtion
but did not strip him of armour, for he admired him in his heart.
He burned the body with its elaborate weaponry
and heaped up a funeral mound over it. And the mountain nymphs

planted elm trees around it, those daughters of aegis-bearing Zeus.
My seven brothers were in the palace;
all of them went down to Hades in a single day.
Swift-footed Achilles slew them all,
while they were with their shambling-footed cattle and shining white sheep.
And my mother, who was queen under wooded Plakos,
her they led off here, along with his other possessions.
Achilles released her again, after taking a handsome ransom,
but Artemis, releaser of arrows, shot her in the halls of her father.
Hector, you are father and honoured mother to me
and brother, for you are my vigorous husband.
Come now, take pity and remain here on the rampart;
don't make your child an orphan and your wife a widow.
Station your troops beside the fig tree, where the city ramparts are most
open to being scaled and the wall most open to attack." (392–434)

Then great Hector of the shining helmet answered her.
"All these things are on my mind, my wife. But in great measure I
would feel acute shame before the Trojan men and the Trojan women with their
long robes
were I like a coward to shrink away from the fighting.
My spirit does not bid me do this, since I learned to be valiant at all times
and to fight among the foremost with the Trojans,
winning great glory for my father and for myself too.
For I know this well in my heart and in my soul:
there will come a day when sacred Ilion (Troy) will perish
along with Priam and the people of Priam of the strong ash spear.
But I am not as preoccupied with the pain for the Trojans that is to come
nor for Hecuba herself or for King Priam
nor for my brothers who, although numerous and valiant,
would fall in the dust at the hands of hostile men,
as much as I worry about you, when some one of the bronze-clad Achaeans
leads you off weeping, stealing from you your day of freedom.
In Argos you would weave at the loom of another woman
and you would carry water from the spring Messeis or Hypereia
much against your will, but strong necessity will lie upon you.
And at some point someone will say as they look upon you weeping,
'This is the wife of Hector, who excelled among the horse-taming Trojans
as he fought, when they battled around Ilion.'
This is what someone will say. But there will be fresh grief for you
being in need of this husband to fight off the day of slavery for you.

But may a pile of earth hide me when I am dead
before I hear you cry out as you are dragged off.'
So speaking glorious Hector reached out to his child.
But the baby shrank back to the breast of his well-belted nurse
crying, panicking at the sight of his own father,
frightened at both the bronze and the helmet with its crest of horse-hair,
thinking it was nodding dreadfully down from the crest of his helmet.
His dear father and mother laughed aloud.
Straightway glorious Hector removed the helmet from his head
and laid it down, all shining, on the ground.
Then he kissed his beloved son and rocked him in his arms.
He spoke, praying to Zeus and the other gods:
'Zeus and the other gods, grant that this child of mine
may become, as I am, pre-eminent among the Trojans,
this powerful in strength, and rule over Ilion in strength.
And let someone say one day, "This fellow is much better than his father
when he returns from fighting. Let him kill an enemy,
bring back the bloody armour and delight the heart of his mother."'
So speaking he placed his child in the arms of his beloved wife. She took him
to her fragrant breast, smiling through her tears. Her husband pitied her as he saw
her
and caressed her with his hand, then spoke to her and called her by name:
'Wondrous woman, don't be overly troubled in your heart on my account.
No one will hurl me to Hades beyond my destiny.
I say that there is no one among men who has escaped his fate,
no coward, no valiant man, once he has been born.
So go back to the house and attend to your own tasks,
the loom and distaff, and instruct the handmaids
to ply their work. War will be the concern of men,
for all of them, those who have been born in Ilion, but mainly for me."'
(*Iliad* 6.440–493)

Hector returns to battle and is eventually killed by Achilles, who drags his body
ruthlessly behind his chariot around the walls of Troy. Eventually the gods
put an end to this cruel display and assist King Priam in retrieving the corpse
from the Greeks for burial. When Troy is eventually sacked the boy Astyanax
is hurled to his death from the walls by the Greek herald and Andromache is
carried off as a concubine for Achilles' son Neoptolemos.

The setting of the *Odyssey* provides a different backdrop for the interactions
of its characters, mortal and divine. This is peacetime, 10 years after the fall of
Troy, although the dramatic action is anything but peaceful. Penelope, bereft of

her husband Odysseus for 20 years, has all but given up hope of his return from Troy, while a host of would-be suitors has invaded the palace on Ithaca hoping to take his place. Their son Telemachus has just come of age as the poem begins, and attempts to assert his youthful authority over his mother and the suitors – with mixed success. From the outset, and throughout the poem, we see her breaking down in tearful distress at her situation.

As the poem begins we are presented with the situation on Ithaca. Telemachus at the behest of Athena has decided to go in search of his father, but first sits with the suitors who are listening to a singer recount the seafaring difficulties being encountered by the Greeks who are returning from Troy. Penelope descends from her chamber and, distressed at the subject of the song, attempts to persuade the singer to change his words for a story more soothing to the soul. Telemachus intervenes, telling his mother to harden her heart and listen, then to leave the men, for he – not she – is in charge.

Mother of mine, why do you begrudge this excellent singer's
bringing pleasure wherever his mind directs him? It is not the singers who are to blame,
but Zeus is at fault, who gives men
who labour for bread just however he wishes, to each man.
There is no reprisal for this man for singing about the evil fate of the Greeks.
People praise the song more
when it is the newest to circulate among the listeners.
Let your heart and your spirit brace themselves to listen.
For Odysseus is not the only one to lose his day of homecoming
at Troy. Many other mortals lost this too.
Go back into the house and take up your own work,
the loom and the distaff, and order the handmaidens
to be busy about their work too. Discussion is the concern of all men,
but especially my concern. For the power in the household is mine.
(*Odyssey* 1.346–359)

When Odysseus eventually returns to Ithaca, he is in disguise. Not only does he take this precaution in order to surprise the suitors, but he had been warned by the ghost of Agamemnon (with whom he had conversed in a visit to the Underworld during his journey home) to be cautious in his dealings with Penelope. Agamemnon's death had been brought about by his own wife Clytemnestra upon his return to Mycenae, and while he does not foresee that Penelope will do the same, he advises Odysseus to be vigilant.

So don't you be altogether naïve when it comes to your wife.

Don't divulge the whole story, all that you know.
Tell her part of it but keep the rest hidden.
(*Odyssey* 11.441–443)

So it is that upon Odysseus' return to Ithaca, Penelope describes her grief to a "stranger," her husband in disguise.

Soon it will be the hour for pleasant sleep – that is, at least,
for anyone whom sweet sleep would overtake – although they may be full of care.
But for me some divinity has given endless grief.
By day I get relief in lamenting over my woes,
seeing to my household work and that of the handmaids in the house.
But when night comes and sleep takes hold of everyone else,
I lie in my bed, and constant and bitter anxieties upset me
while I grieve in my throbbing heart.
(*Odyssey* 19.510–517)

At other times Penelope wavers between surrendering to her grief and attempting to devise some stratagem to take control. The best known of these is the one she contrives at her loom, pretending to weave a shroud for Odysseus' father. Once again, she is speaking to the "stranger," reporting the circumstances that prompted her to do this.

Stranger, the immortal gods destroyed my distinct qualities – my beauty and stature –
when the Argives set sail for Ilion,
and with them went my husband Odysseus.
If he were to come back and look after my life
my fame would be greater and thereby more glorious.
But now I am pained – so many evils has some spirit unleashed upon me.
(*Odyssey* 19.124–130)

She enumerates the places from which nobles from Ithaca and the surrounding area have come to seek her hand, then relates her current strategy for dealing with them:

For this reason I take no notice of strangers nor suppliants
nor heralds who are public servants,
but pining for beloved Odysseus I waste away in my heart.
They are pressing me into marriage, but I spin out some deception.
First, some god inspired me with the idea of a garment,

to set up a great loom in the main hall and to weave
a mantle, finely-spun and very large. Straightaway I said to them:
"Young men, my suitors, since noble Odysseus is dead
stay here eager for my marriage, until I finish this garment,
lest my threads be wasted and spun in vain.
(This is) a shroud for the hero Laertes, against the time
when the dire fate of death, bringer of long-lasting woe, seizes him.
I am afraid that some Achaean woman in the community would reproach me
if he, who has earned many possessions, should lie (there) without a funeral
shroud."
This is what I said, and their proud hearts were persuaded.
Then by day I would weave away at the great loom,
but at night I would undo it when I set up torches beside me.
And so for three years I outwitted them and persuaded the Achaeans.
But when the fourth year came and the seasons came around
and the months came and went, and many days had come to a close,
even then did they – with the conniving of the irresponsible serving women –
break in on me and catch me, and threaten me with words.
So I finished it, unwillingly but by necessity.
(*Odyssey* 19.134–156)

At the end of their conversation, which lasts for most of the night, Penelope
announces that she will propose to the suitors a "bride contest". She will
retrieve from the palace the bow that Odysseus had used when he was still
in Ithaca, one that only he had the strength to string. She would set up a row
of axes inside the hall, challenging the young men to string the weapon and
shoot straight through the row as her husband used to do. As it turns out, it
is only the "stranger" who accomplishes this. He then turns the weapon on
the suitors.

   After Penelope is told that this man is in fact her husband, she is still reluctant
to respond as his wife until she establishes the fact for herself. She describes her
state of mind to Telemachus, who accuses her (after the successful routing of
the suitors) of having a heart of stone for not welcoming her husband home. She
replies with reference to the intimacy that only the two of them know.

My child, the heart in my breast is amazed,
and I am unable to speak directly to him nor ask him a question,
nor look him directly in the eyes. But if Odysseus has truly come home
then we will recognize each other for sure.
For we have signs that we know which are hidden from others.
(*Odyssey* 23.105–110)

There is one principal "sign" shared by the two of them that Penelope uses to test whether the man is truly Odysseus. She asks the housekeeper to bring out from the bedroom the bedstead that Odysseus had made himself, and prepare it for him to sleep on. Odysseus bursts out with the objection that it could not be moved, since he had built the bedroom around an olive tree, using the trunk for a bedpost. Penelope is finally convinced and rushes into his arms. Their bed is prepared, they make love and spend the night recounting to each other the trials they had undergone during their twenty-year separation.

The poet gives us another glimpse into the intimacy that characterizes a good marriage. Odysseus had ended his adventures with one last visit abroad before returning to Ithaca, when he reached the island of the Phaeacians after being shipwrecked. In his sea-worn state, he encounters the lovely young daughter of the local king and queen, Nausicaa, whom he addresses respectfully as someone's future bride. He is hopeful of obtaining fresh clothing and the means to get home.

May the gods grant you everything that you desire in your heart –
a husband and a home, and may they extend to you both a noble oneness of mind.
For nothing is more powerful or better
than for man and wife to keep a household with a shared way of thinking.
This brings grief to their enemies, and joy
to those who care about them; they themselves are the ones who know this blessing best.
(*Odyssey* 6.180–185)

Nausicaa belongs to a ruling family in which her mother enjoys considerable prestige. Although it is her father Alcinous who will ultimately arrange for Odysseus' return to Ithaca, her mother Arete (whose name means "courage," "excellence") is the person whom Nausicaa advises Odysseus to approach first, to present his request for assistance. The goddess Athena, watching out for the hero, disguises herself as a young girl of the island, guiding him to the palace and informing him about the nature of the royal family. Arete, she tells him, is highly regarded – not only by her husband, King Alcinous, but by the whole community:

Alcinous made her his wife
and respected her as no other woman on earth is respected –
of all the women who keep a household for their husbands.
In this way she has been honoured whole-heartedly and is still so respected –
by her own children, by Alcinous himself
and by the people who, looking upon her as a goddess,

welcome her with their speech as she walks through the town.
For in no way is she lacking in noble thinking.
With her fine disposition she resolves for them even the quarrels of men.
(*Odyssey* 7.66–74)

What of the non-elite women in the *Odyssey*? We get a glimpse of the different female slaves through the loyal old family nurse Eurycleia as well as the disloyal young women who enjoy sexual relations with the suitors. As the poet tells us, Eurycleia had been purchased by Odysseus' father as a young girl.

She brought the flaming torches to him, prudent Eurycleia,
daughter of Ops the son of Peisanor,
whom Laertes bought with his wealth
when she was still in the prime of her girlhood, and he gave the worth of 20 oxen
for her. He honoured her as much as he did his prudent wife in his palace,
but he never had sex with her, and avoided the wrath of his wife.
(*Odyssey* 1.428–433)

Eurycleia became the nurse of Odysseus then of his son Telemachus. When Odysseus returns to the palace in disguise and Penelope asks her to wash the feet of the "stranger" the old woman observes a close resemblance to the man she knew so well, reflecting that Odysseus, wherever he is, must be exposing himself to the same kind of taunting that the Ithacan serving women (whom she refers to as "bitches") have leveled at the "stranger". She lifts his bare leg and recognizes a scar identical to one that Odysseus had received on a boar hunt as a boy. She drops the leg in astonishment, spilling the water in the washing bowl and turns to share the revelation with Penelope. Odysseus silences her roughly:

Odysseus,
reaching with his right hand, took hold of her throat,
and with the other he drew her nearer to him and said,
"Old Nanny, why do you want to destroy me? You yourself suckled me
at your own breast. Now after suffering much grief
I have come back to my native land twenty years later.
Since you perceived this, and some god has put it in your mind,
be quiet about it, lest someone else in the palace learn of it.
I will tell you this straight out, and it will be realized:
if some god subdues the illustrious suitors
through my hands I will not keep my hands off you, even though you are my nurse,
when I kill the other women in the palace."
(*Odyssey* 19.479–490)

Eurycleia assures Odysseus that she can keep a secret, and volunteers to name the slavewomen who have been disloyal to him. This offer he bluntly rejects, saying he is capable of sizing them up himself. After his successful performance in the bow contest and his slaughter of the suitors, however, he listens as Eurycleia points out twelve guilty women. Odysseus turns to Telemachus and his faithful swineherd to carry out their punishment.

Begin carrying out the bodies and give orders to the women (to help).
Then wipe down the very beautiful chairs and tables
with water and perforated sponges.
But when everything in the house has been put to order
lead the serving women outside the sturdy palace
between the round building and the tight fence of the courtyard.
Strike them with your long pointed swords
until you deprive them of their life and they forget the love-making
which they enjoyed with the suitors, having sex with them in secret.
(Odyssey 22.437–445)

During his journey back to Ithaca Odysseus had found himself in bed with women other than Penelope – non-mortal creatures like the bewitching Circe and the nymph Calypso, both of whom wished to detain him as their lover.

When Odysseus and his crew first reached Circe's island, they saw smoke rising through the woods and Odysseus sent a group of the men ahead to investigate. They came upon the nymph in her house, which was surrounded by tame lions and wolves – men whom Circe had drugged and turned into beasts. Odysseus' men heard her singing as she was weaving at her loom inside her house and came near. Before long the men were turned into animals, all but one who hid and rushed back to report the fate of his comrades to Odysseus. The hero set off with his sword and was met by the messenger god Hermes, who gave him a drug to ward off the effect of Circe's drugs. Hermes also gave him some important advice:

When Circe strikes you with her huge wand
then draw the sharp sword from your thigh
and dart at Circe as if you are intending to kill her.
She will be terrified and call you to bed with her.
At this point do not any longer turn down making love with the goddess,
so that you may release your companions and safeguard yourself as well.
But order her to swear a great oath by the gods
that she will not contrive any other evil misfortune for you,
nor – when you are naked – make you feeble and unmanned.
(Odyssey 10.293–301)

Odysseus complies, his men are set free, and they all remain with Circe for a year, enjoying her hospitality until the crew remind Odysseus of their need to return home. He climbs into her bed once more, makes his plea to her on his knees, and she gives them the wherewithal for the next stage of their journey.

Calypso (whose name means "Concealer") managed to keep Odysseus captive for seven years, at a time when he had lost all his men and was adrift at sea after a shipwreck. Despite the paradise-like surrounds and her promise to make him immortal if he stayed with her, Odysseus was homesick and a reluctant lover. The goddess Athena persuaded Zeus to send Hermes to instruct Calypso to release the hero. Hermes reached her at her loom, singing. The nymph became angry when she heard the injunction from Olympus:

You merciless gods are the most jealous creatures of all,
who bear a grudge against goddesses having sex with mortal men
openly, when one of them makes (a man) her special bedmate.
(*Odyssey* 5.119–120)

She listed the unhappy fates of two such goddesses, the Dawn Goddess who took the hunter Orion as a lover only to have Artemis kill him, or Demeter who made love with Iasion in a field, before Zeus blasted him with a thunderbolt. Calypso continued her protest, distressed at the injustice of her case but ultimately bowing to the inevitable:

Just so now, gods, you resent me for being with a mortal man.
It was I who saved him when he had been floating on the ship's keel
all alone, when Zeus caught his swift ship and shattered it
with his shining thunderbolt in the midst of the wine-dark sea.
Then all the other noble companions perished
but the wind and the wave carried him and brought him here.
I loved him and looked after him, and kept saying
that I would make him immortal and ageless for all time.
But since there is no way for another god
either to circumvent the mind of aegis-bearing Zeus or to nullify it,
let him go, if that god urges and presses him
over the barren sea.
(*Odyssey* 5.129–140)

Other non-mortal women are both seductive and dangerous. It was Circe who warned Odysseus about the Sirens' singing – bewitching and deadly.

First you will come to the Sirens, who enchant all men

who come near them, whatever man approaches them.
Whoever comes upon them unsuspecting and hears the voice
of the Sirens will never be one whose wife and children
crowd around him and rejoice at his returning home.
But the Sirens bewitch him with their clear-toned song
as they sit in a meadow with a great heap of bones all around,
belonging to decomposing bodies of men, while the flesh around (their bones)
shrivels.
(*Odyssey* 12.39–46)

Circe advised Odysseus how to sail past the Sirens without becoming entranced and caught by them: he should stop up the ears of his sailors with wax. Knowing that Odysseus would want nonetheless to hear the song, she advised him to listen but to have himself bound to the mast until they had rowed past danger. He followed her instructions but struggled against the ropes as he heard their summons.

Come here, world-famous Odysseus, great glory of the Achaeans,
stay your ship so that you can hear our voice at closer range.
For no one has ever sailed past here in his black ship
before listening to the honey-sweet song from our lips.
He leaves filled with delight and knowing more than before,
for we know everything that the Achaeans and Trojans
suffered in broad Troy by the will of the gods,
and we know everything that happens on the all-nourishing earth.
(*Odyssey* 12.184–191)

Another danger facing Odysseus and his men was posed by Scylla and Charybdis, deadly female creatures who inhabited two rocky cliffs between which the sailors had to pass. As Circe tells him, Scylla inhabited a cave halfway up one of the rocks.

Therein dwells Scylla, howling fearfully.
Her yelping is that of a young puppy
but she is a terrible monster. No one would be
happy to look at her, not even were a god to encounter her.
Her forelegs are twelve tentacles and wave in the air,
and there are six very long necks, and on each
a frightful head. Inside are crammed three rows of teeth,
closely packed together and full of black death.
Her midriff is tucked inside the hollow cave,

but she sticks out her heads into the terrible abyss
in which she fishes, scouting over the headland
for dolphins and sea-dogs and, if ever she can, a larger creature – a sea-monster –
the myriad creatures that the moaning Amphitrite (i.e., the sea) sustains.
No sailors have ever yet boasted that they escaped unharmed
past her in their vessel, for with each head
she snatches up a man out of his dark-prowed ship.
(*Odyssey* 12.85–100)

On the facing rock was Charybdis, lurking under a large fig tree. Circe warns
Odysseus to steer closer to Scylla than to this deadly creature, who would be
sure to swallow them into her depths.

Beneath (the tree) divine Charybdis sucks down the black water.
Three times a day she belches it out and three times she swallows it down,
terribly. Don't happen to be there whenever she is sucking it down.
For no one would save you, not even the Earth-Shaker (Poseidon).
(*Odyssey* 12.104–107)

Sexual passion entangled mortals, semi-divine creatures and gods alike in
the *Odyssey*. While Odysseus is staying with the Phaeacians and waiting for
them to escort him back to Ithaca, he enjoys the hospitality of King Alcinous.
This includes being entertained by the blind singer Demodocus, who sings of
an adulterous divine pair, Aphrodite the goddess of love and the Wargod, Ares.
Aphrodite is married to the lame Smithygod Hephaistus, who learns of their
affair and takes action. He constructs a finely spun gold web above the bed
where they will make love and pretends to depart from Olympus, which will
encourage the couple to have sex. Once they are entwined together the gold
chains drop down and ensnare them. Hephaistus comes back to the bedroom
and summons the other gods from Olympus.

Father Zeus and the other blessed gods who live forever,
come here! Come so that you may see some action that is both laughable and
intolerable – how Aphrodite, daughter of Zeus, always brings dishonour upon me
for being lame,
but loves the destructive Ares,
because he is handsome and sound of foot, whereas I
was born a weakling. No one else is to blame for my state
but my two parents who ought never to have given birth to me.
But you will see how these two, climbing into my own bed,
sleep in a loving embrace. When I look at them I am full of pain!

I don't expect them to lie like this even a little bit longer,
however much they are passionate lovers. Soon the two of them won't want
to sleep together, but my contrivance and snare will pen them in
until her father gives me back every last bit of the bride-price,
all I gave him as betrothal, for the bitch-faced girl –
his beautiful but insatiable daughter.
(*Odyssey* 8.306–320)

The gods, including Poseidon, Hermes and Apollo, come to see the captured lovers and the enraged Hephaistus. (The goddesses stayed at home out of modesty.) Hermes and Apollo exchange some banter, then Apollo asks Hermes whether he would be willing to be caught up in chains if he could lie with Aphrodite. Hermes is quick to answer.

If this were to come to pass, far-shooting Lord Apollo,
let three times as many inescapable chains hold me all around
and let all you gods and goddesses look on.
I would still lie beside golden Aphrodite!
(*Odyssey* 8.339–342)

This provokes an uproar of laughter among the gods –with the exception of Poseidon, who felt Ares should be released after paying compensation. Hephaistus does not trust the Wargod to pay up, so Poseidon offers to act as guarantor and the two lovers are released. The song concludes with the return of Aphrodite to Cyprus.

She, laughter-loving Aphrodite, went to Cyprus,
to Paphos. Her shrine and her fragrant altar are there.
Then the Graces washed her and anointed her with ambrosial oil
such as coats the gods who live forever,
and they clothed her in lovely garments, a wonder to behold.
(*Odyssey* 8.362–366)

FURTHER READING

Bergren, A. 1979. "Helen's Web: Time and Tableau in the *Iliad*," *Helios* 7, 19–34

Bertolín, R. 2008 ed. *Penelope's Revenge: Essays on Gender and Epic*. Phoenix 62.1, 1–114

Brown, C.G.B. 1989. "Ares, Aphrodite, and the Laughter of the Gods," *Phoenix* 43, 283–293

Cohen, B. 1995. *The Distaff Side. Representing the Female in Homer's* Odyssey. Oxford/New York

Doherty, L. 1995. *Siren Songs. Gender, Audiences, and Narrators in the Odyssey*. Ann Arbor MI

Felson-Rubin, N. 1994. *Regarding Penelope. From Character to Poetics.* Princeton

Helleman, W.E. 1995. "Homer's Penelope: A Tale of Feminine Arete," *Echos du Monde Classique* 14.2, 227–50

Holmberg, I. 1995. "The *Odyssey* and Female Subjectivity," *Helios* 22, 1–21

Katz (Arthur), M.B. 1981. "The Divided World of *Iliad* VI," in H. Foley ed. *Reflections of Women in Antiquity*, 19–44. New York

Meagher, R.E. 2002. *The Meaning of Helen. In Search of an Ancient Icon.* Wauconda, IL.

Murnaghan, S. 1986. "Penelope's Agnoia: Knowledge, Power and Gender in the *Odyssey*," *Helios* 13, 103–115

Roisman, H. 2006. "Helen in the *Iliad. Causa Belli* and Victim of War. From Silent Victim to Public Speaker," *American Journal of Philology* 127, 1–36

Thalman, W.G. 1998. "Female Slaves in the *Odyssey*," in S.R. Joshel and S. Murnaghan (eds) *Women and Slaves in the Greco-Roman Culture: Differential Equations*, 22–34. London/New York

Winkler, J. 1990. "Penelope's Cunning and Homer's," in *Constraints of Desire. The Anthropology of Sex and Gender in Ancient Greece*, 129–161. New/York/London

4

Women and gender in the melic and lyric poets

While the epic poems and hymns were being composed and performed during the 7th and 6th centuries BCE, poets were also working in another genre, creating shorter verses that expressed personal feelings and ideas – which may or may not be those of the poet. We refer to these poems as "lyric" or "melic," reflecting the fact that they were songs, whereas the epic compositions were most likely performed in a lilting voice, like operatic recitativ. Some of the earliest examples of these songs surviving in written form come from the 7th century BCE.

Alcman was a poet composing in Sparta around the middle or later half of this century. We possess fragments of a few of his choral songs for young girls who would sing them at festivals for divinities overseeing their transition from girlhood to womanhood, as preparation for marriage. The songs are called *partheneia* ("maidens' songs").

The following is taken from a *partheneion* performed at an all-night festival in Sparta in which it seems that two semi-choruses of girls were performing competitively – singing, dancing, probably racing, all the while displaying their beauty in public. The girls sing as if in one voice: the praise of their chorus leaders compares their excellence to that of racehorses. References to their beauty are tinged with homoeroticism. The fragmentary nature of the papyrus text and the difficulty of identifying some of the specifically Spartan references leave us with questions of interpretation, but it is clear that the girls are focusing on the physical attributes of the chorus leaders, and that female beauty is on their mind. After a mythical account of a battle between cousins engaged as rivals in the courtship of two Spartan sisters, the girls sing of the beauty and strength of their female chorus leaders.

I sing of the light of Agido.
I see her as the sun, which Agido
calls as witness to shine upon us. Our glorious chorus-leader does not
permit me either to praise or blame her
in any way, for on her own she seems
pre-eminent, just as if one were to set
a horse among the grazing herds,

a strong one, prize-winning, with clattering hoofs –
one of those in winged dreams. Don't you see?
One is a Venetic race-horse. But the hair
of my cousin Hagesichora gleams
like unmixed gold.
And her silver face –
why should I speak openly of it?
Such is Hagesichora.
And the second in beauty after Agido
races like a Colaxian horse beside an Ibenian.
The Peliades, (or Pleiades) fight
against us as we bring a robe (or plough) to (the goddess) Orthria,
rising through the ambrosial night
like the dog-star Sirius.
For there is certainly not an abundance
of purple to defend us,
nor an intricate serpent (bracelet?),
all-gold, nor a Lydian head-band –
the adornment
of dark-eyed maidens,
nor Nanno's hair,
nor again Areta, like to the gods,
nor Sylakis nor Cleësisera.
You would not go to Ainesimbrota's house and say,
"May Astaphis be mine,
and may Philylla look upon me,
and lovely Damareta and Vianthemis.
But it is Hagesichora who watches over me."
(Alcman, *Partheneion* 1.39–77)

In another of Alcman's *partheneia* (even more fragmentary) the girls sing of
shaking sleep from their eyes, hence are likely performing again at an all-night
festival. An ancient source tells us that the particular garland carried by their
chorus leader Astymeloisa was offered to the goddess Hera, honoured in many
rituals as patron of marriage. It is between the girls and Astymeloisa, however,
that gentle erotic desire is expressed. As in the above song, the girls sing with
one voice.

[W]ith limb-loosening desire
she looks at me more tenderly than sleep or death,
nor in vain is she sweet.

Astymeloisa does not answer me at all,
but holding the wreath
like a star flying through radiant heaven
or like a young golden plant, or a soft feather
… she moves through on slender feet
… the moist, delectable perfume of (Cypriot) Cinyras
clings to her maiden locks.
(Alcman, *Partheneion* 3.61–72)

The grace and soft sensuality expressed by the young girls in the *partheneia* of Alcman is often compared to the lyrics of Sappho, the most famous female poet coming down to us from antiquity. She was born on the island of Lesbos and her songs have been dated to the end of the 7th century BCE. We know little of life in Lesbos at the time, apart from the fact that it experienced political turbulence as individual strong men struggled with each other for political control. There is some ancient evidence indicating that Sappho's family belonged to the aristocratic class, and that during some of the Lesbian political turbulence family allegiances led to her being exiled to Sicily. Most of her surviving songs (and all but one are in fragmentary form) are expressed in the personal voice. Whether the voice was intended to be Sappho's own or projected onto a poetic persona we cannot be sure. Many of her songs assume a female listener or audience, and various ideas have been proposed for the context in which they were originally performed. Some have alleged that she was the leader of a female chorus performing at festivals, others that she was a teacher of young women. That some songs express the pain of loss and separation from other women have led some readers to claim that Sappho educated (and became attached to) girls who were on the threshold of marriage and then left her to become wives.

All readers, ancient and modern, are struck by Sappho's poetic mastery. Her aesthetic richness and crystalline imagery, her ability to transform anguish and loss through the poetic imaginary render her verses almost as powerful in translation as in the original Greek. Not infrequently the anguish arises from the absence of another woman, and the homoerotic content of some of these songs by Sappho of Lesbos have given us the word "lesbian" for same-sex female bonding.

Ancient sources tell us that Sappho composed wedding songs, and some scant fragments from these survive. The following short excerpt (a two-line dialogue, all we have of the song) suggests that the bride experiences marriage as an event that takes away from her something that is precious.

(Bride) Maidenhood, maidenhood where have you gone – leaving me behind?
(Maidenhood) Never will I return to you, never will I come (back).
(Sappho, fr. 114V)

The following fragment, which belonged to another wedding song, implies that maidenhood in all its beauty will be dealt with harshly.

Like the hyacinth that the shepherd-men trample
with their feet in the mountains, and the purple blossom
lies on the ground ...
(Sappho, fr. 105cV)

In another fragment from a wedding song, Sappho portrays maidenhood as a fruit that men were eager to pluck.

As the sweet apple ripens on the topmost bough,
on the very topmost one, but the apple-pickers have missed it;
no, they didn't miss it, but they could not reach it.
(Sappho, fr. 105aV)

In a single-line fragment Sappho expresses the poignancy of maidenhood lost.

Do I still yearn for virginity?
(Sappho, fr. 107V)

This fragment, however, offers a gentler picture of the man who gains a bride.

Blest bridegroom! Your wedding has come to pass,
just as you prayed, and you have the maiden you prayed for ...
you are handsome in form, and your eyes ...
gentle, and love is poured over your beautiful face
... Aphrodite has honoured you beyond the rest.
(Sappho, fr. 112V)

The following two songs express the pain of separation between women who are aching for the closeness they once knew. When Sappho inserts her own name we are tempted to understand the composition as reflecting her own experience.

"I simply want to die,"
she said, weeping as she left me.
Much else and this she said to me:
"Alas what horrible things we have experienced,
Sappho. It is certainly true that I leave you unwillingly."

I answered her as follows:
"Go and fare well,
and remember me, for you know how we have cared for you.
But if you don't, I want to remind you
... and we experienced beautiful things.
With many garlands of violets
and of roses and crocuses too
... you placed yourself beside me,
and many woven neck-wreaths
made with flowers
you cast around your tender throat,
and with much ... precious unguent
you anointed yourself, even with royal perfume.
On a soft couch
you ... released your longing
for a tender ...
There was no ...
nor any shrine nor ...
from which we were absent,
nor grove ... dance ..."
(Sappho, fr. 94V 1–28)

In the following (excerpted) fragment, the poet is consoling a woman named
Atthis, who is suffering from the loss of a female companion now in Sardis,
Lydia, on the mainland across from the island of Lesbos.

Sardis ...
often keeping her mind on you
... (she thought of) you like a well-known goddess,
and took particular joy in your song.
But now she stands out among Lydian women,
like the rose-fingered moon
when the sun is setting,
surpassing all the stars.
The light extends over the briny sea
as much as over the fields abundant with flowers.
The dew is poured about in beauty,
roses are blooming and soft chervil
and flowery sweet clover.
She roams back and forth constantly,
calling to mind lovely Atthis,

her tender heart consumed by your fate …
(Sappho, fr. 96V 1–17)

In the next song, Sappho highlights the poignancy of separation from one's beloved by contrasting a woman's assessment of what is most beautiful with the appraisal of men. She cites as a mythical archetype Helen, whose reputation for beauty was unsurpassed, but it is the Spartan queen's passion for Paris that becomes the point of comparison with the "beauty" of desire for the absent Anactoria.

Some men say that a host of cavalry, others of foot-soldiers
and others of ships constitute
the most beautiful thing on the black earth,
but I say
it is what one loves.
It is utterly easy to make this understood
by all, for she who excelled beyond all mortals
in beauty, Helen, … leaving behind
the best of men,
sailed off and went to Troy,
not in the least keeping in mind her child nor her own parents,
but … (Paris? Aphrodite?) carried her off
… And now I remember Anactoria, who is not with me.
I would rather (see) her lovely step
and the sparkle of her face, radiant to look upon,
than the chariots of Lydia and the infantry in arms.
(Sappho, fr. 16V 1–20)

One of the most admired poems to come from Greek antiquity is the song in which Sappho describes the physical symptoms of despair/desire at watching a beloved enjoying a tête-à-tête with a man.

He seems to me to be the equal of the gods
– whoever he is – who sits across from you and listens close by
as you talk sweetly
and laugh enticingly. But for me
this has always set my heart trembling in my breast.
When I look at you for a moment
then it is no longer possible for me to speak.
But my tongue is fractured,
a thin fire straightway steals under my skin,
I see nothing with my eyes,

my ears hum,
sweat pours down (my body) and trembling
seizes me all over. I am paler than grass
and I am little short of dying,
as it seems to me.
(Sappho, fr. 31V 1–16)

In the only one of Sappho's songs to survive in its entirety, the poet engages in conversation with Aphrodite, enlisting her aid as if she were summoning the goddess in a hymn of invocation, to help with a situation where her love is unrequited.

Immortal Aphrodite on your intricately-crafted throne,
child of Zeus, weaver of guile, I beseech you:
do not crush my heart with pain and anguish,
Queen.
But come here, if ever on other occasions too
you heeded my calls,
hearing me from afar. Leaving the golden home
of your father
you came, yoking your chariot.
Beautiful sparrows drew you over the black earth,
whirring on fast-beating wings down from heaven
through mid-air.
They arrived in an instant. And you, oh blessed one,
smiling with your immortal face,
asked what it was that I had suffered this time,
and why I was calling this time,
and what it was in my maddened heart
that I most wanted to happen:
"Whom am I to persuade this time
to draw you back to her love?
Who, Sappho, is wronging you?
Now even if she flees, soon she will pursue;
if she does not receive gifts – well, she will give them;
if she does not love, she will soon love,
even against her will."
Come to me now also, and release me
from my woes, and as much as my heart desires,
bring this about. You, yes you –
be my ally!
(Sappho, fr. 1V)

In another song, Sappho invokes Aphrodite in a very different mood. The poet creates a dream-like reverie in which all the senses are invited to savour the spell of the love goddess.

Come hither to me from Crete, to your holy shrine
where there is a delightful grove
of apple-trees for you and altars smoking
with incense from Lebanon.
Herein cold water ripples through the apple branches,
and the whole place is shaded
with roses. A trance-like sleep
descends through the shimmering leaves.
In this place a horse-pasturing meadow blooms
with spring flowers. Breezes
waft gently
… You, Cyprian one, taking nectar in golden cups,
pour it mingled
with our festivities.
(Sappho, fr. 2V)

The erotic ambience she evokes in this fragment is not the only way in which Sappho characterizes the experience of love. Sometimes it could strike like a violent seizure.

Eros has shaken my wits,
like a wind sweeping down from the mountain and plummeting into the oak trees.
(Sappho, fr. 47V)

Being "shaken" by love can be less violent than by a storm, although it renders one no less captive. Such captivity is not altogether unpleasant, however.

Once again Love, limb-loosener, sets me awhirl –
sweet-bitter, irresistible creeping thing.
(Sappho, fr. 130V)

Sappho's words addressed to others could be bitter as well as sweet. The following fragment condemns to oblivion another woman who lacks poetic talent, to which she refers as "roses from Pieria." By roses she means the gifts of the Muses, the nine female divinities who inspired poets and musicians, and who lived on the mountains of Pieria (near Mount Olympus). Hesiod describes them as the daughters of Mnemosyne ("Memory"), and Sappho was one of several poets who were confident that their own artistry would ensure their immortality, since listeners/readers (like ourselves) would recall their words.

Once you die you will lie (there) and there will be no memory of you,
never, not even later. For you have no share in the roses
from Pieria but, invisible in the house of Hades too,
you will wander among the feeble dead, having fluttered off.
(Sappho, fr. 55V)

If Sappho were indeed a teacher/mentor of young girls (and a 2nd-century BCE papyrus fragment found recently seems to confirm this) the following criticism-in-song could reflect the fact that her instruction included lessons in personal dress and deportment, delivered in a teaching style that could at times be harsh.

What farm-girl has bewitched your mind? ...
wearing the clothes of a bumpkin ...
and not trained to pull her dress up above her ankles?
(Sappho, fr. 57V)

Recently there have come to light two fragments of Sappho's verses, found on a papyrus roll that had been used as mummy wrapping in Egypt. One of these expands a fragment already known, in which an aging woman (Sappho?) regrets the loss of her youth, with its gifts of song and dance and feminine beauty.

[L]ovely gifts, girls, from the (Muses?) of the violet breast-band
the clear-voiced tortoise-shell lyre that loves song
... but already old age ... my skin that once was ...
and my hair has become (grey?) instead of black.
My heart has been made heavy, and my knees do not carry me,
those that once were as agile in the dance as fawns.
I bewail this all the time. But what can I do?
It is not possible for a human to become ageless.
For once, they say, rosy-armed Dawn,
out of love mounted the cup (of the Sun) carrying Tithonus ... to the ends of the earth,
he who was young and handsome. But nevertheless in time
hoary old age snatched him, he who had an immortal wife.
(Sappho, P. Köln 21351 fragments 1 and 2, published in ZPE 147 [2004] 1–8)

Whereas Sappho's verses highlight the delights and despair that came with love relationships, her contemporary and fellow poet from Lesbos, Alcaeus, joined other male poets in the tradition who condemned Helen, the archetypal female who left her husband and followed her heart. The following song is often contrasted with Sappho's fr. 16 (above, p. 37).

[A]nd aroused the heart in the breast
of the Argive woman, Helen, crazed by the man from Troy,
host-cheater, and followed him
over the sea in his ship
leaving her child in her home ...
and the richly-covered bed of her husband.
Her heart persuaded her to (yield to) love,
(and so did) the daughter of Zeus
... many of (Paris') brothers the black earth
holds, brought down on the plain of the Trojans
because of that woman.
And many chariots (fell) in the dust
and many quick-glancing (warriors)
were trampled,
... slaughter.
(Alcaeus, fr. 283V 3–17)

Greek lyric/melic poets in the 7th and 6th centuries shared a number of themes and images in their compositions, recording a range of perspectives on the mythical tradition they had inherited and the experience of love they had known personally or observed in others.

Stesichorus lived and composed songs in the Greek west, and is associated with the colonies that had been founded in southern Italy and Sicily beginning in the 8th century BCE. His life spanned the last third of the 7th century and the first half of the 6th. Ancient sources claim that he was made blind as a result of having composed a song in the Homeric tradition that condemned Helen for her adultery with Paris. He then composed a second song (a "palinode") in which he redeemed her by saying that the real Helen spent the period of the Trojan War in Egypt, and only a ghostly imitation of her went to Troy. As a result of this, Plato tells us, his sight was restored (*Phaedrus* 243a).

In another song, he (to some degree) exonerated both Helen and her sister Clytemnestra for their marital infidelity by explaining that a ritual offence of their father Tyndareus committed against Aphrodite caused his daughters to be "twice and thrice married" and "husband abandoners" (Stesichorus, fr. 223*PMG*).

Ibycus was also born in the Greek west, in southern Italy, but travelled to the Aegean island of Samos to become a poet in the court of the tyrant Polycrates in the latter part of the 6th century BCE. This was an environment (one it shared with Athens) in which many men enjoyed homosexual as well as heterosexual relations. Their description of the love experience has much in common with Sappho's and Alcman's. This is clear from the following fragments of Ibycus.

In spring the Cydonian
apple-trees are watered by river streams,
where stands the
unviolated garden of the Maidens,
and the vine-blossoms bloom,
opening under the shadowy vine-leaves.
But for me Eros
is at rest during no season.
Blazing with lightning
a Thracian north wind,
darting from Aphrodite's Cyprus
with scorching fits of madness,
dark, fearless, it shakes (?) my heart with force,
right from the bottom.
(Ibycus, fr. 286PMG)

Eros, glancing meltingly at me once again
from under his dark eyelids,
casts me into the endless nets
of the Cyprian, with all sorts of magical spells.
I assure you, I tremble at his coming,
like a prize-winning race-horse bearing his yoke and nearing old age
goes unwillingly into the fray with his swift chariot.
(Ibycus, fr. 287PMG)

Euryalus, offspring of the gleaming-eyed Graces,
precious charge of the fair-tressed Hours(?),
you the Cyprian and soft-eyed Persuasion
nursed among rose-blossoms.
(Ibycus, fr. 288PMG)

Anacreon was a poet contemporary of Ibycus, who moved from the East Greek mainland to join Polycrates' court, as Ibycus had done. In the following song, he describes the love-allure from a boy as "maidenly."

O boy, glancing like a maiden,
I am seeking you out but you do not listen,

not knowing that you are
the chariot-driver of my soul.
(Anacreon, fr. 360PMG)

The following song by Anacreon, set in the form a hymn to Dionysus, recalls
Sappho's appeal to Aphrodite to become her ally in pursuit of a beloved. (It
could also suggest that wine would help in the lover's quest.)

Divine lord, with you the tamer Eros
and the dark-eyed Nymphs
and sea-blue Aphrodite
play, while you haunt
the high peaks of mountains.
I beseech you, and do you come to me
with a kindly spirit and, if it pleases you,
hearken to my prayer:
be a good advisor to Cleoboulus,
that he accept my love, Dionysus.
(Anacreon, fr. 357PMG)

Anacreon also composed songs about the male pursuit of young girls. In the
following, he likens a maiden giving chase when pursued to an untamed female colt.

Thracian filly, why do you
look askance at me,
stubbornly running away? Do you think
that I have no skill?
Know this – that I would artfully
throw the bridle on you and,
holding the reins, I would swerve you
around the final turn of the racetrack.
But now you feed on grassy meadows
and play, leaping nimbly,
for you don't have
a skilled rider to mount you.
(Anacreon, fr. 417PMG)

A recent publication of a papyrus from the 2nd century CE has released
the following fragment of Archilochus, a poet from the island of Paros who
composed his lyrics in the 7th century BCE. In this poem, we have an explicit
description of male sexual aggression. Many of Archilochus' poems are "iambic,"

composed in the iambic metre and characterized by invective. The fragmentary remains of this poem pick up a reported dialogue between a reluctant young woman and an impatient lover.

"[H]olding back completely.
And in like manner (I will be?) be full of resolve ...
But if you are eager and your passion drives you
there is in our house
someone who is now full of great desire,
a beautiful tender maiden. In my view
she has a body that is without fault.
Make her your lover."
Such were the things she said. And I answered her:
"Daughter of Amphimedo,
who was a noble and ... woman,
whom now the dank earth possesses,
many are the delights of the goddess
for young men
besides the divine act. One of these will suffice.
But at leisure
whenever it is dark
I and you will take counsel with the god about this.
I shall comply with what you urge me to do.
A great ... me ...
beneath the cornice and under the gates,
don't begrudge me at all, Sweetheart.
I shall aim for the grassy gardens.
Now, understand this.
Let another man take Neobule.
Good grief, she's over-ripe! Twice your age!
Her girlhood flower has disappeared,
along with the grace she possessed in times past.
For there is no satisfying her –
the raving woman has revealed the full measure of her desire.
Let her go to hell! ...
... lest in having such a wife
I become a laughing-stock to my neighbours.
I really want you,
for you are neither untrustworthy nor duplicitous,
whereas she is utterly driven,
and makes many men her lovers.

I fear lest if I move in haste
I, like the bitch, will engender offspring
that are blind and untimely-born."
This is what I said. And taking the girl
in the blossoming flowers
I laid her down. Covering her with a soft cloak,
holding her neck in my arm
as she ceased ...
like a fawn ...
I gently laid my hands on her breasts;
she revealed her young skin,
the early sign of her girlhood prime.
Feeling over her whole beautiful body
I let go my manly force,
touching her golden hair.
(Archilochus, fr. 196M-W = P. Köln 58.1–35, ZPE 14 [1974] 97–112)

Another iambic poet was Hipponax, who lived in Ephesus and composed his verses a century later than Archilochus. Some of his invective that survives is directed against two sculptors, with a few fragments containing crude metaphors for women's sexual positions and actions. The following pair of lines could be read as a capsule of misogyny or, contrariwise, a poignant comment on the situation of women.

There are two days in a woman's life that are sweetest,
whenever she is married and whenever she is carried out dead.
(Hipponax fr. 68W)

Semonides, from the island of Amorgos, probably composing his verses in the 7th century BCE but a generation later than Archilochus, was another iambic poet. The following is an extended fable-like tirade against women, reminiscent of Hesiod.

First the god made the mind of woman a thing apart (or "of various sorts").
One (he fashioned) from the bristly sow.
Throughout her house everything lies soiled with mud,
unkempt, rolling around on the ground.
She herself is unwashed, and in unwashed clothes
grows fat as she sits in the dung.

Another one the god made from a knavish vixen,

a know-it-all woman. Nothing bad
escapes (her calculation) nor anything better.
For of these she often says the latter is bad
and the former is better. She has moods that vary from one moment to another.

This one he made malicious, from a bitch, a copy of her mother.
She hears everything and wants to know everything,
peeping everywhere and wandering around
yapping, even if she sees no one.
A man would not stop her by threatening her,
not even if he were to get furious and dash out her teeth with a stone,
nor by using honey-sweet speech –
not even if he were to come across her sitting with guests.
She keeps up her unmanageable barking non-stop.

Here is one whom the Olympians moulded out of earth
and gave as a feeble creature to man.
Such a woman knows nothing, wicked or good.
The one thing she does know how to do is eat.
And whenever the god produces a harsh winter
then she shivers and draws her stool nearer to the fire.

He made one from the sea, and she has a disposition of two sorts.
One day she laughs and is cheerful;
a visitor who sees her in the house will praise her (saying),
"There is no other wife more desirable than this one,
nor one more beautiful among all humankind."
Then on another day to cast your eyes on her
or to approach her is intolerable; she rages terribly then
just like a bitch around her pups;
she becomes equally rough and unpleasant
to enemies and friends alike.
Just so the sea often stands still without a ripple,
harmless, a kindly delight for sailors
in the summer season, but she often rages,
heaved up by loud-thundering waves.
Such a woman seems most like this
in her temperament: the sea has an erratic nature.

Another he made from the (grey?) ass, oft-beaten.
Under compulsion and after angry threats

she grudgingly puts up with everything, and does her work
satisfactorily. All the while she eats away in the corner,
by day and by night; she also eats by the hearth.
Likewise, when it comes to the act of love-making
she takes as her partner anyone who comes to her.

He made one from a weasel, a disastrous and miserable sort.
Nothing of her is beautiful or desirable,
nothing delightful or pleasant.
She is raving mad for sex,
but she makes the man who is with her sick to his stomach.
She does much harm to her neighbours with her stealing,
and often devours the sacrifices that are unburnt.

This one was born a mare, with a delicate mane.
She circumvents slavish work and misery
and would never lay hands on the mill
nor lift a sieve nor sweep the dung from the house,
nor sit up to the oven, since she avoids the soot.
She makes a man her lover by compulsion.
She washes off the dirt (from herself)
two, sometimes three, times every day, anointing herself with unguent.
She always wears her thick hair combed out
and shaded with garlands of flowers.
Such a woman is a fine sight
for other men but for the one who has her she is a terrible thing,
unless the man is a tyrant or a sceptre-bearer,
someone whose spirit exults in such things.

Another one comes from a monkey.
Zeus sent this one as absolutely the greatest catastrophe for men.
Her face is the ugliest. Such a wife
goes through town a laughing-stock for all.
Short in the neck, she has trouble moving,
no buttocks, all legs. Ah, wretched fellow,
the one who embraces such a disaster.
She knows all sorts of schemes and strategies,
just like a monkey, and she doesn't mind being the butt of laughter.
She wouldn't do a good turn for anyone, but this she pays heed to,
and schemes with this in mind every day, how she might do the greatest harm.

But this one comes from a bee. Whoever gets her is lucky,
for on her alone no blame alights.
One's livelihood flourishes and grows at her hand.
She grows old, in love with a husband who loves her,
and produces offspring handsome and famous.
She stands out among all other women,
and a godlike loveliness encircles her.
She takes no pleasure sitting with other women,
where they talk about sex.
With such women Zeus favours men –
the best and the wisest.

By the devising of Zeus these various other types
are all with men and stick with them.
Zeus made this the greatest burden for men –
women. Even if they seem to be of some benefit,
for the one who has them they become the greatest problem.
For he never goes through a full day carefree;
the one who finds himself with a woman will not easily keep Hunger from his door,
a hateful housemate, an enemy of the gods.
Whenever a man seems most to be enjoying himself
at home, thanks to a fair portion conferred by a god or man,
she arms herself for battle, finding fault with him.
Whoever has a wife would not welcome with enthusiasm
a visitor coming to his house.
The woman who appears to be the most sound-minded –
it is she who turns out to cause the worst ruin.
For while he is incredulous his neighbours
take delight in seeing how he too is off the mark.
Every man will call to mind and praise his own wife,
but will find fault with the wife of another.
We do not recognize that we all have the same fate.
For Zeus made this the greatest calamity
and has fastened around (us) an unbreakable bond, shackles.
Because of this the House of Hades welcomed those men –
fighting over a woman.
(Semonides, fr. 7W)

FURTHER READING

Auanger, L. and N. Rabinowitz. 2002 (eds) *Among Women: From the Homosocial to the Homoerotic in the Ancient World*. Austin, TX

Clark, C.A. 1996. "The Gendering of the Body in Alcman's Partheneion 1: Narrative, Sex, and Social Order in Archaic Sparta," *Helios* 23.2, 143–172

Gerber, D. 1997 ed. *A Companion to the Greek Lyric Poets*. Leiden/New York/Cologne

Greene, E. 1996a ed. *Reading Sappho: Contemporary Issues*. Berkeley, CA

—1996b ed. *Re-reading Sappho: Reception and Transmission*. Berkeley, CA

—and M. Skinner 2009 (eds) *The New Sappho on Old Age: Textual and Philosophical Issues*. Cambridge, MA

Klinck, A. 2008. *Woman's Songs in Ancient Greece*. Montreal/Kingston/London/Ithaca

Lloyd-Jones, H. 1975. *Females of the Species. Semonides on Women*. Park Ridge, NJ

North, H.F. 1977. "The Mare, the Vixen, and the Bee: Sophrosyne as the Virtue of Women in Antiquity," *Illinois Classical Studies* 2, 35–4

Robbins, E. 1994. "Alcman's Partheneion: Legend and Choral Ceremony," *Classical Quarterly* 44.1, 7–16

Schear, L. 1984. "Semonides Fragment 7. Wives and their Husbands," *Echos du Monde Classique* 28, 39–49

Snyder, J. 1997. *Lesbian Desire in the Lyrics of Sappho*. New York

PART 2

THE CLASSICAL PERIOD

5

The lived experiences of girls and women

The following excerpts record some of the features of the lived reality of girls and women in ancient Greece, primarily in Athens but also in other places around the Mediterranean where Greeks had settled. (There are significant differences in the situation of the Dorian women of Crete and Sparta, and these will be considered separately.)

Unfortunately, it is sometimes necessary to have recourse to texts that were composed much later than the experiences they describe, when there are no contemporary records available. This temporal disjunction is mitigated somewhat by the fact that many patterns of social behaviour are slow to change, particularly when reinforced by ritual – as were many experiences of Greek girls and women.

CHILDBIRTH

Probably because of the blood that issues with the newborn, the mother was considered ritually impure, both "polluted" and "polluting." This could last for several days, as we learn from a sacred law from the Greek colony of Cyrene, in North Africa (4th century BCE).

The woman who has just given birth pollutes the house; she pollutes anyone inside the house, but she does not pollute anyone outside the house, unless he comes inside. The person who is inside shall be polluted for three days, but he will not pollute anyone else, no matter where this person goes.
(RO 97iv)

An important figure in childbirth was the woman who assisted the mother in labour and delivery. This could be the mother of the pregnant woman, but was often a woman who specialized in this – a midwife. In his *Theaetetus*, Plato refers to the fact that the mother of Socrates was a midwife, giving the philosopher a familiarity with the credentials and skills of this important figure.

[Soc.] Consider, then, how it is with midwives, and you will easily learn what I want you to. You know, I suppose, that none of them ever tends other women in childbirth so long as she herself can conceive and bear other children, but only when they are unable to give birth.

[Theaet.] Certainly.

[Soc.] They say that the reason for this is Artemis who, being childless, is patroness of childbirth. She did not allow barren women to be midwives, because human nature is weaker than such as would be able to acquire skill in things of which it has no experience. She assigned the privilege to women who were unable to give birth because of their age, out of respect for their likeness to herself.

[Theaet.] That's reasonable.

[Soc.] It is likely, is it not, and inevitable, that pregnant women can be detected by midwives better than others?

[Theaet.] Certainly.

[Soc.] Moreover, in administering drugs and using incantations midwives are able to bring on the labour-pains and make them gentler if they wish, and to bring on the birth from a difficult labour, and at an early stage cause a miscarriage if it seems best to miscarry.

[Theaet.] This is the case.

(Plato, *Theaetetus* 149b–d)

On an Athenian tombstone (mid-4th century BCE) erected for the midwife Phanostrate, the woman is shown seated, clasping the hand of the mother she served, and surrounded by children. Carved on the stone is a couplet that characterizes her as both a midwife and a physician.

Midwife and physician, Phanostrate lies here,
A trouble to no one, but missed by everyone in her death.
(Pleket 1 = Kaibel 45)

On the fifth day after birth the child was carried around the family hearth, a ceremony known as the *Amphidromia*, during which the father would decide whether the newborn would be kept or exposed. The *Suda*, a Byzantine encyclopedia (10th century CE) that drew its information from earlier sources, supplies evidence for this ritual, which took place along with a purification ceremony for the women who had assisted the new mother.

They hold it for newborns on the fifth day, on which they purify the hands that have had contact with the delivery, and they carry the newborn around the hearth, running, and the kinfolk send presents.
(*Suda*, s.v. "amphidromia")

The 4th-century comic playwright Eubulus makes reference to competitive dancing by women at the tenth-day feast after the birth (when the father named the child).

(Probably spoken by the father) So then, women: see now that through the whole night
you dance on the tenth day festival for the baby.
I will lay out the winning prize – three fillets,
five apples and nine kisses.
(Eubulus, *Ancylion* fr. 2 PCG)

CHILDHOOD

From birth to death a freeborn female in Athens was under the supervision of a *kyrios*, the man who was responsible for her maintenance and upbringing as a child, and for all situations in which she would interact with the public, such as marriage or legal transactions. At birth, the girl child's *kyrios* would be her father or, if he had died, her father's brother or her paternal grandfather. At marriage, her husband became her *kyrios*. If she became widowed or divorced, she returned to her original *kyrios* if he was alive, or came under the *kyreia* of her son or the nearest male relative.

Another important figure to a child reared in a house of sufficient means was the nurse. Nurses were often, but not always, wet nurses, and many remained important figures during the adult life of their charges. Such evidence as we have suggests that most were slaves and foreigners, although some were free women forced into the position by economic necessity. The following grave epigram, said to have been found in the Athenian port city of Peiraeus, was for "Malicha", a slavewoman who had been brought to Athens from the Peloponnese. Despite her social status, she is remembered with respect.

Here the earth holds the nurse of the children of Diogeites from the Peloponnesus,
she who possessed the highest moral character, Malicha of Kythera.
(*IG* II² 9112)

The affectionate bond between the nurse and those for whom she cared is reflected in this tombstone epigram, where the woman was depicted seated on a stool and facing her young protegée. It was found in Athens.

Here the earth conceals the loyal nurse of Hippostrate; she now longs for you.
While you lived I loved you, nurse, and still now I honour you
even as you are under the earth, and I will honour you as long as I live.

I know that for your part, even beneath the earth,
If there is a reward for the good,
honours lie in store for you first, in the realm of Persephone and Pluto.
(*IG* II² 7873)

NUBILE YOUNG WOMEN (*"PARTHENOI" OR "NYMPHAE"*)

At the prospect of their nubile energy being harnessed and confined at marriage girls could well have experienced the sense of loss expressed by Sappho's bride who laments the permanent departure of her maidenhood, or Sappho's image of the trampled hyacinth (see above, p. 35).

The apprehension felt by young girls facing marriage is reflected in the many myths in which they are carried off by men – while they are engaged in play with Artemis and her other "nymphs" or (like Persephone) are picking flowers with their girlfriends.

Plutarch (2nd century CE) preserves the story of the abduction of Helen as a girl, when she was dancing in honour of Artemis Orthia.

(Theseus and his friend Peirithöus) went to Sparta together and, seizing the girl when she was dancing in the temple of Artemis Orthia, they fled. Since those who were sent after them in pursuit had followed them no further than Tegea, once they were free they passed through the Peloponnesus and made an agreement, that the one who obtained her by lot should keep Helen for his wife but would assist the other to obtain another wife.
(Plutarch, *Life of Theseus* 31.2)

Apollodorus (2nd century BCE) in his compilation of myths in *The Library* gives us the story of Callisto who, with her son, supplied the names for the constellations Great Bear and Little Bear (Ursa Major and Ursa Minor), the Big and Little Dipper. Callisto was playing with the other nymphs in the company of Artemis when she was raped by Zeus. Intriguingly, the god (in one mythical tradition) disguises himself as the goddess in order to woo her.

She was a huntress with Artemis, wearing the same outfit, and swore an oath with her to remain a *parthenos*. But Zeus, impassioned, made love with her against her will, likening himself – as some say – to Artemis, but as others say, to Apollo. Wishing to escape the notice of Hera, he changed her into a bear. But Hera persuaded Artemis to shoot her with her bow, as a wild beast. There are some who say that Artemis shot her because she did not defend her maidenhood. When Callisto perished, Zeus snatched her child, named it "Arcas"

and gave it to Maia in Arcadia to rear. But Callisto he turned into a star and
called it the Bear.
(Apollodorus, *The Library* 3.8.2)

MARRIED LIFE

A marriage was initiated by the *kyrios* of the future bride. He selected her future
husband and contracted the betrothal with the pledge of a dowry (in all but
the most impoverished families). That the ultimate purpose of marriage was
the continuation of the family is reflected by these words found in a play of
Menander's (4th century BCE) that sealed the pledge. The purpose of marital sex is
likened to sowing seeds in the earth, an image that recurs in several ancient texts.

[Pataikos] Listen to what I say: I give you this girl for the plowing of legitimate
children.
[Polemon] I take her.
[Pataikos] And a dowry of three talents.
[Polemon] I'm grateful to you.
(Menander, *Perikeiromene* 1012–1015)

The wedding ceremony did not include a legal registration of the marriage.
Proof of this bond, if required, was sought from those who had been present
at a series of events culminating in the procession that took the bride from her
family home to that of the groom.

    Some time after the betrothal the bride and groom met and the bride lifted
the veil from her face, in the richly symbolic act of the *anakalypterion*. She was
no longer hidden from his view. A Greek mythical account of the wedding
between the Skygod Zas (= Zeus) and the Earth goddess Chthonie was recorded
by the 6th-century philosopher Pherecydes of Syros. After the marital house
was arranged Zas presented a robe to his bride, embroidered with the principal
elements of the cosmos. This initiates the "unveiling."

When everything was ready they held the wedding. And then came the third day
of the wedding; at this moment Zas made a robe, large and beautiful, and on it
he embroidered the Earth, Heaven and the domain of Ocean. [*The text is broken
here.*]… "Wishing to marry you I honour you with this. Greet me and be my wife."
This, they say, was the first unveiling (*anakalypteria*). From this it became a custom
among gods and men. She replied, receiving the robe from him. [*The text breaks off
again at this point.*]
(Pherecydes of Syros, Schibli 68 = fr. 2DK)

The wedding procession was an occasion for a public display of the nuptial couple. Some descriptions indicate that it took place at night by torchlight and with a certain amount of noise, together with ritual singing by unmarried girls.

In the *Iliad* the poet describes the shield of Achilles that was forged by Hephaistus to replace the armour that the hero had lost in the battle at Troy. On the shield,the smithy depicts wedding processions in a way that highlights their public nature and the commotion they stir.

On it he fashioned two beautiful cities of mortal men.
In the one there were weddings and feasts.
They were leading the brides from their maiden chambers
with blazing torchlight through the city, and a great sound of the bride-song started up.
Youths whirled as dancers, and among them
the pipes and lyres kept up their sound. The women
standing in the doorways marveled, each one,
and there was a crowd of people assembled in the market-place.
(*Iliad* 18.490–497)

Sappho, in a song whose metre and language reflect epic style, describes the wedding procession of Hector and Andromache, when the Trojan prince is introducing his bride to the city. (The text is fragmentary.)

Hector and his companions are bringing the quick-glancing girl
from holy Thebe and Plakia ...
gentle Andromache, in their ships over the briny sea.
There are many golden bracelets
and purple (scented?) garments, elaborate adornments,
countless silver drinking-cups and ivory.
So (the herald) spoke. Nimbly his dear father rose up
and the news went to his friends through the city with wide dancing places.
Right away the descendants of Ilus led the mules
to the smooth-running women's carriages, and the entire throng
of women and maidens with them, (slender?)-ankled. ...
And the sweet-sounding pipe and the (lyre?) were mingled together,
and the sound of castanets. All the while maidens sang
a hymn, and a wondrous sound reached the sky.
(Sappho fr. 44V 5–15, 24–26)

Like the modern tradition of showering the bride and groom with confetti or rice the spectators of the Greek wedding procession pelted the couple with flowers and fruit, signifying their wish for the couple's fertility. This is captured in a fragment of Stesichorus (7th–6th century BCE) that describes the wedding of Helen and Menelaus.

Many were the Cydonian apples they threw at the chariot of the king
and many leaves of myrtle
and rose-garlands and braided wreaths of violets.
(Stesichorus fr. 187PMG)

The last song in Sappho's book of wedding songs would have been sung outside the door of the nuptial bedroom.

[M]aidens …
celebrating the all-night vigil …
let them sing of your love and
that of the violet-sashed bride.
     But awake! Go to the bachelors
who are your age-mates, so that
we may see less sleep
than the clear-voiced (songbird).
(Sappho, fr. 30V)

The next day gifts would be brought, primarily to the bride. This was called the *epaulia*, and the gifts would consist of such items as clothing, perfumes, chests, toiletry bottles etc.

When a young Athenian woman married she was expected to observe strict sexual fidelity to her husband. He would not be so constrained, however, and would have ready access to a variety of sexual partners, including the household slaves (male and female), adolescent boys and prostitutes (male and female). A much quoted expression of the various services offered married men by the different categories of women available to them (wife, concubine, prostitute) is found in the courtroom speech that ends a legal challenge involving the courtesan/freedwoman Neaera (see below, p. 113).

What was life like for a married woman in an Athenian household (one with enough means to afford slaves)? From the *Oeconomicus* composed by the historian Xenophon (5th/4th century BCE), we have a purported conversation between Socrates and the newly-married Athenian Ischomachus, about his expectations for his young bride.

[Soc.] I would be very pleased to know from you, Ischomachus, whether you yourself taught your wife to be the sort of woman she needed to be or whether you took her when she had learned from her father and mother how to manage her affairs in a household.

[Isch.] Socrates, what could she have learned when I took her to wife, she who came to me when she was not yet 15 years of age, and had lived in the previous period under a watchful eye so as to be seen and heard and to ask questions as little as possible? Does it not seem appropriate to you for her to come to me knowing only how to take wool and produce a cloak, and to have seen how spinning tasks are given to the female slaves? As for eating, Socrates, she came well trained in every respect, and as for me, I think that is very important instruction for a man and woman alike.

[Soc.] Ischomachus, did you train your wife in other respects so that she would be capable of taking care of other matters that concern her?

[Isch.] No, by Zeus, not before I sacrificed and prayed that I would manage to teach, and she to learn, what was best for us both.

[Soc.] Well, then, did your wife sacrifice with you and pray with you for these same things?

[Isch.] Very much so, and she vowed to the gods that she would become the sort of wife she should be. She was clear that she would not be careless when it came to the things that she had been taught.

[Soc.] By the gods, tell me what you began to teach her first, since I would rather hear you give an account of this than describe the finest performance in athletics or horse-training.

[Isch.] Socrates, since she was already submissive and domesticated sufficiently to converse with me, I asked her something like the following:

"Tell me, wife, have you ever thought about why I married you and why your parents gave you in marriage to me, given that there was no problem in (finding) someone else with whom we might share a bed – I know that this is obvious to you as well. For my part I considered, and your parents considered on your behalf, who would be the best partner for us to choose for a household and children. I chose you, and your parents – it seems – chose me from among the other potential partners. Were the god to grant us children one day, then we will consider how we shall train them in the best way. This will also be of benefit for both of us, to obtain the best allies and caregivers in our old age. But at the present moment this household is one we jointly share. I declare everything I have I contribute to our common property, and you have deposited everything you brought as jointly owned. We don't need to reckon with accuracy which one of us has contributed more, but we ought to be well aware of this, that whichever one of us proves to be the better partner is the one who contributes what is of greater value."

In reply to this my wife answered the following, Socrates. "What could I do to assist you? What ability do I have? Everything is in your hands. My mother said that my task was to exercise self-control."

"By Zeus, Wife," I said, "my father told me the same thing. But self-control, surely, for man and wife amounts to acting so that the property will be in top condition and that more will be added to it, as much as possible, by noble and just means."

"And what," my wife said, "do you see that I might do that would improve the estate?"

"By Zeus," I said, "What the gods gave you by nature to be able to do, and what the law approves of your doing – try to do this as well as possible."

"And what is that?" she said.

"I suppose," I said, "that these are not inconsequential things, unless you were to think that the queen bee in the hive attends to chores that are inconsequential." "Wife," I said, "the gods seem to have put together this yoke which is called male and female with the greatest prudence, so that it would be most beneficial for each in the partnership. For first, the yoke is in place so that the race of living creatures not fail, as the couple produces children with each other. Then the acquiring of caregivers in old age is afforded to them by this yoke, at least in the case of humans."

"Then the lifestyle for humans is not as it is for herds in the open air, but the fact that they need a roof over their heads is obvious. There is need, however, for those who intend to have something they (can) bring into the shelter, to have someone working at the outdoor tasks. For plowing, sowing, planting and herding – these are all outdoor chores. From these the necessities of life come about. Moreover, whenever these things are brought into the house then someone is needed to conserve them and to do the work that must take place under the roof. Shelters are needed for the nursing of newborns, and shelters are required for the production of bread from grain. Just so is the production of clothing from wool. Since both indoor and outdoor chores require effort and care, I think the god designed the nature of woman right off, as it seems to me, for indoor tasks and concerns, and that of men for outdoor work. He designed the body and soul of a man to better endure the turns of cold and heat and traveling and military campaigns. Thus he assigned outdoor work to the man. But having created the body of a woman as less able to endure these, the god – it seems to me – evidently assigned the inside tasks to her. Knowing that he had implanted in the woman and assigned her the nurturing of newborn children, he apportioned to her a greater share of affection for infants than he gave to a man. Since he had assigned to the woman the guarding of what is brought inside, knowing that being fearful is not a particularly bad thing for guarding, he apportioned a greater share of fear in the woman than in the man. And knowing that the person doing the outside work would need to act in defence if someone was committing a wrong, he apportioned a greater share of courage in him."

"Because it is necessary for both to give and take, he implanted memory and attentiveness in both in equal measure. The result is that you would not be able to decide whether the female sex or the male exceeds in this. And to be self-controlled when this is required he established it in equal measure in each; whichever one was better in this, the man or the woman, the god granted the privilege of carrying off more of the advantage derived from it. Since the implanting of natural ability is not of the same quality in all respects, because of this they need one another more and the yoke becomes more beneficial to each, inasmuch as the one falls short where the other is able."

"Now, Wife, knowing what has been assigned to each of us by the god, we must try, each of us, to carry out our duties as well as possible. The law agrees with this, for it yokes husband and wife, and just as the god made them partners in parenting, so does the law establish them as partners in the household. The law endorses as honourable in what respects the god has enabled each to excel. For the wife it is more noble to remain inside than to be outdoors, but for the husband it is more shameful to stay indoors than to take care of things outside. If someone does something contrary to what the god implanted by nature, perhaps in rebelling he will not escape the notice of the gods and will pay the penalty for neglecting the chores assigned to him or for doing the work of his wife. It seems to me that the queen bee toils away at the tasks laid out by the god."

My wife asked, "In what way does the queen bee resemble in her work the tasks which I must do?"

I said, "It is because she remains in the hive and does not allow the bees to be lazy, but sends those who must work outside out to their labour, and she knows what each of them brings back in and takes it from them and preserves this until it is necessary to use it. When the time comes for using it, she distributes a fair share to each one. She supervises those inside who are weaving the wax combs, so that they are woven beautifully and swiftly, and she pays attention to the offspring, seeing that they are nurtured. When the young ones have been reared and are able to work, she sends them off to found a home with a leader for the new brood."

My wife asked, "Will it be necessary for me to do this too?"

I said, "Certainly it will be necessary for you to remain inside and to send outside those of the household slaves whose work is outdoors; those whose work must be done inside you must supervise. You must receive what is brought in and distribute what of this must be consumed, but what one must keep as surplus you need to think ahead and guard, lest the supply for a year be consumed in a month. Whenever wool is brought in to you, you must take care that there are clothes for those who need them. You must take care that the dry grain is good and edible. One of your responsibilities will perhaps seem to be unrewarding, namely that if one of the slaves becomes ill you must be concerned about nursing any of them."

"Not at all," said my wife. "It will be most rewarding if those who are well nursed will be grateful and will be better disposed toward me than before."

I was thrilled with her answer. (7.4–38)

Ischomachus returns to the analogy with the beehive, and his wife concurs that her role will be to process and care for the goods he brings in from the outside. He then turns to other tasks he expects of her.

"There are other particular responsibilities belonging to you that turn out to be pleasant: whenever you take a slave who knows nothing about spinning and make her skilled and she becomes twice as valuable to you; whenever you take one who doesn't know how to manage housekeeping and serving and she is made a skilled and loyal servant and you then have one who is invaluable; and whenever you can reward the prudent and helpful ones in your household, and you are able to punish one who appears to be a trouble-maker. But this is the sweetest experience of all – if you appear to be better than I, and make me your servant. You mustn't fear lest as your youthfulness passes you by you will become less honoured in the household, but believe that as you age to the degree that you both become a better partner for me and a better guardian of the property for our children, you will have that much more honour in the household. Noble and good things are not the result of youthful bloom but they increase for humans by their excellence throughout their life." (7.41–43)

Ischomachus continues his instruction, requesting that his wife avoid disorder and confusion in the household: like order in the military or on board a ship, everything is to have its place. After a tour of the house, where he demonstrates that the door to the women's quarters is locked and bolted to keep it separate from the men's, he points out the location of the domestic tools and the importance of the housekeeper. The wife will be overseer of all, like the inspector of a garrison. When the wife agrees to these terms, Socrates comments that she has a "masculine mind" (10.1). As a demonstration of her obedience to his word, Ischomachus highlights the following example:

One time, Socrates, I saw that she had rubbed her face with a lot of white lead so that she might appear paler than she was, and a great deal of alkanet (red colouring), so that she might appear rosier than she really was, and she wore sandals with elevated heels so she might seem taller than she was by nature. "Tell me," I said, "wife, whether you would decide that I was more worthy of loving as co-owner of our possessions were I to show the property as it is, and neither boasted that I had more nor concealed any of it – or were I to try to deceive you by saying that I had more than I have, and by showing counterfeit money and gilt wooden necklaces and purple-dyed raiment that would fade, claim that they were the real thing?" And she answered right away: "Hush!," she said, "don't be like that, for I certainly would not be able to love you from my heart if you were such a man."

"Wife," I said, "was it not the case that we came together as a couple sharing our bodies with each other?"

"That's what people say," she said.

"Well then," I said, "would I seem to be more deserving of love as a sexual partner if I were to try to offer you my body, looking after it so that it was healthy and fit, and because of this sporting the actual complexion for you to see? Or if I showed myself to you smeared with red ochre and coating my eyes with flesh-coloured paste and I presented myself to you and made love to you while deceiving you, offering you red ochre to touch and see instead of my skin?"

"I would not enjoy," she said, "touching red ochre rather than you, or seeing flesh-coloured paste rather than your own skin, nor would it be pleasurable to see your eyes made up rather than healthy."

"Wife," (he said) "reflect that I too would not take pleasure in the colour of white lead or rouge rather than your own colour, but just as the gods have made horses more attractive to horses, cattle to cattle and sheep to sheep, so do humans think of the human body as most attractive when it is unadulterated. These deceptions might be able to deceive strangers, I suppose, since they have no proof, but it is inevitable that those who are always together will be caught if they try to deceive each other. For either they are found out when they get up from bed before they get dressed, or they are caught out by sweat or put to the test by tears or recognized for who they really are when they bathe."

[Soc.] What, by the gods, did she say in answer to this?

[Isch.] What indeed, except that she never put on any of that get-up after that, but tried to present herself unadorned and in an appropriate manner. She asked me, however, if I might have some advice on how she might appear really beautiful, and not only seem to be. And I advised her, Socrates, not to always sit down like a slave, but with the gods' help to try to stand over the loom like a mistress and teach whatever she knew better than another, and to learn what she knew less well. She should oversee the baker, stand beside the housekeeper when she was measuring out supplies, and go around keeping an eye on whether everything was in the place where it ought to be. These tasks, it seems to me, take care of both responsibilities and getting exercise. I told her that mixing flour and kneading bread and shaking and folding clothing and bedding were good exercise. I said that when she had exercised in this way eating would be more pleasurable and she would be healthier and she would really have better colour. The appearance of a wife, when rivaling that of a servant-girl, a wife who is not dolled-up and is more suitably dressed, becomes more enticing, especially when she is also willing to please instead of submitting under compulsion. (10.2–13)
(Xenophon, *Oeconomicus*)

It may be that Ischomachus' lessons ultimately fell on deaf ears. From the 5th century orator Andocides (*On the Mysteries*, 124–127) we are told that our Ischomachus' wife was named Chrysilla, and her daughter married the well-known Athenian Callias. Within a year of the marriage Callias was having sex with both the daughter and her mother. The daughter, after trying to hang herself, fled, and Chrysilla had a son by her son-in-law.

WOOL-WORKING

Working at the loom, as Ischomachus reminded his bride, was an essential activity of women in the Greek world. Girls, wives and household slaves transformed raw wool by carding, spinning and weaving it into clothes and textiles for the household. Wool working also provided a source of income when this was required. The intricacy of weaving and the fact that women worked together at the loom led to its metaphorical association with story-telling but also with guile (comparable to the intricate fabric they produced). The chorus in Euripides' tragedy *Ion* are slaves working at the loom of their mistress Creusa, and reflect on the tales that were told and retold as they worked.

Is he the one whose tale was told as I stood beside my threads,
shield-bearing Iolaos who joined the son of Zeus in shouldering his labours?
(196–200)

And further:

Neither with shuttle in hand nor in the tales (woven) did I hear a story
that children born of gods shared good fortune with mortals.
(Euripides, *Ion* 506–508)

The myth of the sisters Philomela and Procne reflects the fact that the activity of weaving provided women with a means of telling their own stories when they were otherwise silenced. Unable to speak, Philomela weaves the story of the cruel treatment she suffered at the hands of her sister's husband, and Procne takes revenge. The story is told here by Apollodorus.

(Pandion) gave Procne to Tereus in marriage. From her he had a son Itys and, falling in love with Philomela he raped her, saying that Procne had died, hiding her in the country. He cut out (Philomela's) tongue. But she, weaving images in a robe, by these means she brought to Procne's attention her own circumstances. Procne, having sought out her sister, killed her son Itys, boiled him and set him out as dinner for the unsuspecting Tereus. Then she fled in haste with her sister.
(Apollodorus, *The Library* 3.14.8)

Xenophon, in his *Memorabilia*, describes a conversation between Socrates and Aristarchus, an Athenian citizen who was obliged to take in his female relatives when he was suffering financially under the constraints of wartime. Aristarchus was ill equipped to support them and he seeks advice from Socrates when household tensions were running high. Socrates' advice is to get them engaged in the traditional work of women – weaving:

What they know how to do seems to be the most honourable and the most proper for women. And they all work at what they know how to do with the greatest ease and speed, work that is most beautiful and brings the greatest pleasure. So don't hesitate to introduce to them something that will bring profit both to you and to them, and it is likely that they will take up your proposal with enthusiasm. (2.7.10)

The proposal is implemented, and Xenophon reports on what happens:

As a result capital was provided, wool was purchased and they worked while eating lunch, then stopped at dinnertime. Instead of being ill-tempered they were

delighted; instead of being jealous they looked at each other with smiles. They loved (Aristarchus) as a guardian, and he loved them for they were useful.
(Xenophon, *Memorabilia* 2.7.12)

An inscription (after mid-4th century BCE) accompanies a dedication to Athena (patron of crafts), reflecting the fact that some women could support their families with the work of their hands.

Melinna, having raised her children with her hands and through the skills applied to her labours, and through righteous undertakings, set up this memorial to you, Athena, goddess of handiwork, offering a share of the possessions she earned, in honour of your favouring.
(*IG* II² 4334 = *CEG* 774)

PREGNANCY

For success in becoming pregnant and for safe delivery in childbirth, married women turned to the gods. They might travel to a sanctuary of the god of healing, Asclepius (son of Apollo), for help with conception and birth. The following inscription comes from the god's large shrine at Epidaurus, in which suppliant women would, with others seeking healing, sleep, and via this "incubation" hope to be successful in their petition. The following inscriptions, erected at Epidaurus and dated *c.* 320 BCE – despite their fantastical elements – attest to this practice.

Cleo was pregnant for five years. When she had been pregnant for five years she came as a suppliant to the god and slept in the inner room. As soon as she went out from here and was away from the shrine, she gave birth to a son. He, straightway after he was born, washed himself off from the spring and immediately crawled around his mother. In receipt of these things she wrote on the dedication: "Not the size of this tablet is the wonder, but the divinity, since Cleo was pregnant with the weight in her womb for five years, until she slept in the shrine and (the god) made her healthy."
(*RO* 102.3–9)

A second inscription also describes a successful incubation at Epidaurus, where the god appears to be a little pedantic.

A three-year pregnancy. Ithmonica of Pellene arrived at the shrine because of offspring. Lying down to sleep she saw a dream: it seemed to her that she asked the god that she might conceive a daughter, that Asclepius said that she would get

pregnant, and if she asked for anything else that this too would be granted to her. But she said that she had need of nothing else. Becoming pregnant she carried a child in her womb for three years, until she approached the god as a suppliant over giving birth. Lying down to sleep she saw a dream. It seemed that the god inquired of her whether all she had asked for had not happened and had she not become pregnant? About the birth of the child she had added nothing (in her request). And he had asked her this, whether she needed anything else, and he had said that he would do this also. But since she was now present as a suppliant over this he said that he would accomplish this for her too. After this she left the inner room in haste. When she was outside the sanctuary she gave birth to a daughter.
(RO 102.10–22)

That many Greek women died in childbirth is widely attested. Whether they survived or died, their clothing might be dedicated to Artemis. If they did not survive, this was often referred to as being struck by the arrows of the goddess. The following epigram commemorates a successful birth.

Artemis, the son of Cichesias has dedicated these sandals to you,
and Themistodike her simple folded robe
because, Lady, you held your two hands over her gently
when she was in labour, coming without your bow.
Artemis, grant to Leon that he yet see his infant son
grow into a youth strong in limb.
(AP 6.271)

CONCUBINES (*PALLAKAI*)

A concubine (*pallake*) was most likely a free woman without the status that would enable her to obtain a legal marriage, such as a foreigner ("metic", see below, pp. 94–7). She could still be in a common-law relationship with a man that was established by contract (whether formalized or not), parallel to a marriage sealed with a dowry and the appointment of a man as the woman's *kyrios*. The orator Isaeus confirms this in a courtroom speech.

Even men who give their female relatives into concubinage first come to an agreement about what will be given to them as concubines.
(Isaeus, *On the Estate of Pyrrhus* 39)

It would seem from the law on homicide quoted in Demosthenes' speech *Against Aristocrates* that concubines could be mothers of legitimate children (although Pericles' citizenship law of 451/450 BCE stipulated that for this to happen both parents had to be legitimate Athenians). Concubines were treated no less than wives as sexual property.

If a man kills another unintentionally in the athletic games, or by overcoming him on the road, or in battle while not recognizing him, or while (he is having sex) with his wife or mother or sister or daughter or with the concubine whom he kept for producing legitimate children, he shall not go into exile for the killing on these grounds.
(Demosthenes, *Against Aristocrates* 53)

The text of Aristotle's will, recorded by Diogenes Laertius, makes it clear that at least by the mid-4th century BCE not only wives but concubines could inherit property.

The executors and Nicanor remembering me and also Herpyllis, who has been attentive to me, should take care of her in other ways and if she wishes to take a husband, shall give her to someone not unworthy of me. In addition to the other things that she has received earlier they should give her a talent of silver from the estate, and three handmaids, those whom she wishes, along with the female slave that she has now, and the slave Pyrrhaeus.

And if she wishes to live in Chalcis, she is to have the guesthouse by the garden. But if she prefers to live at Stagira, she is to have my father's house. Whichever of the two she chooses, the executors are to equip it with furniture that seems to them suitable and that is sufficient in Herpyllis' view.
(Diogenes Laertius, *Lives of Famous Philosophers* 5.13–14)

WIFE-ABUSE

Because Athenian married men had ready access to a variety of sexual partners outside marriage without incurring the charge of adultery (unless they engaged in sexual activity with a married woman) wives were often passed over in favour of others. A flagrant display of this comes up for criticism in court, when Demosthenes attacks Apollodorus, son of Archippe and Phormio (the defendant).

Now you wear a soft cloak, and you have freed one *hetaera* and given another in marriage – and doing this when you have a wife – and you go around with three boys for your attendants, and live wantonly for all to see.
(Demosthenes, *For Phormio* 45)

The behaviour of Alcibiades toward his (wealthy) wife Hipparete was, like many of his other actions, notorious.

Hipparete, a well-behaved and affectionate wife, grieving over (Alcibiades) on account of his liaisons with courtesans – foreign and local – left the house and went to live with her brother. Alcibiades did not mind this, but lived wantonly. So she had to place her plea for divorce before the archon, and do it not through others but in person herself. When, therefore, she was out in public to do this in keeping with the law, Alcibiades came up to her and seized her and went bringing her home through the marketplace, with no one daring to confront him or take her away. She remained with him nonetheless until her death, and she died not long afterward when Alcibiades went and sailed to Ephesus.

This violence did not appear to be at all outside the law or inhuman. For the law seems to have this purpose, that the woman who wants a divorce goes ahead to the court in person, so that the husband may come upon her and get possession of her.
(Plutarch, *Life of Alcibiades* 8.4–6)

ADULTERY

A courtroom defence speech composed by the orator Lysias exposes a marriage in which the wife is engaged in an adulterous relationship. Her husband Euphiletus, whom Lysias is defending, has killed her lover, Eratosthenes. Some details of the speech imply that the prosecution is alleging that Euphiletus lured the lover into the bedroom, having other motives for murdering him. The defendant is careful to make it clear to the jury that he can provide witnesses for his actions. The speech is delivered by Euphiletus.

Members of the jury, when I decided to marry and I brought my wife to the house, at that time then I conducted myself so as not to harass her – but she was not to do for herself whatever she wanted to. I kept watch over her as much as possible, and paid attention to her, as was appropriate. When a child was born I trusted her and I handed over all my possessions to her, thinking that this was a marriage that was ideal. At first, men of the jury, she was the best of all women, a clever house-keeper, good at economizing and scrupulous at managing everything. But when my mother died, her death became the source of all my troubles. At the procession to the tomb, as she was accompanying the body, my wife was seen by this man, and in time she was seduced. He kept a lookout for the maid who goes to market and propositioned her, corrupting her.

First of all, gentlemen, for I should explain this to you, I have a little house with two floors, equal in size, with the women's quarters upstairs and the men's quarters downstairs. When the baby was born his mother nursed it. So that she not risk having to go downstairs whenever she had to bathe him I lived upstairs and the women downstairs. And so it was customary for my wife to leave often, to sleep with the baby so that she could give it her breast and it wouldn't cry. And thus it went on for a considerable time and I was never suspicious, but I was so foolish that I thought that my wife was the most virtuous woman in the city.

But time went on, and once when I came in unexpectedly from the farm after dinner the baby began crying and whimpering – because it had been deliberately provoked by the housemaid to do this. The man was inside, you see. Later I learned it all. I told my wife to go and nurse the baby, to stop it from howling. At first she refused, alleging that she was glad to see me after being away for so long. Then I got angry, and ordered her to go.

"Oh sure," she said, "so that you can get your hands on the young maid here! On an earlier occasion too, you got drunk and mauled her."

I laughed. She stood up and went out, closing the door, pretending to be playful, and drew the bolt.

I didn't worry about this at all, nor was I suspicious, being eager for sleep after coming in from the farm. When it was near daybreak she came and opened the door. I asked her why the doors were making a noise during the night. She said that the lamp beside the baby had gone out, so she got a light from the neighbours. I said nothing and thought this was really the case. She seemed to me, gentlemen of the jury, to have put makeup on her face, although her brother had been dead not yet thirty days. Nevertheless, despite this, saying nothing about this matter I left and went out, in silence.

After this, gentlemen, a period of time went by, while I was totally unaware of the troubles surrounding me. An old slave-woman approached me, sent by a woman with whom that man was committing adultery, as I later found out. The woman was angry and thought that he had wronged her because he no longer visited her as often, and she was keeping a watch on him until she figured out the cause. The slave-woman, who had been on the lookout for me near my house, approached me. "Euphiletus," she said, "don't think that it is from a desire to interfere that I have come to you. The man who is committing adultery with your wife happens to be an enemy of ours. If you grab the housemaid who goes to the market and waits on you, and you question her, you will learn the whole story. It is Eratosthenes from

Oea," she said, "the one doing this, who not only has corrupted your wife but other women as well. He makes this his business."

Saying this, gentlemen, she went off. I was immediately upset. Everything came back to my mind, and I was full of suspicion, upset at being locked in the bedchamber, recalling that during that night the inner door creaked, as well as the outer one – something that has never happened – and how it seemed to me that my wife was wearing makeup. All this came into my mind, and I was full of suspicion. Going home, I ordered the housemaid to follow me to the market, but I led her instead to the house of one of my friends, saying that I had learned everything that had taken place in the house. "It is up to you," I said, "to choose one of two options, either to be flogged and be thrown into the treading-mill and never to be released from being bound to these tortures, or to confess the whole truth and suffer no punishment but to be forgiven by me for your mistakes. "Don't lie about anything, but tell the whole truth."

At first she denied it, and told me to do what I liked – for she knew nothing. But when I drew her attention to Eratosthenes, and said that he was the one visiting my wife, she was struck dumb, thinking that I had learned every last detail. Then, falling at my knees and exacting from me a pledge that she would suffer no harm, she accused him first of following (my wife) after the funeral procession and then (confessed) how finally she acted as go-between, and how over time my wife was persuaded. She described the means by which he got in, and how she had gone to the temple at the Thesmophoria with his mother when I was away at the farm. And she related all the other events that had happened in detail. When she had told everything I said, "See to it that no one knows about this; otherwise, nothing of the agreement I made with you will be in place. I think it is a good idea for you to show me these things actually happening; I have no need of words; I want the deed to be exposed, if it is as you say."

She agreed to do this and four or five days went by [text missing], as I will show you with important evidence. First I want to relate the events of the last day. Sostratos was a neighbour and friend of mine. I met him at sunset, as he was coming home from the farm. Knowing that in coming home at that time of day none of the necessities would be available I invited him to dine with me. Coming to my place, we went upstairs and dined in the upper storey. When he had had enough to eat, he got up and left, and I went to sleep.

The dinner with Sostratus would provide Euphiletus with the alibi that he was occupied when Eratosthenes came into the house, and could not have been actively engaged in luring him into the house. The narrative continues:

Now, gentlemen, Eratosthenes came in, and the housemaid woke me and immediately told me that he was inside. I told her to take care of the door, and I went downstairs and outside quietly. I came to the house of this and that person; some I found inside, others were not at home. Taking as many as I could from those who were available I proceeded. Getting torches from the shop nearby we went inside. The door had been opened, as pre-arranged with the housemaid. Opening the door of the bed-chamber, the first to go in saw him lying beside my wife, and those who came after saw him standing naked on the bed. I, gentlemen, struck him and knocked him down, then pulled his hands around behind his back and tied them. I asked him why he was committing this outrage against me, entering my house. He admitted that he was guilty, but he begged me and entreated me not to kill him, but to settle for some money. But I replied, "It is not I who am killing you but the law of the city, which you in disobeying considered less important than your own pleasure. You preferred to commit such a crime against my wife and against my children rather than to obey the laws and to be decent."

So, gentlemen, the man met with the outcome that the law prescribes for men doing such things. He was not seized off the street nor having taken refuge at the hearth, as these men say. For how could it be, when the man who was struck in the bedroom fell at once, and I tied his hands behind his back? When there were so many men inside that he could not escape, and he had neither iron nor wood, nor anything else with which he could have defended himself against those who entered the room? But, gentlemen, I think and you know that those who commit a wrong do not agree that their opponents speak the truth, but by lying and contriving such arguments they arouse the anger of the listeners against those doing what is right. First, then, read the law. (6–28)

The Homicide Law, inscribed on the pillar of the court of the Areopagus, was read at this point. It permitted the *kyrios* of the woman a choice among possible penalties, including killing her lover. Witnesses were brought into the courtroom, presumably those whom Euphiletus had fetched after his dinner with Sostratus. He points out to the jurors that capital punishment was endorsed by the law.

You hear, gentlemen, that it has been decreed explicitly by the Court of the Areopagus itself, which – as both traditional and contemporary – has been granted the right to try cases of homicide, that one cannot convict a man for murder when he catches an adulterer with his wife and inflicts this punishment. And the Lawgiver thought so firmly in the case of lawfully wedded wives that these provisions were just that he put in place the same punishment in the case of concubines, who are of less worth. And further, it is clear that if he had had access to a more severe punishment in the case of married women he would have put it in place. But as it stands, not being able to find a more serious penalty than this in the case of those women, he thought best that there be the same one as applied in the case of concubines. Now read the law, please. (30–31)

The Law on Rape is read, and Euphiletus explains the reason behind the fact that the punishment for seduction of a married woman is more severe than that for rape.

You hear, gentlemen, that the Lawgiver orders in the case of a free man or boy raped by force, double the fine is owing (compared to the case of slaves). If it is a wife, gentlemen, a class in which it is permitted to kill (the violator), he is liable to the same indemnity. Thus, gentlemen, he thought that rapists were liable for a lesser penalty than seducers. For the latter, he prescribed the sentence of death, but for the former double the fine, holding that those who carried out the deed by force were hated by the victims, but that those who use persuasion corrupt their victims' minds so as to make other men's wives more intimate with them than with their own husbands, and the whole household is in their power. It is not clear to whom the children happen to belong – the husbands or the seducers. (32–33)

With rhetorical force Euphiletus now points out that this case has broader implications not only for himself but for the city at large.

I do not think, gentlemen, that this punishment was inflicted on my behalf but on behalf of the whole city. For those men doing such things, seeing such "prizes" awarded for crimes of this sort, will be less inclined to commit them against others if they see that you too hold the same opinion. If not, it would be much better to annul the laws in place and to put others in place which would penalize those keeping guard over their own wives, but give full amnesty to those wanting to corrupt the women. This would be far more just than to trap citizens by the use of the laws, laws that order someone, if he catches a person committing adultery, to do with him whatever he wants, yet for those who are wronged trials are in place more terrible than for those who dishonour the wives of others. I now am at risk when it comes to my body, my property and everything, because I obeyed the laws of the city. (47–50)
(Lysias, *On the Murder of Eratosthenes*)

In another courtroom speech, the orator Aeschines refers to some severe regulations of Solon intended to curtail the adultery of women.

Solon, the most illustrious of lawgivers, prescribed – with the gravity appropriate to this earlier period – regulations for the proper conduct of women. He forbade all adornment for a woman caught in adultery, and she was not to attend public sacrifices, lest in mingling with proper women she corrupt them. And if she attended these, or dressed herself up, he ordered someone who came across her to tear her clothes and remove her jewellery and to beat her. He forbade them to murder her, or to leave her maimed, rather dishonouring her and setting her up for a life that was intolerable. (Aeschines, *Against Timarchus* 183)

LOWER CLASS WOMEN

Aristotle observed that in a democracy it was impossible to prevent the women of the poorer classes from going out to work.

The legislation of boys or women, even if there were some other magistrate in charge of such a thing, is more suited to an aristocratic government, for in a democratic one how is it possible to prevent the wives of the poor from going out? (Aristotle, *Politics* 1300a4–7)

In a prosecution speech against Eubulides, Demosthenes mounts a defence of those women who, like his mother, were obliged to seek employment outside the home.

Now I will speak concerning my mother (for they are slandering me through her) and I will call witnesses to support my claims. And yet, men of Athens, Eubulides, in discrediting us for working in the marketplace, has acted not only contrary to your decree but also contrary to the laws. These pronounce that someone who makes business in the marketplace a reproach against anyone – a male or a female citizen – shall be liable to the penalty for slander. (30)

When the citizen status of Demosthenes is challenged, on the grounds that his mother had once worked as a nurse, he counters with the observation that many women and men are forced into menial labour through poverty.

For even if being a nurse is a lowly occupation I do not avoid the truth. We have not been charged with wrong-doing on the grounds of being poor, but for not being citizens. The present trial is not about our circumstances or our money, but about our lineage. Penury forces free persons to undertake many slave-like occupations, and for these it is more just that they be pitied, rather than brought to ruin in addition. For, as I hear, many women have become nurses, and workers at the loom and vineyard workers because of the misfortunes of the city in those times – citizen women. (45) (Demosthenes, *Against Eubulides*)

An inscription from Athens (4th century BCE) pays tribute to female as well as a male grocer.

Callias the grocer in the neighbour's street and his wife Thraitta ... Glycanthis whom they call Malthace ... Mania the (female) grocer near the spring. (*IG* III.iii.87= *DTA* 87a)

Julius Pollux, who composed a Greek thesaurus in the 2nd century CE, mentioned that the comic playwright Menander (4th–3rd century BCE) referred to a women's market in his "Women Who Take Breakfast Together" (Pollux *Onomasticon* 10.18).

Inscriptions from Athens (4th century BCE) attest to women engaged in a number of professions. From their gravestones, we have a record of the following:

Good Theoxene, wet-nurse (11647)
Good Paideusis, wet-nurse (12387)
Good Pynete, wet-nurse (12559)
Elephantis, cloak-seller (11254)
Thraitta, perfume-boiler (11688)
Melitta, salt-vendor (12073)
Philyra, wet-nurse (12996)
Choerile, wet-nurse (13065)
(*IG* II²)

In 1935 a marble fragment inscribed on two sides was found in Athens recording the manumission of some women who pursued their trades as freedwomen.
On Side A were recorded:

Onesime, sesame-seed seller (l. 221)
Lampris, wet-nurse (ll. 255–256)
Eupeithe, her child, wet-nurse (l. 259)
Lyde, wool-worker (ll. 328–329)
Rhodia, wool-worker (l. 468)
Thraitta, grocer/tavern-worker (l. 493)
Itame, wool-worker (l. 497)
Demetria, harpist (l. 505)
Olympias, wool-worker (l. 518)

On Side B were recorded:

One (female) horse-tender (l. 93)
Atta, pulse vendor (ll. 112–113)

Malthace, wool-worker (ll. 114–115)
… rityra, *aulos* player (l. 212)
Echo, wool-worker (l. 214)
(These were published by D.M. Lewis in *Hesperia* 1959, 208–38.)

Other occupations are documented for women in the record of their manumission.

Midas, sesame-seed seller and Soteris, sesame-seed seller (1561.22–23, 26–27)
Philoumene, honey-seller (1570.73)
Melitta, frankincense-seller (1576.15–17)
(Female) shoe-seller (1578.5)
(*IG* II²)

Women were also employed as entertainers, dancers and musicians, particularly at men's symposia, the after-dinner gatherings providing opportunities for discussion, and also erotic activity. In his *Symposium*, Xenophon (5th century BCE) describes an entertainment troupe from Syracuse who performed at the house of Callias. The players include a dancing girl who was also a skilled juggler, and she was accompanied by a female aulos player.

I saw this dancer stand up and someone hand hoops to her. After that another woman played the *aulos* for her, and someone stood beside the dancer and one-by-one handed her twelve hoops. She took them and at the same time danced, and threw the hoops up spinning, estimating how high she had to throw them in order to catch them in time to the music.
(Xenophon, *Symposium* 2.7–8)

SLAVEWOMEN

Female slaves in an Athenian household were under the control of the *kyrios* of the household, but able to circulate in public, performing errands for their mistresses who were largely confined. They would also be privy to the household secrets and, as in the case of the slavewoman who had acted as a go-between for the wife of Euphiletus, evidence could be sought from them (as from male slaves) by torture. In another Athenian courtroom speech, Isaeus explains why.

You are of the opinion that in both private and public affairs inquiry by torture is the most accurate form of cross-examination. When slaves and free men are available and it is necessary to establish something under investigation you do not

need the testimony of free men but by putting the slaves to torture you seek in this way to find out the truth about what happened. This is reasonable, gentlemen of the jury. For you know that some witnesses before now have appeared not to be giving a true testimony, but none of those who have been examined under torture has ever been convicted for not speaking the truth under torture.
(Isaeus, *On the Estate of Ciron* 12)

The same argument for the superiority of truth obtained from slaves under torture is made by Demosthenes (*Against Onetor* 37), although Aristotle felt that the possibility of a strong slave withstanding the pain of torture rendered the process fallible (*Rhetoric* 1376b–1377a). It was often the case that the torture of slaves, like oaths in exchanges between free men, was invited by the prosecutor or defendant as a legal challenge, which might or might not be accepted. For example, there is no evidence that the threat was carried out in the case of the slavewoman threatened with torture by Euphiletus as proof of his wife's adultery (see above, pp. 70–4), or those of Neaera by Apollodrus in order to establish the true parentage of her children (see below, p. 113) . The orator Lycurgus, in a speech of prosecution against Leocrates, turns to the jury after issuing such a torture challenge to the defendant.

It is far from my intention to prosecute Leocrates unjustly, inasmuch as I was willing, at my own risk, for the proof to be established through the torture of the household slaves, male and female. But he, aware of his guilt, did not accept this, but rejected the offer. And yet, gentlemen, the male and female slaves of Leocrates would have more readily denied any of these facts than to have falsely charged their master with untruths.
(Lycurgus, *Against Leocrates*, 30)

By the middle of the 4th century BCE we begin to hear of the manumission of slaves, as attested in Aristotle's will. (He died in 322 BCE.)

Let Nicanor see that the young slave Myrmex is brought back to his family, with the remaining property that we took from him – in a manner worthy of me. Let Ambracis also be freed, and when my daughter marries give to her five hundred drachmas and the slave-girl that she has. Give to Thale, in addition to the slave-girl she has, the one she bought, one thousand drachmas and a female slave. And for Simo, apart from the money previously given to him for another slave, either buy a slave or give him the money (for this). Tycho shall be free whenever my daughter marries, along with Philo and Olympius and his son. Don't sell any of my slaves who looked after me, but use them. When they come of age let them have their freedom, as they deserve.
(Diogenes Laertius, *Lives of Famous Philosophers* 5.14–15)

OLDER WOMEN

Women past the age of childbearing are almost invisible in the historical record of the Classical period. Nonetheless, some priesthoods were reserved for older women, including the highly influential Pythia, who channelled the voice of Apollo at Delphi. Diodorus (1st century BCE) gives us an account of the reasons why she was chosen from this sector of the population.

It is said that in former times virgins gave out the oracles because of the incorruptibility of their nature and because of their resemblance to Artemis. For they are well suited to guarding closely the secrecy of the revelations of the oracles. In more recent times, however, they say that Echecrates the Thessalian, when he was present at the oracle and caught sight of the virgin delivering the prophecies, lusted after her because of her beauty and abducted and raped her. The Delphians, because of the disastrous occurrence passed a decree that in the future no longer would it be a virgin who gave the oracles but a woman older than 50 years of age who would do the prophesying. She dresses in the clothing of a maiden, as a reminder of the prophetess of olden times.
(Diodorus Siculus, *Historical Library* 16.26.6)

Older women doubtless acted as helpers and attendants within the family. This grave monument was set up in the Kerameikos cemetery in Athens commemorating a grandmother. With the poignant inscription is an image of a seated woman holding a child in her arms.

AMPHARETE.
I am holding this dear son of my daughter; when we were alive we looked with our eyes on the rays of the sun. I held him on my lap, and now in death I hold him, dead.
(*IG* II² 10650)

It may be because of the important role that older women played in the family that in the last play of his *Oresteia* trilogy Aeschylus has Athena specify that female elders should join with girls and women in escorting the pacified Erinyes, depicted as hate-filled hags earlier in the play, to their new subterranean shrine in Athens. The converted Furies will in the future use their dark energy to ensure reverence for justice in the city.

I will send you (Eumenides) by the light of gleaming torches to the depths below, the underworld places, with the attendants who guard my image, and rightly so. Let the jewel of the entire land of Theseus come out, a famous contingent ... of

girls, women, and a procession of elder women ... give them honour, clad as they are in robes dyed in purple.
(*Eumenides* 1022–1028 [passage somewhat corrupt])

Old women did not always enjoy respect. Some literary texts reflect a stereotyping of them as hags desperate for drink and sex. (One might recall that many women were widowed young, the result of their being married to men much older than they and the fact that many men died prematurely on the battlefield.)

In Aristophanes' play *Assemblywomen* (produced *c.* 390 BCE), the women of Athens, fed up with the way the men have been running the city, take over the Assembly by stealth (dressing as men and outvoting the number of men who turn up). One of the decrees that they pass obliges every young man to have sex with older women before he can have access to a young one. At the end of the play a young man Epigenes is pursued by three old women and complains:

[Epig.] I'm damned three times over, if I have to screw a rotten hag all night and all day! And then, when I escape from her I get an old toad holding her funeral urn next to her jaws. Now, am I not doomed? A man under heavy damnation, by Zeus the Saviour, and out of luck – a guy hemmed in by such beasts. Nevertheless, if I suffer a pile of misfortunes again and again, sailing back in under these two floozies, bury me right at the mouth of the entrance. And as for this one, cover her with pitch right from the top of her body, while she is still alive, and then fix her two feet in molten lead, circling around her ankles, and place her as a substitute over my grave, instead of a funerary urn.
(Aristophanes, *Assemblywomen* 1098–1111)

From the 1st century CE comes an epigram in the same vein, by the (often satirical) Greek poet Nicarchus.

The old woman is not bad-looking, wouldn't you say? You know she was when she was young. Then she asked for money
    but now *she* is willing to pay out some cash when she is being mounted.
You will find her full of tricks; when she drinks then you have her
    more submissive – however much you want.
For she drinks three or four pints, if you are up for it,
    and she is all over the place as a result.
She clings, she teases, she plays the passive role in sex.
If someone gives her something she takes it; if not, just having sex is her payment.
(Nicarchus, AP 11.73)

Old women were also scorned for their participation in rituals, especially those given to emotional excess.

Sabazius was a Phrygian god who was imported to Greece during the 5th century BCE and identified with Dionysus. The cult, with initiatory and ecstatic elements, was greeted with some suspicion in Athens. It admitted the participation of older women, which may have helped to fuel the derision it received from contemporary writers. The Athenian politician and orator Demosthenes attacks his political opponent Aeschines in a speech by accusing him of officiating with his mother in these rites.

When you became a man you read out the books and helped your mother with the other preparations when she performed the initiation rites. During the night you robed the initiates in fawn-skins, mixed the wine, washed the bodies of the initiates, and wiped them off with clay and bran ... In daytime you led your handsome band through the streets, with their heads garlanded with fennel and white poplar, squeezing the red-brown snakes and brandishing them over your head, now shouting "euoi sabaoi," now dancing to the beat of "hues attes, attes hues," hailed by the old hags as Master of Ceremonies, Instructor in the Mysteries, Ivy-Bearer, Winnowing-Fan Carrier.
(Demosthenes On the Crown 259–260)

But not all older women were scorned for their public religious activity. A tombstone near the sanctuary of the Great Mother [Cybele] in the Peiraeus, 4th century BCE) honours "Chairestrate," a woman who is depicted with her grand-daughter who is holding a small drum used in the rites of Cybele.

Ministrant of the Mother of all Children, the august and revered Chairestrate lies in this tomb, a woman whom her husband adored while alive and grieves for now as she is dead. But she left the light a fortunate woman, having seen her children's children.
(IG II² 6288)

The famous priestess of Athena Polias, Lysimache, served the goddess for a remarkable 64 years, dying at the age of 88. Her statue was found near the south wall of the Acropolis with this inscription:

Lysimache, whose father was Dracontides, lived through 88 years. In all she served Athena for 64 years, and saw four generations of children. Lysimache, mother of ... Phlya. Demetrios made this.
(IG II² 3453)

DEATH AND FUNERALS

Contact with a corpse, as with birth, was polluting, reflected in this sacred law from the island of Keos (5th century BCE), where a limited number of women were permitted to attend the body.

Carry the corpse in its shroud, in silence, until you get to the tomb. Execute the preliminary sacrifice according to tradition. Bring the bier and the covers back inside the house from the tomb. On the next day thoroughly sprinkle the house, first with sea-water then scrub it with earth and wash it. When it is thoroughly clean, then the house is purified, and sacrifices are held on the hearth. (10–17)

Where one has died, after (the body) has been carried out, no women are to go into the house other than those women who are (already) polluted. Those women polluted are the mother, the wife, the sisters and daughters, and in addition to these not more than five other women, children of the daughters and cousins; beyond this no one. Those who have been polluted, once they have been washed all over including with water poured from jugs over their heads, they are purified. (23 –31)
(*LSCG* 97A)

As women were closely tied to activities surrounding birth, so did they look after the corpse and frequently led the mourning rituals. There is evidence that some women were hired for these tasks, in addition to performing as family members. The washing and dressing of the corpse was followed by the laying out of the body (*prothesis*), after which women joined men in the procession to the place of burial (the *ecphora*). The identification of women not only with the care of the body but with dramatic gestures of grief is reflected in clay reliefs and vase paintings from the Mycenaean through the Archaic and Classical periods, in postures that change little over the thousand years. These public demonstrations by women had apparently led to tensions among social factions in Athens during the Archaic period, in response to which the lawgiver Solon passed a restrictive law in the final years of the 6th century BCE. The following law reflects Solon's prescriptions for the position, age, number and kin affinity of the women who participated.

The deceased shall be laid out inside, in whatever way is wished. They shall carry out the deceased on the day after which they lay out the body, before sunrise. The men shall walk in front when they carry out the body, and the women behind. No woman younger than 60 years of age is permitted to enter the room of the

deceased nor follow the deceased when the body is carried to the tomb, except those who are at least as closely related as daughters of a first cousin. Nor shall any woman enter the room of the deceased when the corpse is being carried out except those who are at least daughters of first cousins.
(Demosthenes, *Against Macartatus* 62)

The following record of Solon's legislation governing the conduct of women at funerals was preserved by Plutarch, in his biography of Solon.

He also established a law governing women's coming out into public, their mourning and their festivals, putting a stop to their lack of discipline and their licence. He ordered them, to go out with no more than three cloaks, carrying no more than three obols' worth of food and drink, nor a basket larger than a cubit, nor to travel about at night except in a wagon, with a lamp lighting the way. He forbade the lacerating of skin by those beating (their breasts) and prepared lamentations, and the shrieks of grief over someone at the burial of other people.
(Plutarch, *Life of Solon* 21.5–6)

At Delphi, the priestly clan of the Labyadai instituted restrictions in the late 5th century on the value of grave offerings and the behaviour of the mourners, among whom we assume women were and had been prominent. The following is a fragmentary record of a sacred law from Delphi.

Let the corpse be carried out veiled, in silence, and at the crossroads they are not to lay it down anywhere, nor wail outside the house, before they come to the tomb. (13–19)

Around the gravesites of those who have died before there is not to be mourning nor wailing aloud, but each one is to go home. (21–26)
(*LSCG* 77C)

    That women's role in performing burial rites could provoke social tensions is at the heart of the dramatic crisis in Sophocles' tragedy *Antigone* (produced c. 442 BCE). Children of Oedipus, Antigone's two brothers fought over possession of the throne in Thebes. One of them invaded the city to claim his share of the rule, and both were killed in the battle that ensued. Their uncle (Creon) takes charge, declaring that the invading brother is a traitor and must not receive burial; anyone who undertakes this will be stoned to death. Antigone feels the burial is a familial and religious obligation. When she fails to enlist the help of her sister in this, she declares to her that she will risk death for what she considers a pious duty.

You be the sort of person that seems best to you, but that man
I will bury. For me it is noble to die doing this.
As his own I will lie with him, one who is my own,
having committed a crime of piety.
(Sophocles, *Antigone* 71–74)

When Creon accuses Antigone of disobeying the law she replies that in burying
her brother she was responding to an ordinance that had greater force than a
political decree. (Her words are quoted below, pp. 138–9)

In 430 BCE the Athenian leader Pericles was chosen to deliver a public eulogy
for soldiers who had died in the first year of the Peloponnesian War. His focus
was not so much on the glorious dead as on the Athenian way of life for which
the men had fought, and on the need for all present to dedicate themselves to
this cause. At the end of the speech he turned to the women present, who had
lost husbands.

If it is incumbent upon me to bring to your attention something about the excellence of women, for those of you who will now be in widowhood, I will make my
point with a brief piece of advice. Your reputation is great if you do not fall short of
the real nature you have been given: glory is awarded to her of whom there is the
least report among men, either of praise or blame.
(Thucydides, *The Peloponnesian War* 2.45.2)

The grief of a mother for her daughter is reflected in the following epitaph that
accompanies a statue on the grave of a girl from Amorgos (*c.* 450 BCE).

I lie here a statue of Parian marble instead of a woman,
a remembrance of Bitte and of her mother's tearful grief.
(*CEG* 153)

The following epitaph (*c.* 360 BCE) was found in the Piraeus, commemorating
a mother.

WORTHY XENOCLEA
Leaving behind two young unmarried girls, Xenoclea, daughter of Nicarchus, lies
here dead; she mourned the bitter death of her son Phoenix, who died out at
sea when he was eight years old ... Who is so ignorant of grief, Xenoclea, that he
doesn't pity your fate? You left behind two young girls and died of grief for your
son, who has a pitiless tomb, lying in the dark sea.
(IG II² 12335)

FURTHER READING

Alexiou, M. 1974. *The Ritual Lament in Greek Tradition*. Cambridge

Barber, E.J.W. 1994. *Women's Work: The First 20,000 Years. Women, Cloth and Society in Early Times*. New York

Bonfante, L. 1997. "Nursing Mothers in Classical Art," in A.O. Koloski-Ostrow and C. Lyons (eds) *Naked Truths. Women, Sexuality and Gender in Classical Art and Archeology*, 174–196. London/New York

Brock, R. 1994. "The Labour of Women in Classical Athens," *Classical Quarterly* 44, 336–346

Carey, C. "Rape and Adultery in Athenian Law," *Classical Quarterly* 45.2, 407–417

Cohen, A. 2007. *Constructions of Childhood in Ancient Greece and Italy. Hesperia* Supplement 41

Cohen, D. *Law, Sexuality and Society. The enforcement of Morals in Classical Athens*. Cambridge

Cox, C. 1998. *Household Interests: Property, Marriage Strategies, and Family Dynamics in Ancient Athens*. Princeton

Demand, N. 1994. *Birth, Death and Motherhood in Classical Greece*. Baltimore, MD

Fletcher, J. 2009. "Weaving Women's Tales in Euripies' *Ion*," in J.R.C. Cousland and J.R. Hume (eds), *The Play of Texts and Fragments. Essays in Honour of Martin Cropp*, 127–139. Leiden

Henderson, J. 1987. "Older Women in Attic Old Comedy," *Transactions of the American Philological Association* 117, 105–129

Joshel, S.R. and S. Murnahan. 1998. *Women and Slaves in the Greco-Roman Culture: Differential Equations*. London/New York

Keuls, E. 1993. *The Reign of the Phallus. Sexual Politics in Ancient Athens*. Berkeley, CA

Kosmopoulou, A. 2001. "'Working Women': Female Professionals on Classical Attic Gravestones," *Annual of the British School at Athens* 96, 218–319

Lewis, D.M. 1959. "Attic Manumissions," *Hesperia* 28.3, 208–238

Lewis, S. 2002. *The Athenian Woman. An Iconographic Handbook*. London

Neils, J. and J.H. Oakley. 2003 (eds) *Coming of Age in Ancient Greece: Images of Childhood from the Classical Past*. New Haven, CT

Oakley, J. and R. Sinos. 1993. *The Wedding in Ancient Athens*. Madison, WI

Patterson, C. 1985. "Not Worth the Rearing. The Causes of Infant Exposure in Ancient Greece," *Transactions of the American Philological Association* 115, 103–123

Pomeroy, S.B. 1994 ed. *Xenophon Oeconomicus. A Social and Historical Commentary*. Oxford

Rawson, B. 2011 ed. *A Companion to Families in the Greek and Roman Worlds*. Chichester

Schaps, D.M. 1998. "What Was Free about a Free Athenian Woman?" *Transactions of the American Philological Association* 128, 161–188

Scheidel, W. 1995. "The Most Silent Women of Greece and Rome. Rural Labour and Women's Life in the Ancient World," Part 1. *Greece and Rome* 42, 202–217

Wolpert, A. 2001. "Lysias 1 and the Politics of the Oikos," *Classical Journal* 96, 415–424

6

Women and property

The surviving laws recorded in Athenian courtroom speeches indicate for the most part that an Athenian woman could not control property of any size. Once married, her husband-*kyrios* managed her dowry. He could not sell any of this property or spend any of the funds transferred, but he could use this as, for example, security for a mortgage. If he did so, it would be indicated on one of the "mortgage stones" (*horai*) found throughout Attica. The amount would be returned to the wife's family in the event of the death of the husband or divorce.

The following is the text from one of these *horai*, placed near the Areopagus:

Boundary-stone of the land and house, security for the dowry belonging to Stratonike.
(*IG* II² 2665)

The following inscription describes the wife's full dowry as divided in half, with a mortgage serving as security for a portion that remained unpaid by her father but would be supplied two years later (the two archonships cover 305–304 and 303–302 BCE respectively).

In the year Euxenippus was archon. Boundary-marker of the lands and houses, securities for the dowry of Xenariste, daughter of Pythodorus of Gargettus; this is half, together with the interest coming to her, 2720 drachmas, until the year Leostratus is archon.
(*IG* II² 2679)

It was normal practice for the wife to retain the personal effects she had brought into the marriage as a bride. The following comes from a speech of Isaeus and refers to a divorce instigated by a husband because of his wife's childlessness. The husband asks her kin to find her another husband, to whom he would transfer the dowry, and he permits his wife to keep her trousseau.

Menecles gave over her dowry to him ... and the clothing which she had had when she came to him, and the jewelry, whatever there was, he gave to her.
(Isaeus, *On the Estate of Menecles* 9)

It was normal for the woman's guardian (*kyrios*), if she were a widow or divorced, to arrange another marriage for her, in which case the dowry would be under the new husband's control.

Athenian women could conduct commercial transactions, but the size of this was limited by law, as we learn from several sources, such as the following.

For the law explicitly forbids permitting a child or woman to perform a transaction more than (the value of) a medimnus of barley.
(Isaeus, *On the Estate of Aristarchus* 10).
(A medimnus of barley was roughly equivalent to three bushels. The value of this amount of barley has been calculated as the price of feeding an average family for approximately one week.)

The fact that the law considered women as minors in this way appears to be contradicted, however, by several cases in which women engaged in cash transactions. In the following speech the orator Lysias prosecutes a man who had been elected to public office. This man had proven himself an unworthy citizen and even his mother did not entrust her burial to him, which would involve giving him the necessary funds.

She refused to entrust herself to him once she had died, but having confidence in Antiphanes, who was no relation, she gave to him three minae of silver for her burial, passing over this man, her own son.
(Lysias, *Against Philon* 21)

A mina was worth 100 drachmas, and the value of three would be 1/20 of a talent.

Two minae could purchase a domestic slave, as we learn from a speech of Demosthenes in which the plaintiff is trying to recover 10 minae, outstanding from the payment of a dowry, from a man who at one point borrowed a significant amount of money from the mother of the bride.

And there are 1800 drachmae, concerning which I don't know what he will have to say that can be justified. For he had borrowed the money from the wife of Polyeuctus, and there are papers which she left behind when she died, and the woman's brothers are witnesses, having been with her for it all and having questioned her about each thing.
(Demosthenes, *Against Spudias* 8–9)

One possible explanation for the discrepancy between the law restricting women's access to money and actual practice could be the fact that the women ignored the law when they were confident that their *kyrios* would not contest the transaction(s). In the case of the woman cited in the speech that follows, her marriage to Phormio had been arranged by her previous husband, the banker Pasio. Pasio's will was read in another speech of Demosthenes, making it clear that this woman, Archippe, had considerable wealth at her disposal.

This is laid down in the will of Pasio of Acharnae. I give my wife Archippe to Phormio, and I give Archippe as dowry a talent from my property in Peparethus [off Euboea] and another talent from my property here [in Athens], a tenement house worth 100 minae, the maidservants and gold jewellery, and everything else in the house, all these I leave to Archippe.
(Demosthenes, *Against Stephanus* 28)

That some Athenian women kept close watch on financial transactions is clear from this, and from the following speech of Demosthenes, in which it is obvious that Archippe clearly acted as a gatekeeper to preserve the arrangements that her deceased husband Pasio had put in place for her from his (significant) accumulated resources. When she died, one of their sons, Apollodorus, took advantage of this to bring a suit against Phormio for some funds (cf. the earlier excerpt, from Lysias *Against Philon*, p. 87).

Indeed, while his mother was alive – she who had scrupulous knowledge of all these arrangements – Apollodorus never brought a charge against this man Phormio. But when she died he demanded as his due three thousand drachmas of silver, in addition to the two thousand drachmas she had given to (her husband's) children.
(Demosthenes, *For Phormio* 14)

Women who felt that they had been victims of the mishandling of property within the family could not sue for justice in their own name, but would need to find a supportive male relative to issue a court challenge. One such woman was the widow of a wealthy Athenian merchant Diodotus, who had been killed in battle. Not a woman easily intimidated, she accused her father Diogeiton, the brother of her deceased husband, of cheating her sons in the distribution of Diodotus' estate, and using the funds due to them as inheritance for enriching his family by his second wife. Her son-in-law represented her in court, reporting that she had sought his help in summoning her father before other male relatives. He tells the jury that she had then asked her father how he could treat his nephew in this way.

With you being their father's brother and my father, their uncle and grandfather! Even if you aren't ashamed in the face of any man, you ought to fear the gods – you who took the five talents my husband left behind as a deposit when he sailed away to war. I am willing to swear the truth of this, on the lives of my sons and the children born later to me, in any place that you name. I am not so desperate, nor do I put such store in money as to end my life having perjured that of my own children, nor would I wish unjustly to steal my father's property. (12-13)

In this meeting she accused her father of stealing seven talents and 4000 drachmas from marine loans, producing the records of these transactions that her sons had located. She also claimed that he had taken 100 minae, interest from a mortgage loan, along with 2000 drachmas invested so as to bring in an annual supply of grain, and valuable furniture. (This all suggests a certain amount of financial, in addition to alphabetic, literacy.) Her son-in-law continues his report of her determined attack on her father, in which she accuses him of claiming that all that remained for her children in the bequest of Diodotus was the amount of her dowry, which had been returned to him upon her husband's death.

Then you dared to say, when you had so much money, that their father had left these children 2000 drachmas and 30 staters – the amount that was left to me and that I gave you when my husband died. And you thought it appropriate to turn these children, being your grandchildren, out of their own house in worn-out clothes, without shoes, with no attendant and with no bed-clothes, no cloaks and without the furniture that their father left them and without the deposit he had left with you! Meanwhile you are bringing up the children you have had by my step-mother in the lap of luxury. You are justified in doing that, but you dealt unjustly with my children because you threw them out of their house in dishonour and were determined to turn them into beggars instead of people of means. And with actions such as these you are not afraid of the gods, nor are you ashamed that I am conscious of what you have done; you are not mindful of your brother, but you think of us all as less important than money. (15–17)
(Lysias, *Against Diogeiton*)

The woman is unnamed, because it was not permitted to name respectable women in court.

Because there were no official records kept of marriages, a woman who needed to prove that she had been legitimately married (for example, for public acknowledgement of the legitimacy of her children, or to establish lawful inheritance for them and for herself when her husband died) had to have recourse to other means. These could include an appeal to the eye witnesses at her marriage party, the acknowledgement of her sons by her husband's tribe (*phratry*), or her own participation in a religious festival such as the Thesmophoria, which was open to lawfully wedded women whose husbands belonged to a citizen group (*deme*). One such attempt to assert legitimacy is made by a woman who is attempting to lay her claim to the estate of her deceased father, Ciron. Her son conducts the suit in court.

Therefore it ought to be clear from what I have shown that not only is our mother the legitimate daughter of Ciron, but also it should be clear from this what our father has done for us as well as from the way that the wives of his demesmen have acknowledged her. When our father took her in marriage, he held a wedding feast and summoned three of his friends in addition to his relatives; he also gave a marriage banquet to the phratry according to their established customs. After this the wives of his demesmen also chose our mother to preside at the Thesmophoria along with the wife of Diocles of the deme Pithus and to conduct the ceremonial rites together with her. In addition to this, when we were born, our father introduced us to the phratry, swearing an oath according to the established customs that he was introducing children born from a perfectly legitimate Athenian woman and a lawfully betrothed wife. None of the members of the phratry objected or disputed the fact that this was true, although there were many of them and they investigated such matters carefully.

Surely you cannot suppose that if our mother was the sort of woman that these opponents allege our father would have given a wedding-feast or a marriage banquet! Rather, he would have hidden the whole affair and the wives of other demesmen would not have chosen her to conduct the rites with Diocles' wife and put her in charge of the sacred objects. Rather, they would have turned to some other one of the wives for these matters. The members of his phratry would not have admitted us; they would have accused our father and challenged his claims, if it had not been agreed on all sides that our mother was the legitimate daughter of Ciron.
(Isaeus, *On the Estate of Ciron* 18–20)

THE HEIRESS (*EPIKLEROS*)

In the event that a father died without a will and leaving only a daughter, she could inherit property but only in the sense that it was attached to her body and would be passed on to her husband at marriage, to be preserved for male children who would inherit this directly. (The same was true for her sisters if she had any.) There would be pressure on the *epikleros* to marry, and in such a way as to preserve the property within the family. If there were no daughters, the property passed directly to males within the family in a prescribed order.

Whoever dies without having made a will, if he leaves female children his property shall go (via marriage) with these women. If not, the following will be in possession of it: if there are brothers of the same father and if there be legitimate sons of the brothers they take their father's share ... Males and the offspring of males shall take precedence, if they are descendants from the same forbears, even if they are more distant kin. If there are no relatives of the father closer than the children of cousins, males on the mother's side are the heirs in the same manner. If there is no one on either side within this degree of kinship then the nearest relative on the father's side shall be heir.
(Demosthenes, *Against Macartatus* 51)

The marriage of a poor heiress (when her father has died intestate) was encouraged by the mandatory provision of a dowry by male relatives, and by the state's enforcing her marriage if need be. The amount of the dowry was calculated in keeping with the social class of the man responsible for her marriage.

As for heiresses from the class of serfs (*thetes*) if the nearest of kin does not wish to marry her let him give her in marriage, providing 500 drachmae if he is of the class of Pentacosiomedimni (the wealthiest class); if he is of the class of Knights, 300; if he is from the Zeugitae 150 – in addition to whatever she has of her own. If there is more than one kinsman each shall contribute a share to the heiress. But if there are several heiresses it is not necessary for a single kinsman to give more than one heiress in marriage, but the nearest in kin shall give her in marriage or marry her himself. If the nearest of kin does not marry her nor give her in marriage let the archon compel him to marry her or give her in marriage. If he does not compel the kinsman, let him be fined 1000 drachmae and dedicate them to Hera. Let anyone who wishes denounce to the archon the man who does not want to do this.
(Demosthenes, *Against Macartatus* 54)

The sister of a man who died without children and without a will could inherit the property of the deceased brother, or a share of this if she has another brother who is childless. (This property was "hers" only in the sense that she preserved it to pass on to a husband and male heirs.)

There is a law that lays it down that if a brother by the same father dies childless and without a will, his sister and a son born from another sister, if there is one, shall be equal heirs of the property.
(Isaeus, *On the Estate of Apollodorus* 19)

An heiress who was already married might be obliged to leave her husband and marry a family member at her father's death. This would not be necessary if there were sons born of her first husband, as they would have priority as heirs.

Regarding daughters who have been given in marriage by their fathers and are living as wives with their husbands (for who plans better than the father about such things?), even though they have been thus given in marriage, if their father dies without leaving legitimate brothers of the sisters, the law bids them be subject to the legal claims of the nearest male kin. Many men living with their wives have had their own wives taken away from them.
(Isaeus, *On the Estate of Pyrrhus* 64)

Male relatives who qualified to marry the *epikleros* could decline the opportunity. Several factors could contribute to this decision, including the desire of the man to stay with his current wife or to avoid taking on responsibility for a less valuable estate, or even his decision to honour the woman's wishes.

The inherited property of an heiress would not have been hers to use for private gain, but was attached to her until she had sons. Her husband could manage it (as her *kyrios*), but when the sons came of age, they gained possession of it. If she were widowed, divorced, or remarried, this remained the case. The following comes from a courtroom speech on behalf of a son who was contesting the awarding of his grandfather's estate to the adopted son of a cousin of his mother, an heiress. Aristomenes, uncle of the heiress, and his son Apollodorus, had both declined to marry her, and Aristomenes had been instrumental in seeing that the estate fell to his grandson Aristarchus.

It is not possible for Aristomenes or Apollodorus, to whom my mother might have been awarded in marriage (to inherit the estate). If Apollodorus or Aristomenes *had* been married to my mother it would be surprising if it had been possible for them to dispose of the property of an heiress. This is in accordance with the law that does not allow anyone to be *kyrios* of the property of an heiress except her sons, who take possession of it when they are two years past puberty. It will be surprising if Aristarchus is permitted to give her in marriage to someone else and introduce an adopted son as heir to her estate. This would be outrageous!

It was not possible for her father, if no sons had been born to him, to have disposed of (the estate) separately from her. For the law lays down that it is legitimate to give his estate to whomever he wishes, together with his daughters. But when someone has not thought fit to take the heiress in marriage, and it is not her father but her cousin who is introducing an heir, will these actions be valid when contrary to every law?
(Isaeus, *On the Estate of Aristarchus* 12–13)

Rival claims for the hand of an heiress are recorded in several courtroom speeches. Aristotle (*Politics* 1303b18) claimed that even civil wars could ensue over these disputes. Claimants in any case needed to submit their petitions to the archon; this would be made public and others were invited to apply on the basis of being the nearest male relative. (Demosthenes, *Against Stephanus* 22)

PROTECTION OF ORPHANS, WIDOWS AND HEIRESSES

For those without the protection of a *kyrios* there was a law obliging the archon to take over.

Let the archon take responsibility for the orphans and heiresses and the families that are without heirs, and all those women who remain in their homes when their husbands have died and declare that they are pregnant. Let him take charge of these and not permit anyone to do any outrage against them.
(Demosthenes, *Against Macartatus* 75)

FURTHER READING

Cox, C.A. 1998. *Household Interests: Property, Marriage Strategies, and Family Dynamics in Ancient Athens*. Princeton

Foxhall, L. 1989. "Household, Gender and Property in Classical Athens," *Classical Quarterly* 39, 22–44

Johnstone, S. 2003. "Women, Property, and Surveillance in Classical Athens," *Classical Antiquity* 22.2, 247–274

Schaps, D.M. 1979. *Economic Rights of Women in Ancient Greece*. Edinburgh

Whitehead, D. 1986. "Women and Naturalisation in Fourth-Century Athens. The Case of Archippe," *Classical Quarterly* 36, 109–114

7

Foreign women

Many foreign women (metics) came to Athens in the aftermath of wars and political dislocation – including the Persian Wars, the turbulence that resulted from the development of an Athenian empire and the consequences of the protracted Peloponnesian War.

In a speech of Demosthenes delivered in the last quarter of the 4th century BCE we learn of a metic woman who befriended Aristogeiton, a fugitive who owed a large debt to the state and may have been a former lover of hers. She hid him from the police for a time, then provided him with a tunic and cloak and travel money. In the courtroom prosecution of Aristogeiton, we learn of her subsequent ill treatment by him and some details about her general situation as a woman and metic.

This same woman, who had been a benefactor to him in this way, when he was putting on a great show and giving himself airs among you, and when she criticized him somewhat and reminded him of these services, thinking that she should be recompensed, first off he gave her a thrashing and threatened her and turned her out of his house. When she did not stop, but carried on like a woman and went about accusing him among well-known citizens, he grabbed her himself by his hands and led her off to the auction-room at the tax registry for metics. If it had been the case that her tax had not been paid she would have been sold, because of this man for whom she herself had been the means of escape.
(Demosthenes, *Against Aristogeiton* 1.57)

From another speech attributed to Demosthenes we hear again of the registry and tax imposed on metics in Athens. The speaker is arguing that his mother, a ribbon seller, was a legitimate Athenian, not a foreigner, because there were public means of determining whether an individual was not an Athenian.

I presume that it is to be expected that there are many to testify that they know who she is, and not only from hearsay. For, if she were a foreigner they could determine this by examining the official lists in the marketplace, whether she had paid the foreigners' tax, and they could have pointed out from what country she had come.
(Demosthenes, *Against Eubulides* 34)

The best known foreign woman in 5th-century Athens was Aspasia, who came from Miletus and became the partner of the statesman Pericles. A clear picture of her life and status is difficult to obtain because many of the details are reconstructed from the portraits drawn in comedy with the aim of discrediting Pericles, but it is clear that she was a remarkable and prominent figure in her own right. It is likely that she came to Athens c. 450 BCE, just after Pericles enacted a law that would forbid citizen rights to all but those born of two Athenian parents. This would have meant that Aspasia could not anticipate a normal married life and the bearing of legitimate children. While the comic poets referred to her as a courtesan or common whore, and singled out her son born to Pericles as a bastard, the philosophical tradition focused on her intelligence, making her a mentor of the brightest men of Athens, including Socrates. Plutarch, in his *Life of Pericles*, claimed that wives of respectable Athenians also consulted her (24.5).

Two fragments from Cratinus' comedy *Cheirons*, attack both Pericles and Aspasia. The passage probably comes from the parabasis of the play (where the poet speaks directly to the audience through the comic chorus).

Stasis (either "fixedness" or "dissent") and primeval Time, mating with one another gave birth to a very great tyrant whom the gods call "head-gatherer."
And Lewdness bears him Hera-Aspasia, a dog-eyed concubine.
(Cratinus, fragments 258–259PCG)

Aristophanes, in his *Acharnians*, plays with the idea found in Herodotus' introduction to his *Histories*, that major wars were triggered by the abduction of women. Making Aspasia a fellatrix and a procuress was a means of sexualizing the political tensions between Megara and Athens, when Pericles initiated an embargo of Megarian goods during the Peloponnesian War.

But then some drunken, cottabus-playing youths went to Megara and stole the whore Simaitha. Well, then the Megarians were driven garlic-mad by the pain of this, and stole in turn two whores from Aspasia. From this the beginning of the war erupted for all the Greeks – from three strumpets!
(Aristophanes, *Acharnians* 524–529)

Portraits of Aspasia as a philosophical teacher often combine the erotic with the instructional (paedeutic) function, in good Greek fashion. The dialogue called *Aspasia* of Aeschines, composed in the early 4th century BCE, has been reconstructed in part from allusions in later sources. In the dialogue Socrates advises the well-known Athenian figure Callias to approach Aspasia as mentor for his son. The Socratic dialogues of Plato and Xenophon in the early 4th century shifted away from the portrait of a whore-Aspasia to a woman whose wisdom and mentorship informed male discourse about the ideal life. In the following conversation with Callias, Socrates quotes a dialectical conversation conducted by Aspasia with Xenophon and his wife, in which Aspasia advises both marriage partners to become spouses equally worthy of one another. Her advice in choosing a marriage partner, should one have recourse to an intermediary in making the selection, is to consider honesty an essential factor. (It is worth noting that the matchmakers referred to here are female.)

[Soc.] [A]s once I heard from Aspasia. She said that the good matchmakers are skilled at bringing people into a marriage arrangement when the positive things they report (about the individuals) are true. She did not want to praise lying matchmakers. For if (the parties) are deceived they hate each other and the match-maker too. I am convinced that this is correct.
(Xenophon, *Memorabilia* 2.6.36)

That Aspasia's ethical stance in marriage matters struck Xenophon as important could account for his construction of the idealized partnership between Ischomachus and his bride in his *Oeconomicus* (see above, pp. 59–60). In this work, the dialogue between husband and young wife is preceded by this interchange between Socrates and his interlocutor Critoboulus:

[Crit.] About those men whom you say have good wives, Socrates: did these husbands educate their wives themselves?
[Soc.] There is nothing like a close inspection. I will introduce you to Aspasia, who will explain this whole matter to you more knowledgeably than I.
(Xenophon, *Oeconomicus* 3.14)

Socrates, in Plato's dialogue *Menexenus*, during a discussion of the benefits of oratorical training, describes the intellectual debt he owes to this woman. When asked by his interlocutor Menexenus whether he could compose with equal force a eulogy of the Athenians before a Spartan audience, or of Spartans in front of Athenians, he replies that this would be possible because of the superior training he received from Aspasia.

It is no surprise that I would be able to, since my teacher happens to be in no way mediocre at rhetoric, but she has also produced many excellent orators, one of whom who surpassed all the Greeks, Pericles, son of Xanthippus. (235e)

I was listening yesterday to Aspasia going through a funeral speech for these same people. For she heard the same thing that you say, that the Athenians are intending

to choose the speaker. Then she went through the sort of things that should be said, in part improvised and the other part previously prepared from the time when – as it seems to me – she composed the funeral speech that Pericles gave, culling together as much as was left from that speech. (236b)
(Plato, *Menexenus*)

Socrates continues with a recital of the speech of Aspasia. The irony of Plato's installing a foreigner and a woman to compose a speech extolling Athenian manly values – many of which must have been in direct conflict with her ideals – is not lost on modern commentators.

FURTHER READING

Carey, C. 1991. "Apollodoros' Mother: The Wives of Enfranchised Aliens in Athens," *Classical Quarterly* 41.1, 84–89
Henry, M. 1994. *Prisoner of History. Aspasia of Miletus and Her Biographical Tradition*. Oxford
Nails, D. 2002. *The People of Plato: A Prosopography of Plato and Other Socratics*. Indianapolis, IN

8

Prostitutes

We encounter two principal Greek words for a female "prostitute," *porne* and *hetaira*. The former would apply to a slave working in a brothel or on the street, and the latter to a self-employed woman, but *porne* was also a rhetorical and derogative term applied widely, and both terms could be used interchangeably. The lawgiver Solon was credited with organizing state-run brothels, although the documentary source is a reference from comedy (found in Athenaeus 13.569d3–f4). It is likely that with the increased urbanization during the 6th-century BCE prostitution increased, and in some cities, including Athens, was regulated to some degree. In Athens, for example, a prostitution tax was collected from sex workers or their owners.

Resentment over the fees charged by prostitutes is found in many of the sources. Corinth, which supported a lively trade in prostitution that served merchant sailors, gave rise to a proverbial Greek saying:

Not for everyman is the trip to Corinth.
(quoted by Strabo, *The Geography* 8.6.20)

References to the fees charged for a single service seem to range from a few obols to 1000 drachmas. There is a story that the orator Demosthenes approached the beautiful courtesan Laïs for her services, but declined them when she quoted the price of 10,000 drachmas (Aulus Gellius, a Roman writer of the 2nd century BCE, claimed he got this from a Hellenistic source, *Attic Nights* 1.8). According to Athenaeus (13.595c) several of the well-known courtesans charged the same price for all, regardless of their wealth or circumstances – whether because of a price war among them, or for other reasons such as maintaining a large clientele.

A fragment from a comic play by Alexis (5th century BCE) repeats the accusation against prostitutes for their greed, and makes some satirical comments about their professional habits.

First of all, they care about making money and robbing those nearby. Everything else is incidental. They weave traps for everyone. Once they start making a profit they take into their houses new prostitutes who are novices in the profession.

These girls they remodel immediately, so that they no longer carry on with the same manners and looks. Suppose one of them is small; cork is stitched into the soles of her slippers. One of them is tall. She wears thin slippers and goes around with her head tipped towards her shoulder; that reduces her height. One of them has no buttocks. The senior one dresses her underneath in a sewn-on bottom, so the onlookers shout aloud that she has a fine bum. One has a fleshy paunch. There are false breasts on these women, like the comic actors wear; having set such attachments on straight out they pull their dresses away from the stomach to the front as if (held out) with poles. One has tawny eyebrows. They paint them with lamp-black. One happens to be dusky. She smears on white lead. Another is too pale-skinned. She rubs on rouge. A part of the body of one is pretty; she shows it bare. One has nicely-formed teeth. She has to keep laughing perforce, so those present see the mouth she sports so beautifully. If she doesn't like laughing, she spends the day inside, like what is on display at the butcher's when goats' heads are for sale; she keeps a thin branch of myrtle propped between her lips, so that in time she grins, whether she wants to or not.
(Alexis, fr. 103PCG)

In the 6th-century BCE Naucratis in Egypt was a lively trading centre for the Greeks. Rhodopis, also known as Doricha, was a well-known prostitute who was active in this emporium. Herodotus (2.135) reports that she had been brought there as a slave by a man from Samos, but was freed by Charaxus, brother of the poet Sappho, for a large sum. Doricha was then able to establish herself in Naucratis and made a considerable amount of money. Herodotus tells us that after Charaxus freed her he returned to Lesbos, where his sister attacked him bitterly in her poetry. We possess two fragmentary poems of Sappho reflecting her discomfort at his connection with this woman and the shame it has brought her. Aphrodite's epithet "Cypris" ("from Cyprus") is usually supplemented as the first word of the first poem.

(Cypris and) the Nereids, grant that my brother
come here unharmed, and that
everything his heart wishes to come to pass
be fulfilled.

And see that he make amends
for his past errors
and be a joy to his friends
and (a curse) to his enemies, and may no one ever
become a source of grief to us.

May he wish to make his sister
partake of honour.
(Sappho fr. 5V 1–10)

The second poem is more harsh, but also more fragmentary. This may be the one known to Herodotus.

... blessed ...
... fair-tressed (?) ...

Cypris, may he (or she) find you harsh,
and may Doricha not boast, recounting
how he came
a second time for
long-desired love.
(Sappho, fr. 15V 1–2, 9–12)

Herodotus, in the same passage as above, describes Rhodopis as amassing enough wealth from her occupation to be able to present a prominent memorial of herself at Delphi.

Rhodopis wanted to leave a memorial of herself in Greece, by having something made that would not have happened to occur to anyone else, and to have it dedicated in a temple, and set up at Delphi as a memorial of herself. So from one-tenth of her earnings she had a number of iron spits made, as much as the tenth-part would allow, and sent them to Delphi.
(Herodotus, *Histories* 2.135)

A marble fragment belonging to this dedication was found built into the walls of a church at Delphi. The remaining letters seem to read "Rhodopis dedicated ..."
(*SEG* 13.364).

Socrates was not averse to visiting prostitutes. Xenophon describes the philosopher's being intrigued by a woman whose beauty was extolled, and reports that he had urged him (and others) to join him in visiting her. When they arrive at her house they find her engaged in posing for an artist who is painting her portrait. The conversation turns to the pleasurable experience of beholding her beauty, and they all agree that the experience is mutually gratifying.

When the painter had finished, Socrates said, "Men, should we be more grateful to Theodote because she showed us her beauty, or should she be grateful to us because we beheld it? If the display is more advantageous to her then she should be grateful to us, but if the sight of her is more advantageous to us, then are we to be grateful to her?"

When someone said that he spoke fairly, he said "Well, doesn't she already derive some advantage from our praise, and when we spread the report of this to many people won't she benefit even more? We are now eager to touch what we have seen, and we shall go away titillated and shall desire her when we have left. As a result of this it is likely that we are doing her a service, and she is the recipient of this service." Then Theodote said, "My goodness, if this is the case then I ought to be grateful to you for looking at me."
(Xenophon, *Memorabilia* 3.11.2–3)

Before departing, Socrates comments on the sumptuous surrounds in Theodote's house, and learns that her wealth comes exclusively from her profession. He advises her to reciprocate the generosity of her suitors with kindnesses, arguing that this ennobles everyone, and will be good for her business.

Socrates wasn't the only prominent philosopher to consort with prostitutes. Athenaeus (13.589c) reported that the 3rd-century BCE philosopher and biographer Hermippus, in his biography of Aristotle, recorded the fact that Aristotle sustained a relationship with the courtesan Herpyllis until his death, and produced a son with her.

A dedicatory epigram ascribed to Plato adopts the voice of Laïs, the famous courtesan from Corinth who was felt to be the most beautiful woman alive in the 5th century BCE. The poem purports to accompany Laïs' dedication of her mirror to Aphrodite, once she realizes that her beauty has faded with age.

I who laughed arrogantly at Greece,
I who had a swarm of young lovers at my doors back then,
dedicate my mirror to Aphrodite, since I don't wish to look upon myself
as I am, and cannot look upon myself such as I was.
(Plato, *AP* 6.1)

Six hundred years later Julianus, the Roman prefect of Egypt, took up this conceit in several epigrams including the following:

Laïs took Greece captive, which had vanquished the proud shield of the Persians, captive to her beauty.
She was defeated only by old age, and the proof (of this) she dedicates to you, Aphrodite, friend of her youth.
She hates to look upon the irrefutable appearance of grey hair

whose shadowy outline she abhors.
(Julianus, AP 6.20)

Sexual activity of any sort was considered polluting, and it appears that sex with prostitutes was more polluting than sex within marriage. Purification after sex was in order before participants could enter a shrine or engage in ritual. Some sacred laws, such as this one posted in front of the temple of the Great Mother at Metropolis in Asia Minor (4th century BCE), reflect the view that intercourse with prostitutes was more polluting than sex within marriage:

[H]e may perform the rituals two days after intercourse with his own wife, three days after sex with a courtesan. (LSAM 29.4–7)

Evidence for ritual activities of prostitutes is found frequently in connection with the cult of Aphrodite. Corinth, a port city, supported a lively trade in prostitution. There was a large temple of the love goddess on its acropolis, frequented by sailors. When the Persians invaded Greece in 480 BCE, Corinthian prostitutes who considered their trade to be under the auspices of Aphrodite prayed to the goddess for deliverance of Greece from the enemy, and these prayers were believed to have helped in the ultimate defeat of the Persians. The 5th-century poet Simonides composed this epigram to accompany a dedication given to the temple in gratitude for this deliverance:

Women dedicated to the goddess stand praying to the Cyprian
on behalf of the Greeks and her close-fighting citizens.
For divine Aphrodite did not want to give over
The citadel of the Greeks to the bow-carrying Medes.
(Simonides, Epigram 14FGE)

In 464 BCE a Corinthian named Xenophon won first prize in the stadion and the pentathlon at the Olympic games. In a song composed for the victory symposium, the poet Pindar refers in a bemused way to a vow the wealthy victor appears to have made to Aphrodite as he set out for the games:

Young women, hospitable to many strangers,
handmaidens of Persuasion in wealthy Corinth,
who kindle golden tears of fresh green frankincense,
often flitting in your thoughts to the mother of loves,
    to Heavenly Aphrodite –
to you, children, she has extended the plucking of the fruit
of soft youthfulness, in welcome love-making,

without blame.
When under obligation, all is honourable ...
O Mistress of Cyprus, here into your sacred grove
Xenophon has led a hundred-bodied herd of grazing maidens,
rejoicing at the fulfillment of his vows.
(Pindar, fr. 122Sn-M 1–9, 17–20)

Prostitutes were admitted to the initiation rites at Eleusis. The famous courtesan Phryne, who may have been the model for Praxiteles' sculpture "Cnidian Aphrodite," was initiated at Eleusis. In the middle of the 4th century she was prosecuted for impiety, on a charge of introducing rites in honour of a new god but the jurors acquitted her. In the 2nd or 3rd century CE Athenaeus records some details from the trial that were still in circulation – including a striking move by Hyperides, the speaker in her defence. According to Athenaeus, he persuaded the jurors by tearing Phryne's short *chiton* (the obligatory dress of the prostitute) and arousing in them pity and religious fear, to the extent that they acquitted her.

Leading her into full view and tearing off her little outfit he exposed her breasts bare. In addition, he aroused pity at the sight of her, suitable for the peroration and such as to cause the jurors to feel superstitious awe before an interpreter and attendant of Aphrodite, appealing to their compassion not to kill her.
(Athenaeus, *The Learned Banqueters* 13.590d-f = Hyperides fr.178 Kenyon)

Like Rhodopis, it seems that Phryne had a memorial dedicated at Delphi. Athenaeus (13.591b–c) claims that he learned from a report of Alcetas (a general under Alexander the Great) that there was a golden statue of her placed on a marble column base in the sanctuary of Apollo, made by Praxiteles. This was also known to Pausanias (10.15.1).

The poet Nossis (*c.* 300 BCE) from Locri, a Greek city in the south of Italy, composed a dedicatory epigram to accompany another golden statue dedicated to a divinity by a prostitute.

Going to the temple let us look at the statue of Aphrodite,
how it is embellished with gold.
Polyarchis set it up, after reaping the fruits of great wealth
gained from her own glorious body.
(Nossis, A.P. 9.332)

Prostitutes could join other women in celebrating the rites of the Adonia, an informal all-female festival in which women mixed laughter with dirges for the mythical figure of Adonis, a beautiful youth beloved of Aphrodite who died while hunting. We have evidence for the inclusion of prostitutes in this ritual from Menander's comedy *Samia* (produced *c.* 300 BCE), which takes its name from a courtesan from Samos who was kept as a mistress by a wealthy Athenian. The man's son overhears the all-night celebration, which includes the planting of little gardens on rooftops that are destined to wither and die. He takes advantage of the noise to seduce a neighbour's daughter.

The girl's mother was friendly
with the Samian (courtesan) of my father,
and she was often with them; then again
they were at our house. Hurrying back from the country,
as it happened, I came upon them gathered here at our house
with some other women, to celebrate the Adonia.
Since the festivity involved a lot of fun,
as you would expect, I found myself there –
oh dear! – as a spectator.
Their noise made for sleeplessness on my part.
they were carrying some gardens onto the roof,
dancing, spreading themselves about the whole night long.
I shrink from telling the rest. Perhaps I am ashamed
when I needn't be – but I am ashamed nonetheless.
The girl became pregnant.
(Menander, *Samia* 35–49)

A famous courtroom prosecution speech by Apollodorus (composed and delivered by him, although traditionally ascribed to Demosthenes) indicted a non-Athenian and former prostitute named Neaera. The charge was "usurpation of civic rights," since Neaera and her partner Stephanus claimed to be living as legitimate Athenians, as husband and wife. Although the content of the speech focuses on Neaera, the real target was a man named Stephanus – consistent with the way in which prostitutes were rhetorically useful in judicial oratory. This speech strikes a sensitive nerve in the audience by claiming a serious religious violation at an important Athenian festival. Neaera's daughter, assumed to be as sexually unrestrained as her mother, played the role of bride of Dionysus at the Anthesteria.

The speech begins with the story of the origins of Neaera, a non-Athenian slavegirl who received training in prostitution along with six other girls in a brothel.

Nicarete, a freedwoman who had been the slave of Charisius from Elis, and the wife of Hippias, Charisius' cook, bought these seven young girls when they were small children. Nicarete was clever by nature in being able to spot beauty in young girls, and knew this trade, how to bring them up and train them with skill, for she had established this as a profession for herself and had earned a livelihood from them. She used to call them "daughters" by name, so that she might charge the highest fees from those who wished to consort with them, in the belief that they were free girls. When she had reaped the fruits of budding youthfulness in each of them, she sold them as a group, the bodies of all seven of them – Anteia, Stratola, Aristocleia, Metaneira, Phila, Isthmias and this Neaera here. ... The fact that Neaera herself belonged to Nicarete and worked with her body for pay, taken from those who wanted to enjoy her, this is the fact on which I want to focus again. (18–20)

The speaker continues with a report that when the girls were old enough to work as prostitutes the orator Lysias, who was a lover of one of the girls, Metaneira, decided to take her to the Eleusinian mysteries, so that he could arrange for her to be initiated. He asked Nicarete to come to the mysteries and bring Metaneira. Neaera came along. We learn that Lysias observed discretion in housing the women when they came to Athens to go to the festival.

When they came, Lysias did not bring them to his own house, out of respect for the wife whom he had, the daughter of Brachyllus, and his own niece, and for his own mother who was elderly and who lived in the same house. Lysias set them up, both Metaneira and Nicarete, with Philostratus from Colonus, who was still a bachelor and a friend of his. Neaera herself accompanied them, having already been working as a prostitute, although she was young and had not yet reached the age for it. (22)

Philostratus is called to testify that he had accommodated Lysias in housing the women in Athens, and was aware that they had come from Corinth where they worked as prostitutes.

Later, Neaera came again to Athens with Nicarete, to attend the Panathenaic festival. This time she was brought by a Thessalian named Simus. The women were housed with another Athenian named Ctesippus, and Neaera proceeded to entertain a number of men there, drinking and dining with them at symposia. She then returned to her life as a prostitute in Corinth.

After that she worked openly in Corinth, and being a star performer among her lovers were Xenocleides the poet and Hipparchus the actor, and they kept her on hire. (26)

Two other lovers, resenting the high fees charged by Nicarete, eventually arranged to remove Neaera from her bawd by paying a lump sum that would give them exclusive access to her. Next they began the process whereby she could purchase her freedom.

After that two men became her lovers, Timanoridas the Corinthian and Eucrates the Leucadian. These men, since Nicarete was excessive in her demands, expecting to get from them the entire daily expenses of her household, paid down to Nicarete thirty minae as the price for Neaera's body, and purchased her outright from (Nicarete) in accordance with the law of the city, to be their slave. They kept her and used her for as much time as they wanted. But when they were intending to marry they announced to her that they did not want to see her, who had been their exclusive mistress, working as a prostitute in Corinth nor belonging to a brothel-keeper, but that it would be fine with them to take in less money from her than they had put down, and to see her having some of the profit. They said they would give up 1000 drachmas toward the price of her freedom, 500 drachmas each. And they asked her to pay back the 20 minas to them when she found the means. (29–30)

Neaera then raised more funds from a former client in order to secure her freedom and arrange to move back to Athens.

When she heard these words from Eucrates and Timanoridas she summoned to Corinth among others who had been her lovers, Phrynion of Paeania, the son of Demon and brother of Demochares, a man who was living a wanton and extravagant life, as the older ones among you recall. When Phrynion came to her she told him the proposal that Eucrates and Timanoridas had made to her, and gave him the money that she had garnered from her other lovers, having collected it as a contribution toward her freedom, along with whatever she had managed to save on her own. She begged him to advance the rest, whatever was needed to make up the 20 minas, and to deposit it for her as her payment to Eucrates and Timanoridas, so that she would be free. Phrynion heard these words of hers with pleasure and, taking the money that had been brought to her from her other lovers he added the remaining amount himself, then paid the 20 minas to Eucrates and Timanoridas for her freedom, on condition that she not work as a prostitute in Corinth. (30–32)

The speaker describes Neaera's life in Athens as dissolute and abusive.

When he came back here with her, he treated her in a dissolute and reckless fashion. Taking her to dinners, he went everywhere wherever one could drink, always partying right beside her; he had sex with her openly whenever and wherever he wished, with an ostentatious display of his privilege to make the onlookers jealous. He went to the houses of many other men, taking her for reveling, among them to the house of Chabrias of Aexone when, in the archonship of Socratides he was victor in the Pythian Games in the four-horse chariot which he had bought from the sons of Mitys the Argive. When he returned from Delphi he gave the victory feast at the temple of Colias. At this event many other men had sex with her when she was drunk while Phrynion was asleep, even the servants of Chabrias. (33)

Neaera decided to escape from Phrynion and Athens and went to Megara, taking with her some personal property including two maidservants.

So since she was treated with wanton brutality by Phrynion and was not loved as she thought fit, and since he did not pay attention to what she wanted, she packed up the things from his household and as much as she possessed from him – the clothing and jewelry for adorning her body – and two maid-servants, Thratta and Coccaline, and ran off to Megara. This was the period when Asteius was archon in Athens, the time when you were fighting the Lacedaemonians in the latter war. She spent two years living in Megara, a year during the archonship of Asteius and one under Alcisthenes. The prostitution trade did not furnish her with enough money to maintain her household, for she was extravagant but the Megarians were miserly and parsimonious. And there was not a great supply of foreigners in that place because it was wartime and because the Megarians were supporting the Spartans, while you were in control of the sea. It was not possible for her to return to Corinth, because she had been freed by Eucrates and Timanoridas on the condition that she not work in Corinth. (35–37)

Next another lover, the Stephanus involved in the suit, took up with her in Megara, and offererd to bring her back to Athens and protect her from an enraged Phrynion. He also offered to establish her as his "wife," and to arrange for the sons she had borne to become Athenian citizens.

So when peace came during the archonship of Phrasikleides, and the battle between the Thebans and the Spartans was fought at Leuctra, then this man Stephanus, having come to stay in Megara and landed at her house as at the residence of a courtesan, was sleeping with her. She told him everything that had been done, and the brutal treatment by Phrynion. She gave him what she had taken away from his house when she left. She was keen to live in Athens but was afraid of Phrynion because of how she had wronged him, and because he was furious with her. Knowing that his was a violent and contemptuous disposition she took this Stephanus as her patron. This fellow stirred her on while in Megara, by what he said and with his boasting, to the effect that if Phrynion were to lay hands on her he would be good and sorry, but that he himself would take her as his wife and would introduce the sons she had to his clansmen as being his own and would make them citizens. He promised that no human being would wrong her. He came here with her from Megara and with her came her three children, Proxenus and Ariston, and a daughter whom they now call Phano. He took her and the children to the cottage that he had beside Whispering Hermes, between the house of Dorotheus from Eleusis and that of Cleinomachus – the place that Spintharos has now bought from him for seven minae. So the property belonging to Stephanus was this and nothing else. (37–39)

Stephanus planned to avail himself of the revenue not only from the prostitution of Neaera, but of the funds he would receive from blackmailing her clients on the grounds that they were committing adultery with an Athenian wife.

He brought her here for two reasons: so that he would have a beautiful mistress for free and because this work would bring in supplies and maintain his household. For he had no other revenue apart from blackmailing. (39)

Phrynion appeared at Stephanus' door, and Stephanus was forced to post bail when Neaera was brought before the polemarch.

When Phrynion learned that she had moved here and was staying with Stephanus, taking some young men with him and going to Stephanus' house he grabbed her. When Stephanus took her away from him – in accordance with the law, on the grounds that she was a free woman – Phrynion compelled her to give security before the polemarch. (40)

Neaera was released when bail was posted, and she resumed her life as a prostitute-wife, while Stephanus continued to reap the rewards of this arrangement.

When she had been released on bail by Stephanus and was living with him she carried on with the same work no less than before, but she charged greater fees for those wanting to have sex with her, on the grounds that she was now a woman of some status and was living with her husband. Stephanus also participated with his blackmailing; if he caught some unsuspecting and wealthy foreigner as her lover he would lock him up inside on grounds of committing adultery with her and extorted a lot of money from him – naturally, as there was no property belonging to Stephanus or Neaera such as to be able to supply the funds for their expenses day by day. The housekeeping expenses were high; whenever you consider that they had to support him and her and three children which she had when she came to him, and two maidservants and one house-servant. Besides, she had learned to live without restraint, since others had previously furnished the necessities for her. (41–43)

Next Apollodorus directs the accusations against Stephanus, urging that his actions warranted an even greater punishment than Neaera's. The man, he claims, had no legitimate income other than blackmailing and acting as an informant, receiving payment for his public denunciations. (Apollodorus had been among his victims.) Meanwhile, Phrynion continued his prosecution of Stephanus, but the case was settled out of court.

Phrynion brought this suit against him: Stephanus had removed this woman Neaera from him and freed her, and he had received the goods that she had from him when she left him. Their friends got them together and persuaded them to submit their case to arbitration. (45)

The friends and arbitrators are named.

These (arbitrators) met in the temple and when they had heard the facts from both sides and from the woman herself they gave their decision, and these men accepted it: Neaera was a free woman and her own mistress, but what she had taken when she left Phrynion's house she should give back, all except the clothing and the jewelry and the maidservants, which had been bought for the woman herself. She should live with each man on a day-by-day basis, but if they should persuade each other of some another arrangement this would be the valid agreement. The upkeep was supplied by the man who possessed her at a given time. For the future they should be friends with each other and not carry a grievance. This, then, was the agreement recognized by the arbitrators for Phrynion and Stephanus in the case of this woman Neaera. (46–47)

The results of the arbitration with the terms of reconciliation are read aloud.

When the arbitration had been completed, those who supported each side in the settlement and in their affairs did just what I think tends to happen in cases like this, especially when the quarrel is about a courtesan: they went to dine at one or the other's place – whenever he was in possession of Neaera, and she dined and drank with them, since she was a courtesan. (48)

Apollodorus summarizes his argument – that Neaera was a freedwoman, a foreigner and a prostitute. He then turns to the situation of Neaera's daughter, for whom Stephanus had arranged a marriage to an Athenian. The marriage was short lived.

The daughter of this Neaera, whom she brought with her as a small child when she came to Stephanus' house, they called at that time Strybele, but now Phano.

This fellow Stephanus gave her in marriage as if she were his own daughter to an Athenian, Phrastor of Aegilia, and he gave 30 minae as dowry for her. When she came to the house of Phrastor, a labouring man who had collected his means by living frugally, she did not know how to adapt to his ways, but yearned for the habits of her mother and the licentious way of life at her house – having been brought up, I think, in such a wanton fashion. Phrastor saw that she was neither disciplined nor willing to listen to him and at the same time learned for certain that she was the daughter not of Stephanus but of Neaera, and that he had been deceived when the betrothal took place into thinking that he was taking the daughter of Stephanus and not of Neaera – that she was born of an Athenian woman before he lived with Neaera. Angry at all this and thinking that he had been treated outrageously and deceived, he threw the woman out, having lived with her for a year and with her pregnant; he did not return the dowry. (50–51)

Stephanus sued Phrastor for this action, and Phrastor launched a counter-suit.

Stephanus sued him for alimony in the Odeon, in accordance with the law that requires that if someone divorces his wife he must give back the dowry, and if not he has to pay interest on it at the rate of nine obols; it is permitted for the guardian to sue for alimony on behalf of the women in the Odeon. Phrastor brought this indictment against Stephanus before the legislators, on the grounds that he had betrothed to him as an Athenian the daughter of a foreigner, as if she had been his own, contrary to this law. (52)

Once again, a private settlement was reached.

Knowing that he would risk being subjected to the heaviest penalties if he were convicted of pledging in marriage the daughter of a foreign woman, Stephanus came to terms with Phrastor and gave up his claim to the dowry and withdrew his suit for alimony. Phrastor then withdrew his indictment before the legislators. (53)

Phrastor fell sick, and Apollodorus gives an account of the means by which Neaera and her daughter took advantage of the situation.

Now I will provide you with another testimony of Phrastor and his clansmen and relations, to prove that Neaera is a foreigner. Not much later than Phrastor had divorced the daughter of Neaera he fell sick, fell into a sorry state and became completely helpless. Since there was a long-standing rift between him and his own relatives, generating anger and hatred, and in the face of his childlessness, he was beguiled in his feeble state by the ministrations of Neaera and her daughter. They came to him when he was ill and without a caregiver in his sickness, bringing him what was needed for his condition and looking out for him. Now you know yourselves, what value a woman is during illnesses, being at the side of a man who is sick. The son to whom the daughter of this Neaera had given birth – when she had been sent away pregnant, after he learned that she was the daughter not of Stephanus but of Neaera, and was enraged at the deception – he was persuaded to take back and acknowledge as his own. His reasoning was human and what one would expect, given that he was in a precarious situation without much hope that he would recover. Desiring that his relatives would not take what was his nor that he die childless he acknowledged the child, and took him back as his own. (55–57)

But Phrastor recovered, and married an Athenian woman. There follows an account of Stephanus' setting up a former lover of Neaera to have sex with Phano, then blackmailing him for committing adultery. The lover indicts Stephanus on the grounds that he was operating a brothel and that he had therefore not committed adultery with a married woman but a woman working as a prostitute. The matter came to arbitration and the lover agreed to pay a sum of money towards a dowry for the marriage of Phano. Stephanus arranged for Phano to be married to a respectable and prominent Athenian, Theogenes, the King-Archon. An important religious role was played by the King-Archon's wife at the Anthesteria festival.

He then gave (Theogenes) this woman as his wife, the daughter of Neaera, and this Stephanus betrothed her to him as if she were his own daughter. So greatly did he show contempt for your laws. And this woman performed for you, on behalf of the city, the sacrifices that are not to be named, and she saw what is not appropriate for her to see, as a foreigner. Being such a woman as she is, she entered where no one else of the great host of Athenians enters except the wife of the King. She administered the oath to the venerable priestesses, the ministrants for the sacrifices, and was given to Dionysus as his bride. On behalf of the city she conducted the ancestral rites for the gods, which are many and sacred and not-to-be-named. Things that it is not possible for all to hear – how is it an act of piety for a newcomer to Athens to perform them, especially for a woman of such a character and one who has done such things as she has done? (72–73)

The sacred Herald is summoned to testify, and reads the oath taken by the priestesses as they administer the sacrifice, a sacred act overseen by the wife of the King-Archon.

I live purely and am chaste and undefiled, keeping away from other things that are impure, and from having sex with a man; I will celebrate the feast and the Iobacchic festival for Dionysus in accordance with the ancestral customs and at the appropriate times. (78)

The speaker reports that the Council of the Areopagus investigated Phano's background and when this was uncovered they threatened to fine Theogenes for marrying her. Theogenes pleaded ignorance of her family history, claimed he had been deceived by Stephanus and promised to divorce Phano. The Council relented. The clerk is then asked to read the Athenian law on adultery, as it pertained to an adulterous wife.

When (the husband) catches the adulterer, it is not permitted for the one who has caught him to continue to live with his wife. If he does continue to live with her let him be stripped of his citizen rights. And it is not permitted for a wife who has been taken in adultery to attend the publicly-sponsored sacrifices. If she does attend, let her suffer any punishment except death – with impunity. (87)

After a lengthy reflection on the exclusivity of Athenian citizen rights Apollodorus returns in his final remarks to the subject of Neaera, and the threat that she posed to the purity of conduct of Athenian men and women. He asks the members of the jury to do some self-reflection.

Since you all know (the facts) and you have her in your own power and are entitled to punish her, yours is the act of impiety toward the gods if you fail to punish her. What would you say, each of you, when you go home to your own wife or daughter or mother, if you have voted for her acquittal? When she asks you "Where were you?" and you answer "We were trying a case." "Whose?" she will immediately ask. "That of Neaera," you will clearly say, won't you? "Because she as a foreigner lives with an Athenian contrary to the law, and gave her daughter, who has lived a debauched life, to Theogenes the King-Archon, and she performed the sacred rites that are not to be named on behalf of the city and was given as wife to Dionysus." And relating the other facts regarding the charge against her, (you will say that) the prosecution was conducted well and memorably and with attention paid to every detail. And when the women have heard this they will say, "What did you do?" And you will say, "We acquitted her." Now at this point won't the most decent of the women be furious with you, because you maintained that Neaera should have a share like their own in the affairs of the city and in the public rituals? And as for thoughtless women, you will point out that they can clearly do what they want, as being impervious to you and the laws that have been given. For you are making your assessment lightly and with indifference, you yourselves being in agreement with the way of life of this woman. It would be much better if this trial had not taken place than for you to vote for acquittal in light of what has happened. Mark that in that case there will be freedom for prostitutes to live with whomever they like and allege that their children belong to whomever they happen to be with. Your laws will be ineffectual, but the life-style of harlots will legitimize whatever they want to effect for themselves. Look out for the needs of legitimate Athenian women, lest the daughters of the poor find themselves without a dowry. For it is now the case that, even if a girl is without resources, the law provides sufficient dowry for her, if nature has allowed her even a modest degree of comeliness. But with the law dragged through the mud by you and having no effect, while this woman gets off scott-free, then the trade of the harlots will find its way to the daughters of citizens, all those who through lack of resources are unable to marry. The reputation of free women will pass to the courtesans, if they take advantage of the licence available to them to bear children as they wish and share in the rites and sacred rituals and honours belonging to the state.

So let each one of you take thought to cast your vote, one on behalf of his wife, another his daughter, another his mother, others the city and the laws and the religious rituals, lest those respectable women not appear to be held in the same high regard as this whore. Take thought lest those raised by their relatives observing a great deal of noble modesty and attentiveness, who have been given in marriage in accordance with the laws – lest these women appear to be on the same level as a woman who, in many dissolute ways and on many occasions has had sex with many men every day, whenever a man wanted it. (109–114)

Apollodorus tells the jury that he anticipates that Stephanus will argue in his defence that Neaera's children (including Phano) are legitimate, born to him by an Athenian woman whom he had married earlier. To counter this he challenges Stephanus to get the maidservants (slaves) of Neaera to give testimony under torture about the parentage of the children. If the women should testify that the children are legitimate offspring of Stephanus he will withdraw the case. He then reminds the jury of the three distinct categories of women available to Athenian men.

For this is what living together (as man and wife) means – to produce children and introduce the sons to the members of one's phratry and deme, and to give the daughters in marriage to their husbands, as one's own (children). We keep mistresses for our pleasure, concubines for the daily care of our bodies, but wives to produce legitimate children and to have faithful guardians of our property. (122) (Apollodorus [ps. Demosthenes], *Against Neaera*)

FURTHER READING

Davidson, J.N. 1997. *Courtesans and Fishcakes: The Consuming Passions of Classical Athens.* London

Faraone, C. and L. McClure 2006 (eds) *Prostitutes and Courtesans in the Ancient World.* Madison WI/London

Glazebrook, A. and M. Henry 2011 (eds) *Greek Prostitutes in the Ancient Mediterranean: 800 BCE–200 CE.* Madison, WI/London

Milner, J. 2003. "Courtesan, Concubine, Whore: Apollodorus' Deliberate Use of Terms for Prostitutes," *American Journal of Philology* 124.1, 19–37

9

Religious life of girls and women

It is clear from the written as well as the visual record (i.e., that supplied by images on painted ceramics and sculptures) that most of the important events in women's lives achieved definition and recognition through ritual activity. The roles girls and women played in religious performances awarded them a social prominence they could not expect to receive elsewhere.

The following fragment probably belongs to the lost play of Euripides entitled *The Captive Melanippe*, about a young Thessalian woman transported to Metapontium in southern Italy and imprisoned by the jealous wife of the city's founder. In the fragment it is probably Melanippe speaking, making a claim for the overall importance of women's rituals.

And what's more, when it comes to the gods – for I think this is of the first importance – we have the greatest share. For women interpret the mind of Loxias (Apollo) in the temple of Phoebus. By the holy foundations of Dodona beside the sacred oak the female race conveys the thoughts of Zeus to all Greeks who wish to know it. As for the holy rituals performed for the Fates and the Unnamed Goddesses, these are not ordained as holy rituals for men, but among women they thrive, all of them. In affairs dealing with the gods the appointed right of women stands thus.
(Euripides, *Melanippe Captive* fr. 494*TGF*, 12–22)

RITUALS FOR YOUNG GIRLS

A much-cited text used as evidence for the religious activities of pre-adolescent girls is found in the comic play of Aristophanes, *Lysistrata* (produced in 411 BCE). A chorus of old women look back on their childhood performances in public festivals, speaking with one voice.

It is appropriate (to benefit the city) for she nurtured me in luxury, splendidly.
As soon as I was seven, I served as an *arrhephoros*.
Then I was an *aletris* at ten years of age, for the goddess in charge.
Next, wearing the saffron-coloured robe, I was a "bear" at the Brauronia.

As a beautiful young girl I was a *kanephoros* ("basket-bearer") wearing a necklace of dried figs.
(Aristophanes, *Lysistrata* 640–647)

There were four *arrhephoroi*, girls chosen by the King-Archon from Athenian noble families. Two of them performed in the Arrhephoroi festival, during which they descended into an underground sanctuary under the Acropolis with boxes containing sacred objects. This was a re-enactment of an Athenian foundational myth in which Athena entrusted the daughters of the first king with a basket containing the baby Erechtheus. Despite instructions the girls opened the basket, whereupon a snake leapt out, and in fear they jumped to their death from the Acropolis. At the annual Athenian festival two *arrephoroi* deposited the boxes in the sanctuary and returned to the Acropolis with other sacred items.

All four girls, together with the priestess of Athena Polias, spent the year weaving the Panathenaic robe for Athena. In his *Birds*, we find Aristophanes making reference to the civic importance of this religious activity. Produced in 414 BCE – a difficult time for the city at war with the Spartans – the play presents a group of birds that is planning a utopian city, modeled after Athens. The chorus leader comments:

A prosperous construct, this city. Now what god do you suppose
will be the citadel guardian? For whom shall we prepare the peplos?
(Aristophanes, *Birds* 826–827)

The *aletrides* ("grain grinders") were also selected from noble families. They ground meal in sacred mills to make sacrificial cakes.

The Brauronia was held at Brauron, on the east coast of Attica, not far from Athens. Every four years a group of girls between the ages of five and ten were selected to spend an extended time there honouring Artemis, goddess of transitions in the female lifecycle. Among other activities, the girls "played the bear," perhaps engaging in a dramatic rendition of the mythical narrative in which Artemis became angered when a bear had been killed. Many small painted vessels (*krateriskoi*) have been found at Brauron depicting girls nude or wearing short tunics, running and dancing together. From the *Lysistrata* passage it appears that in addition they wore the *krokotos*, a saffron-dyed garment that was the colour of that worn by brides.

The archeological remains at Brauron include mirrors, jewelry etc. but also a considerable amount of spinning and weaving equipment, indicating that the girls' activities also included the preparation of textiles. Dedications of clothing are recorded both at Brauron and in the sanctuary of Artemis Brauronia on the

Acropolis in Athens. The following inscription (4th century BCE) accompanied one collection of these dedications. It was found at Brauron.

Archippe: a spotted, sleeved tunic in a case, during the year Callimachus was archon. Calippe: a little tunic, scalloped and embroidered; it has letters woven in. Chaerippe and Eucoline, a dotted tunic in a box. Philumene a tunic made from (woven) stalks of mallow, in the year Theophilus was archon. Pythias a dotted robe in the year Themistocles was archon. There is an embroidered sea-purple tunic in a box: Thyaene and Malthace dedicated it. An embroidered sea-purple tunic in a box: Eukoline dedicated it. Phile: a woman's belt; Pheidylla a white woman's cloak in a box. Mneso a frog-green garment. Nausis a woman's cloak, with a broad purple border that has a wave design all around.
(*IG* II² 1514, 6–18)

The civic involvement in the Brauronia festival and its importance to the well-being of the Athenian state is reflected in this fragmentary inscription from Brauron (late 4th/early 3rd century BCE), recording a proposal to guarantee public support for the sanctuary.

[S]on of Hierokles of the deme Philaidai proposed: in order that everything in the sanctuary of the goddess at Brauron be safe and sound, and the temple (i.e., the old one) and that of the Virgins; that the dining-rooms should be kept dry, and the chamber of the attendants in which the Bears live and the upper room above the chamber, and the gymnasium and the wrestling-school and the stables and everything else that the city has built and dedicated to the goddess for the salvation of the Athenian people.
(*SEG* 52, 104.2–8)

The *kanephoroi* ("basket bearers") were girls chosen from noble families to carry the ritual baskets containing the sacrificial knife and other objects for sacrifices at various festivals. The girls would be conspicuous in festival processions as nubile virgins, and in fact often led the procession.

In another one of Aristophanes' utopian comedies, *The Acharnians* (produced 425 BCE), an Athenian citizen who is fed up with war-torn Athens makes a private truce with the Spartans, and together with his family celebrates a private version of the rustic festival of Dionysus that involved parading with a phallus pole. His daughter would be the *kanephoros* and his slave the phallus polebearer. His words appear to reflect familiar ritual speech and practice:

Speak words of good omen, speak words of good omen!
Let the *kanephoros* go ahead, a little in front.

Xanthias, hold the phallus pole erect!
Daughter, put down the basket, so that we may begin.
(Aristophanes, *Acharnians* 241–244)

NYMPHAE

As Greek girls approached puberty they were referred to as *parthenoi*, "virgins" – but virgins as much in a social as a physical sense, i.e. not yet under the control of a husband. As nubile, potential brides, they were known as *nymphae*, and remained *nymphae* even after marriage – until the birth of their first child.

Artemis regularly received gifts brought to her various sanctuaries by *parthenoi/nymphae* as they prepared to leave childhood behind and marry. A poignant testimony to this practice is the (anonymous) epigram composed for "Timareta," a *parthenos* who dedicated her gifts to the goddess but died before she could make the transition. Here Artemis, like Persephone before her marriage to Hades, is called a *kore*. *Kore* is usually translated as "girl," but is often one who is being considered particularly as daughter; perhaps for this reason *"kore"* was also the word used for "doll." In this (anonymous) epigram, there is a triple identification of *korae*: Timareta, her dolls, and the goddess.

Timareta before her wedding dedicated her tambour and her lovely ball
    and the hair-net that held her hair;
her *korai* too, a *kore* to a *kore* as is fitting,
    and the clothing of the *korae* to Artemis of the Lake.
Daughter of Leto, do you place your hand over the girl Timareta
    and in purity may you preserve her purity.
(AP 6.280)

A large number of terracotta dolls have been found in sanctuaries of Artemis and in caves/springs dedicated to the nymphs, a testimony to the widespread practice of girls dedicating these along with a lock of their hair and other emblems of childhood to divine figures who meant most to them at this time of life. These were known as *proteleiae*. But the story of Persephone highlights the dark side of this transitional moment – its affinity, real or conceived, with death.

There are several Greek myths in which the narrative runs parallel to the real story of Timareta, where a maiden dies. Perhaps the best known is that of Iphigeneia, daughter of Agamemnon who, in some versions of the myth, was sacrificed by her father to appease Artemis. The goddess, angered at an offence committed against her by the king, would not provide winds favourable for the Greek expedition to sail to Troy and take vengeance for the abduction of Helen. In Aeschylus' *Agamemnon* (produced 458 BCE) the chorus of Argive elders struggle to make sense of the choice made by the king to kill his daughter. She, like the Bears at Brauron, wears a saffron-coloured robe.

So he dared
to become the sacrificer of his daughter,
as a prop for wars fought over a woman,
an offering on behalf of the ships. (*Strikingly, Aeschylus uses the word "proteleia" for this offering.*) They, war-passioned judges, held as of no account
her pleas, her invoking of her father
nor her maiden years.
Her father, after a prayer, ordered his attendants
to take her as she fell forward, with all their strength,
and lift her up wrapped in her robes above the altar, like a (sacrificial) she-goat,
and to check with a restraint
any curse on the house uttered from the beautiful mouth,
with force and the silencing strength of straps.
Dropping her saffron-dyed robe to the ground,
she struck each of the sacrificers
with a pitiful dart from her eyes.
She was lovely as in a painting,
wanting to call out to them as when on many occasions
she had sung amid the hospitable tables of her father's banqueting halls,
and with the pure voice of a chaste maiden
she had lovingly honoured the joyful paean of her dear father
at the third libation.
(Aeschylus, *Agamemnon* 224–246)

In his tragedy *Iphigeneia among the Taurians* (produced *c.* 413 BCE), Euripides presents the sacrifice of Iphigeneia differently. The goddess substitutes a deer for the girl on the altar, and transports Iphigeneia to Tauris on the Black Sea. There she becomes a priestess of Artemis, a position she will retain when she returns to Greece until her death, as the goddess Athena foretells at the end of the play. The text makes clear the connection between Brauron and another, very real, type of death that could await *nymphae*.

You, Iphigeneia, by the holy stairs of Brauron,
must serve as key-bearer to this goddess (Artemis).

You will die and be buried there, and they shall dedicate
as an offering to you dresses of finely woven fabrics,
which wives when they gasp their last in childbirth
leave behind in their homes.
(Euripides, *Iphigeneia Among the Taurians* 1462–1467)

Another sanctuary of Artemis with connections to Brauron was that located at Mounichia, on a hill overlooking the Piraeus, the port city of Athens. The myth associated with the rites at Mounichia contains parallels to the bear story at Brauron and the various accounts of the sacrifice of Iphigeneia, as we learn from the *Suda*. In all of these stories we get the sense that this time of a girl's life was felt to be precarious.

A she-bear appeared in the shrine and when it was killed by the Athenians a famine occurred. The god prophesied that they would be delivered from it if someone sacrificed their daughter to the goddess. Embaros alone agreed, on condition that his clan hold the priesthood for life. He dressed up his daughter, but hid her in the innermost part of the temple and, dressing a goat in clothes, sacrificed it as though it were his daughter.
(*Suda*, s.v. "*Embaros eimi*")

The sexual awakening that would be felt by *parthenoi/nymphai* can explain the homoerotic lyrics in Alcman's songs for *parthenoi* (see above, pp. 32–4) and the prominence awarded to the virginal young women in religious processions, which doubtless also functioned as a display of future brides. References to *parthenoi* dancing at religious festivals are numerous. Not infrequently the festivals commemorate the death of a mythical young man. In Euripides' tragedy *Helen* (produced 412 BCE), the chorus imagine Helen's return to Sparta with Menelaus after the Trojan War, where she would find young women performing at the Hyacinthia, a festival that honoured the young beloved of Apollo who was killed by his lover as they were throwing the discus.

(Helen), you would find the daughters of Leucippus by the rising river
or in front of the temple of Pallas,
when you return at the time of the dances
or the revels of Hyacinthus, and join their night-time festival.
(Euripides, *Helen* 1465–1470)

In *Hippolytus*, another of Euripides' tragedies, King Theseus of Athens brings about the violent death of his son, the virginal Hippolytus who is a devotee of Artemis. The goddess comforts him as he lies dying with the promise that maiden girls will sing laments for him, cutting a lock of their hair in his honour before their marriage, and singing of the illicit passion of his stepmother that led to his death.

[Artemis] To you, unfortunate man, in return for these grievous ills
I will grant the greatest honours in the Troizen city.
Maidens (*korai*) unyoked, before their marriage
will cut their hair in your honour, for you who –
through the long span of time –
will reap the deepest grief of their tears.
The song-making of *parthenoi* will for all time
be directed toward you for its theme.
(Euripides, *Hippolytus* 1423–1429)

The sexual life that awaited brides was represented by mythical nymphs, sexually active females inhabiting the wild areas outside cities. As cult figures they were patrons of springs and fountains, where human *nymphae* came to collect water. The divine nymphs often shared cult honours with the randy goat god Pan. Pan opens Menander's comedy *Dyscolus* ("The Grump," produced 317 BCE) with a description of the daughter of the *dyscolus*. Pan describes her as a *parthenos* who is assiduous in her devotion to the nymphs.

His daughter
has grown up consistent with her upbringing,
not in the least indifferent. But with scrupulous care
and adulation for my cult-mates the Nymphs
she honours us and persuades us
to pay some attention to her.
(Menander, *Dyscolus* 34–39)

It so happens that there is a young man observing as the *parthenos* garlands the statues of the Nymphs at the shrine. He naturally enough falls in love with her and the play proceeds toward their wedding. The nuptial festivities (appropriately) take place in the shrine of the Nymphs and Pan.

An awareness of the loss of independence and fresh sexual potency that came with life as a married woman may also lie behind an Argive ritual that was reported to Pausanias, the religious antiquarian and traveler of the 2nd century CE. He was told that in the spring of Canathus at Nauplia the statue of Hera was bathed annually in a ritual intended to restore her *parthenia* (Pausanias, *Description of Greece* 2.38.2)

MARRIAGE RITUALS

With marriage, Greek *parthenoi* experienced a change in their relationship with Artemis. No longer was the goddess a patron of their childhood. She would oversee their transition to becoming wives and mothers, but there may have been a sense in which the loss of her virginity came with a price. This seems to be reflected in a purification law from the Greek colony in Cyrene (4th century BCE).

Before the bride enters the bedchamber she must pay compensation to Artemis. She will not be under the same roof as her husband nor will she bring on pollution until she comes to Artemis. She who does not do this incurs pollution voluntarily; when she has purified the temple of Artemis she will sacrifice in addition a grown animal, then shall go to the bedchamber. But if she pollutes involuntarily she shall purify the sanctuary.
(*LSCG Supp.* 115B 1–8 = RO 97.B83–90)

The term "*proteleia,*" referring to a gift given to divinities on behalf of future brides, was also the term Athenians used for the day on which a prenuptial sacrifice was held for Athena.

Thus *proteleia* they call the day on which her parents lead a *parthenos* to the Acropolis, to the goddess, and carry out sacrifices.
(*Suda* s.v. "*proteleia*")

Aphrodite, patron of sexual activity and fertility, would also be a fitting goddess to receive a *proteleia*. An early 4th-century BCE Athenian inscription on a treasury box describes its contents (one drachma) in sacrificial terms, a "first-fruit offering" for Aphrodite-of-Heaven.

Treasury-box, first-fruits to Aphrodite Ourania as a *proteleia* for marriage: one drachma. (*SEG* 41, 182)

The nuptial activities involving divinities occurred before the events of the wedding itself. On the day of the wedding (the *gamos*) the bridal bath could be performed with water from a sacred spring, often one protected by nymphs such as the Kallirhoe Spring in Athens. In a procession the bride's attendants would carry the water in special vessels called *loutrophoroi* ("water carriers"). In the sanctuary of the "Nymphe" on the south side of the Acropolis many of these *loutrophoroi* have been found, indicating that they were dedicated after the wedding. *Loutrophoroi* were also placed in tombs, particularly in the graves of girls who died before marriage.

RITUALS FOR WOMEN

One of the best known women's rituals in Ancient Greece involved ecstatic activity in honour of Dionysus. Many vase paintings have survived that depict maenads dancing, their heads thrown back while they shake *thyrsoi* (ivy-covered wands often crowned with a pinecone) – attesting to the fact that the celebrations, which took place outside urban areas, were anything but marginal. Euripides' play, *Bacchae* (likely produced in 405 BCE, just after his death), gives us a mythical account of the effect of Dionysus on men as well as women. While the actual activities of the women while under the influence of the god – such as tearing apart living creatures and eating raw flesh – are doubtless an extreme exaggeration, the description likely had some basis in maenadic ritual.

The play is set in Thebes. The chorus consists of female followers of Dionysus who have travelled with him to Thebes from Lydia in the East, where the rituals were shared with those for the Great Mother Cybele, which also involved ecstatic dancing. In their entrance hymn, the chorus praises the blessed state and mystical knowledge the participant achieves.

Blessed is the one who, happy
in knowing the rites of the gods
lives in purity,
initiating his soul into the mystical band,
celebrating the mysteries of Bacchus on the mountains
in ritual purifications.
Keeping the celebrations of the Great Mother,
Cybele, shaking the *thyrsus* and crowned with ivy,
the votary serves Dionysus. (72-82)

Later in the same song, the chorus of maenads describes an epiphany of Dionysus as he races on the mountains in Lydia, then stops to devour the flesh of a dying goat. Miracles follow.

A welcome sight (is the god) on the mountains
when he falls on the ground, leaving the chase of the ritual band,
wrapped in the sacred garment of fawn-skin,
hunting down the blood of the slain goat,
the delight of raw flesh devoured.
Rushing to the mountains of Lydia and Phrygia
this cult leader Bromios –
Euhoi!
The ground runs with milk, flows with wine,

runs with the nectar of bees. (135–144)
(Euripides, *Bacchae*)

The king of Thebes, nephew of the god, is determined to stop the rituals that Dionysus and his band wish to introduce to the city. He imprisons the god and his band of followers, but they escape. He imagines that the Theban women who have taken to the mountains to celebrate the god are using the occasion as an excuse to drink wine and have sex. Instead, a messenger reports that their actions resemble those described by the eastern maenads.

The pasturing herds of cattle were just ascending to the heights
at the hour when the sun releases its beams
warming the earth.
I saw three dancing bands of women,
of one of them, Autonoë, was the leader,
of the second your mother Agave, and Ino of the third dancing group.
They were all sleeping, their bodies relaxed,
some resting their backs on branches of fir,
others rested their heads on the ground on oak leaves,
at random, completely chaste.
They were not, as you say, drunk on the wine-bowl
or the intoxicating sound of the pipe,
nor were they going off alone into the woods in pursuit of Aphrodite. (677–688)

The messenger continues his report of their benign behaviour, once they are awakened by Pentheus' mother Agave.

They rubbed the deep sleep from their eyes
and stood up straight, a vision of orderliness –
young and old, and young women not yet in the yoke of marriage.
First they let their hair fall loose to their shoulders,
and all the fastenings of the fawnskins that had come undone
they fastened up, and belted the dappled skins
with snakes, who were licking their cheeks.
Some held fawns or wolf cubs from the wild in their arms,
giving them their white milk –
all those who had just given birth, whose breast was still over-full,
having left their newborn at home. They placed on themselves
crowns of ivy and oak-leaves, and flowering bindweed.
Someone, taking a *thyrsus*, struck it against a rock,
and out leapt a dew-wet spring of water.

Another sunk her fennel stalk down into the earth
and right there the god released a fountain of wine.
As many as wished a drink of milk
scraped the earth with their fingertips
and got gushings of milk. From their ivy-entwined *thyrsoi*
dripped sweet streams of honey.
The result of this would have been, had you been there,
that the god whom you now censure
you would have approached with prayers – as you looked upon these things. (692–713)
(Euripides, *Bacchae*)

The tranquility of the scene of miracles and gentleness is broken when a group of cowherds and shepherds make an attempt to capture Agave, Pentheus' mother. As they leap out from an ambush Agave rallies the women to attack the men with their *thyrsoi*. The herdsmen escape, but the women turn to their herds and flocks and tear the animals apart. Then they turn to ravaging the nearby village before returning to their mountain glen, where they wash off the blood of their quarry in the streams provided by the god.

Meanwhile, King Pentheus is overcome with curiosity about the rituals, and is persuaded by the god to dress as a maenad and spy on the women. The Theban women once more are tranquil until they catch sight of the spy. In their state of divine possession, they tear him limb from limb. His mother spears his head on her thyrsus and carries it back to Thebes, glorying in the "lion" she has captured and killed.

While Euripides was clearly fabricating some extreme acts that the Theban women undertook when filled with Dionysiac ecstasy, some of the elements of his account of the ritual seem to be confirmed by an inscription from Magnesia, a fertile city on the Meander river near Ephesus. (The inscription is a Roman copy of one from the Hellenistic period.) The text reinforces the tragedian's focus on Thebes as a home for maenadism, as well as his description of a triad of ritual groups (*thiasoi*) who carried out the ritual. The inscription quotes a Delphic oracle that gave the prescription for establishing the cult in Asia Minor.

Go to Thebes, to the holy plain, so that you may obtain
maenads who are from the race of Ino, daughter of Cadmus.
They will give you both the rites and the noble customs,
and they will establish *thiasoi* for Bacchus in your city.
(*IMagn.* 215[a]24–30)

Near Magnesia, at the mouth of the Meander, was the coastal city of Miletus from which we have a sacred law giving regulations for its maenadic ritual.

The following text suggests that the raw flesh is most likely that belonging to a sacrifice for Dionysus, rather than to the frenzied killing and consuming of an animal.

Whenever the priestess (carries out) the sacred rituals on behalf of the city ... it is not lawful to go out, to deposit raw flesh before the priestess deposits them on behalf of the city. Nor is it lawful for anyone to assemble the *thiasos* before the public one (has been assembled).
(*LSAM* 48.1–4)

In Miletus in the 3rd or 2nd century BCE this epigram was composed for the tomb of a local maenadic leader, a priestess of Dionysus:

Bacchae of the city, say "Farewell,
    Holy Priestess." This is the right tribute for a good woman.
She led you to the mountain, conducted all the rites
    and carried the sacred implements in procession in front of the whole city.
If some stranger should ask her name – Alcmeionis
    daughter of Rhodius, who knew her portion of noble fare.
(Th. Wiegand, *SB* 507 = A. Henrichs, *HSCP* 82 [1978] 148

Pausanias (2nd century CE) reports that women from Attica joined with others from Delphi every other year to travel to Mount Parnassus (near Delphi) and celebrate the mountain rituals for Dionysus, performing dances along the way (10.4.3). Plutarch (1st–2nd century CE) reported that in the year 355 BCE maenads from Phocis (the region of Delphi) came to the city of Amphissa at night, exhausted after vigorous performance of their ritual, and collapsed in the agora and fell asleep. Since Amphissa was hostile territory, the maenads were in danger, but local women came out and stood guard over them until they could escort them to safety (Plutarch *Moralia* 249e–f).

Rituals in honour of Demeter and Dionysus often included obscene language (*aischrologia*) and behaviour. In the *Homeric Hymn to Demeter* (which may have taken written form as early as the 7th century BCE), we have a mythical account of the importance of mockery and what was likely indecent behaviour on the part of a handmaid. The result of Iambe's gesture is that the goddess, previously sombre and uncooperative because of the abduction by Hades of her daughter is moved to laugh, then renews her generosity to mortals.

But Demeter, bringer of the seasons and bestower of splendid gifts,
did not want to be seated on the shining seat.

She remained silent, her lovely eyes cast down
until that moment when Iambe, who knew what was appropriate,
set down a well-built stool and threw over it a silvery fleece.
Seated there (Demeter) held out her veil in her hands.
For a long time she sat without speaking on the stool, sorrowful at heart,
and greeted no one with word or gesture,
but without laughing, without eating, without drinking
she sat, wasting away in her longing for her deeply-belted daughter,
until Iambe, who knows what is appropriate, with jokes
and many mocking gestures turned the disposition of the revered goddess
towards smiling and laughter and the possession of a gracious heart,
Iambe, who later as well cheered her moods.
(*Homeric Hymn to Demeter* 192–205)

In other versions of the story Demeter is made to laugh by "Baubo." An Orphic
fragment describes Baubo's exposing her genitals before the goddess, while the
baby Iakchos (a name applied elsewhere to Dionysus) holds his hands under
her breast and giggles. The goddess' change of mood leads her to accept the
kykeon, a barley drink that was consumed at Demeter rituals, including those
at Eleusis.

So speaking she pulled up her dress and exposed herself,
and showed all of her body, even the hollow that is not suitable for seeing.
The child Iakchos was jostling her and laughed, with his hand under her breasts.
And she, the goddess smiled then – smiled in her heart,
and took the gleaming cup in which the *kykeon* had been poured.
(Orphic fr. 52 Kern)

The most important ritual honouring Demeter in which women played a central
role was the Thesmophoria. It is thought to have been established very early in
Greece, and was extremely widespread. As a "mystery" cult its worshippers
were not to divulge details of their ritual activities, but some elements can
be gathered from scattered references, and from the setting for Aristophanes'
Women at the Thesmophoria (see below, pp. 143–7).

Apollodorus (2nd century BCE), in his *Library*, tells the story of Kore/
Persephone's abduction. (Demeter's daughter is conventionally referred to as
"Kore" ["Maiden," "Daughter"] before her abduction, and "Persephone" after
her Underworld marriage.). He accounts for women's engaging in *aischrologia*
at the Thesmophoria by the fact that Demeter's grief and anger was converted
to laughter through the provocation of Iambe, to whom he refers as a crone
(1.5.1).

Diodorus Siculus (1st century BCE) also comments on this connection, in his description of the festival in his native Sicily, at Syracuse. Believing that the site of the abduction was outside the city of Syracuse, the Sicilians – men as well as women – held a ten-day festival at the time the grain was sown (Sicily was a rich grain-producing area in antiquity), and obscenities were an integral part of the celebration.

In honour of Demeter they chose as the time for the sacrifice the one at which the sowing of the grain is started, and for ten days they hold a festive gathering which takes its name from this goddess, and because of the splendour of its preparation is the most magnificent. In the undertaking of this they imitate the ancient way of life. It is the custom for them during these days to engage in coarse banter as they associate with one another, on account of the fact that the goddess, aggrieved at the abduction of Kore, laughed as the result of obscene speech.
(Diodorus Siculus, *Historical Library* 5.4.7)

An ancient commentator on Lucian's *Dialogue of the Courtesans* (composed 2nd century CE) provides some other details about the festival, linking it to Kore/Persephone's abduction by Hades/Plouton to the Underworld. The description of the rituals of the Thesmophoria provided by this commentator makes clear the Greek association of human with natural fertility. It is worth noting that the Greek word for "piglet" was also used informally to refer to women's genitals, as was "*barathron*," a word that meant "pit."

The Thesmophoria. A festival of the Greeks that included the mysteries, and these same mysteries are called "Skirrophoria." They were conducted in accordance with the more mythological account, namely the one in which Kore was abducted by Plouton while picking flowers. Eubouleus, a swineherd, was pasturing his pigs at the same time and in that exact place, and was drawn into the pit (opened for) Kore. It is in honour of Eubouleus, therefore, that piglets are thrown into the pits of Demeter and Kore. Women called "Fetchers" bring up the rotten remains that were cast into the chasms below, having kept themselves purified for three days, and descend into the sacred spaces. When they have brought them up they deposit them on the altars. They think that whoever takes this and sows it along with the seed will have a good harvest. They also say that there are serpents below, around the pits, who eat most of what is thrown down. For this reason there is a commotion whenever the women do their fetching, and whenever they set those forms down again, so that the serpents will withdraw, those they take to be guarding the sacred spaces. The same rituals are called "Arrhetophoria," and are conducted with the same rationale regarding the growing of produce and the fertility of humans. On the same occasion they

bring sacred things not to be spoken about, prepared from wheat dough – images of serpents and of male genitalia. And they take pine branches because of the prolific nature of that plant. They throw those things into the pits, the so-called sacred spaces, together with the piglets, as I already said, and the latter because of their fecundity, a token of the fertility of vegetation and humankind, as a thanks offering to Demeter.
(Scholion *ad* Lucian's *Dialogue of the Courtesans* 80.2.1 = Rabe pp. 275–276)

Theodoretus, a Christian bishop in Syria (4th century CE), saw the activity at the Thesmophoria as parallel to the Phallophoria. Where men at the latter festival worshipped the phallus of Dionysus, women at the Thesmophoria gave sacred honour to the female sex organ (*Graecarum Affectionum Curatio* 3.84).

From the same collection of scholia on Lucian's *Dialogue of the Courtesans* comes an account of another festival celebrated by women that involved scurrilous speech and their handling models of male and female genitalia. This festival was the Haloa, in honour of Dionysus as well as Demeter and Kore. It was one in which the married women were invited to contemplate adultery.

In this festival, one of the women leads in (the activities) at Eleusis and much playfulness and mockery in speech occurs. Only the women who have come in have their fill of what they want to say. They say the most shameful things to one another at that time, and the priestesses go around to the women on the sly, advising them (i.e. whispering) in their ears to do something unspeakable, to engage in extramarital sex. All the women shout to one another shameful things, while handling the indecent parts of the body, unseemly male and female parts. There is also wine available and tables are laden with all sorts of food from land and sea.
(Scholion *ad* Lucian's *Dialogue of the Courtesans* 7.4.12–27= Rabe p. 280.12–27)

FURTHER READING

Blundell, S. and M. Williamson 1998 (eds) *The Sacred and the Feminine in Ancient Greece.* London/New York

Burkert, W. 1985. *Greek Religion.* Cambridge, MA

Clinton, K. 1996. "The Thesmophorion in Central Athens and the Celebration of the Thesmophoria in Attica," in R. Hägg ed. *The Role of Religion in the Early Greek Polis*, 17–25. Stockholm

Connelly, J. 2007. *Portrait of a Priestess. Women and Ritual in Ancient Greece.* Princeton

Dillon, M. 2002. *Girls and Women in Classical Greek Religion.* London/New York

Dodd, D.B. and C. Faraone 2003 (eds) *Initiation in Ancient Greek Rituals and Narratives: New Critical Perspectives.* London/New York

Foley, H. 1994 ed. *The Homeric Hymn to Demeter: Translation, Commentary and Interpretive Essays*. Princeton

Henrichs, H. 1978. "Greek Maenadism from Olympias to Messalina," *Harvard Studies in Classical Philology* 82, 121–160

Kraemer, R.S. 2004. *Women's Religions in the Greco-Roman World: A Sourcebook*. Oxford

Larson, J. 2001. *Greek Nymphs. Myth, Cult, Lore*. Oxford

O'Higgins, L. 2003. *Women and Humour in Classical Greece*. Cambridge

Parca M.G. 2007. *Finding Persephone. Women's Rituals in the Ancient Mediterranean*. Bloomington, IN

Sourvinou-Inwood, S. 1988. *Studies in Girls' Transitions*. Athens

10

Gender performed on the Athenian stage

Beginning in the later decades of the 6th century BCE the Athenian City Dionysia, a springtime festival for the god Dionysus, became the occasion on which dramatic competitions were held. Competing tragic playwrights developed plays based on traditional mythological material and submitted their texts in the hope of gaining approval for production. Three tragedians would be chosen, each supplying three tragedies and one "satyr" play, a mythological burlesque. In 487 BCE comedies were introduced to the festival, when five comic poets were selected, each presenting one play (the numbers were reduced during the Peloponnesian War.) Another Athenian festival for Dionysus hosted dramatic performances too. This was the Lenaia, a winter festival that mounted five comedies each year beginning in 442 BCE, then added two tragedies a decade later. (Those numbers were also curtailed during the war.)

For all roles in those plays that were chosen male actors and dancers were trained. Female characters, then, were played by men. While there may have been some women in the audience at the actual performances, there is no firm evidence for this, and although it would seem that the dramas were essentially intended to be a form of entertainment by and for men, questions can be raised about the intentions of the playwright and the impact on the audience, when traditional expectations of marriage and gender roles come into question and a woman's voice is heard.

TRAGEDY

In *Prometheus Bound*, a play that some ascribe to Aeschylus, the playwright works with mythical material from Argos. Io, a local nymph and priestess of Hera in Argos, tells Prometheus the story of her rape by Zeus, foretold to her in a dream:

You will learn clearly by my story everything that you want to know.
And yet even as I speak I am ashamed to speak
of the storm, god-sent, and the ruin

of my beauty, how it swept down over me, a wretched one.
Over and over again in my maiden apartments
nocturnal visions would visit and beguile me
with smooth words: "O most fortunate maiden,
why do you lead a virginal life for so long, when it is possible
for you to obtain the greatest of marriages?
Zeus has been heated by a weapon
of desire for you, and wishes to partake of love with you.
Don't, my child, spurn the bed of Zeus
but go to the deep meadow of Lerna,
where the flocks and cattle-steadings of your father are found.
Go, so the eye of Zeus may be relieved of its desire."
("Aeschylus", *Prometheus Bound* 641–654)

Her father learns of her visions and consults Delphi, where he is told that he is to send Io out of the house to an isolated place, or the thunderbolts of Zeus would destroy his entire family. Io's shape is transformed, and she grows cow horns. She is pursued by a gadfly over the earth, finally settling in Egypt, where Zeus impregnates her.

Euripides, in his *Ion*, worked with the myth of the daughter of the king of Athens who was raped by the god Apollo. Creusa exposes the child when he is born, and later confronts her divine lover with the consequences for her of the love he forced on her.

You, making the seven-stringed cithara
to sing, which produces on the lifeless horns
of the rustic creature
its tuneful hymns of the Muses –
against you, son of Leto,
I shall address my reproach in this light of day.
You came to me, flashing with your hair of gold
at the time when I was plucking
saffron-coloured petals into the folds of my cloak,
reflecting their golden light with their bright hue.
You took me by the pale wrists of my arms
to a bed in the cave,
while I let out a shriek, "Mother!" –
you a divine lover,
granting a favour for shameless Aphrodite.
And I, poor wretch, bore you a son
whom, out of fear of my mother,

I threw on your covers,
on the bed of misery
where you had lain with me, miserable.
Oh, woe! And now he is gone,
snatched by the winged creatures for their feast,
my child – and yours,
you brazen one. And you, playing on the lyre
and singing your paeans!
(Euripides, *Ion* 881–906)

The mythical material used by Aeschylus in his *Suppliants* connected Argos with Egypt. Danaus and Aegyptus were two sons of the Egyptian king; the former had 50 daughters and the latter 50 sons. After a quarrel with his brother, Danaus fled with his daughters to Argos. When an Egyptian herald is spotted arriving in Argos the girls realize that they will be forced to marry their cousins. Rather than accept the inevitable, the Danaids see death as preferable to marriage:

No longer could this evil be averted.
My heart is shaken, and turns black.
My father's lookout has caught me; I am undone, by terror.
I would prefer to meet my doom
in the braids of a noose,
rather than have an abominable husband touch this skin of mine.
Before that may Hades be my overlord, as a dead woman!
(Aeschylus, *Suppliants* 784–791)

The various myths associated with the city of Thebes circulated in epic poems, parallel to those that were narrated in the Trojan saga. After the death of Oedipus, the king of Thebes, Eteocles violates an agreement made with his brother and refuses to relinquish the throne to Polyneices. The latter gathers a force from Argos under seven military leaders to invade Thebes. Aeschylus' play incorporating this story opens with the arrival of the Argive host and the initial clashes of the two armies. The chorus of young Theban maidens sing songs of terror and pray wildly to the gods to protect their city. King Eteocles attempts to silence their disruptive energies.

I ask you, unbearable creatures,
is this the best means of saving the city?
Does it give confidence to our beleaguered army,
falling upon the images of our city's gods

to howl and shout – an anathema to people of sound mind?
Neither in difficult nor in easy times
may I live with the female sex!
When a woman is in charge, her boldness is intolerable to be around,
but when she is fearful she is an even greater menace to the household and city.
Just so now, with this frenzied running around in flight
you are instilling weakness and faint-heartedness in our citizens by your clamour.
You are advancing the success of the enemy outside as best you can,
and we are being ruined by our own side from within.
Such is the result you would get by living with women!
(Aeschylus, *Seven Against Thebes* 182–195)

The expressed wish of men to live without women, implicit in Hesiod's story of Pandora, occurs in several Greek tragedies. In Euripides' *Medea*, Jason defends his decision to marry the Corinthian princess on grounds of expediency, and in accusing his wife Medea of acting outrageously from jealousy he attacks the female sex as a whole.

For me it is profitable to benefit my living children
by having children in the future. Now is this bad planning?
Now not even you would say so, if it were not *sex* that is chafing you.
But you women have arrived at such a point that if all is well in the bedroom
you think you have everything.
But if some disaster occurs in your sexual life
you regard what is best and ideal for you as the most inimical.
Mortals ought to beget children from somewhere else,
and there should not be a female sex.
Then there would be no trouble for mankind.
(Euripides, *Medea* 566–575)

In *Hippolytus*, Euripides picks up the story of Theseus, when his third wife Phaedra has fallen in love with her stepson, born of Theseus' former (Amazon) wife. Hippolytus has devoted himself to the celibate life in the service of Artemis, and is horrified at the revelation of his stepmother's passion.

Oh, Zeus! Why did you set women to dwell in the light of the sun,
an evil counterfeit for mankind?
If you had wanted to reproduce the race of mortals
you should not have provided this from women,
But men could have deposited in your temples
bronze or iron or a great weight of gold

purchasing the seed of children,
each man the amount fitting his estate,
and so they would have lived in their homes freed from women. (616–624)

It is clear from this that a woman is a great evil.
The father who begat her and raised her
pays out a dowry and sends her away to live, so that he can be rid of this evil.
But the man in turn who receives the baneful creature into his house
takes pleasure in adding adornment to this idol –
a fine overlay on the basest thing of all, and he finishes her off with garments,
and the poor wretch by degrees drains his house of its wealth. (627–633)

Both Hippolytus and Jason express their disgust for women who demonstrate cleverness. Hippolytus continues his rant with the following:

It is easiest for the man who has a nobody, but it is still a harmful thing,
a wife who is set up as a simpleton in his house.
But I hate a clever woman. May there not be in my house
a woman who has more intelligence than a woman ought to have.
Aphrodite engenders more mischief in clever women,
but a helpless woman
is deprived of folly because of her simple thoughts.
(Euripides, *Hippolytus* 638–644)

In Sophocles' play *the Women of Trachis*, we meet what many people would regard as a model wife who is a victim of circumstance but in some sense also a murderer. Deianeira, wife of Heracles, has been left alone in the city of Trachis, where they were exiled for one of the hero's acts of violence. While he is away on his exploits, or serving time for other misdemeanours, his wife is full of anxiety, as she confesses to the chorus of young local women.

You are here, as it seems, having learned
of my misfortune. May you not learn by suffering how my heart agonizes,
for right now you lack experience.
What is young gets nourishment
in such places as are its own, and the heat of the Sungod,
the rain, and none of the breezes disturb it,
but it lifts its life aloft in pleasures,
(for a female) untroubled up to the point when one is called a woman
rather than a girl. At night-time she gets her share of anxieties –
fearful on behalf of her husband or children.

Then a person would see, by examining her own circumstances,
with what evils I am burdened. (141–152)

When Heracles arrives back it is as a conqueror, and amidst the trappings of his
victory is a group of captive women, including the daughter of the king whose
city he had sacked. It becomes clear to Deianeira that her husband has fallen in
love with the young princess. Her initial response is a generous one. She speaks
of love as a disease, one that can affect anyone.

Whoever stands up to Eros
as if wielding the hands of a boxer is not in his right mind.
This creature rules even the gods, just as he pleases,
and he rules me too. How would he not rule another woman like he rules me?
So that if I blame my husband who has been afflicted by this disease
I am certainly raving mad,
or if I blame this woman for being an accessory –
she who has done nothing shameful or bad to me –
impossible! (441–449)

As Deianeira was leaving home as a young girl to marry Heracles she was
threatened by the sexual advances of a centaur. Heracles dispatched the creature
with a poisoned arrow, but before dying the creature gave her some of the blood
seeping from his wound, advising her to keep it safe in case at some time she
needed a love charm. After the arrival of Heracles with his captive lover Deianeira
decides that the time has come to use it, and anoints a robe with it before sending
it to Heracles as a gift. When the tuft of wool that she had used to apply the
centaur's blood to the robe disintegrates instantly on being exposed to sunlight she
fears the worst, and confesses to the chorus that this might have been a deadly gift.

So I don't know, wretch that I am, into what corner of my thoughts I should tumble!
I see that I have wrought a terrible deed.
Why ever, or in gratitude for what, would the beast have shown
kindness to me as he was dying, and I the cause of his death?
Impossible! But he was beguiling me,
wanting to finish off his attacker. I grasp the implication of this
when it is no longer of any use.
I alone – unless my judgement is false –
am the unfortunate one who will completely destroy him.
For I know that the arrow that struck (the centaur)
also undid Cheiron, a god,
and it kills a whole host of beasts – whomever it touches.

Since this was the black poisoned blood
issuing from the wounds of this creature
why would it not destroy (Heracles) too? At least that is my way of thinking.
Well, I have made a decision. If he is overthrown
it will be by the self-same impulse that I die along with him.
For it is intolerable to live with a bad reputation –
if one is a woman who prefers not to be evil by nature.
(Sophocles, *The Women of Trachis* 705–722)

In Euripides' *Alcestis* the woman of that name sacrificed her own life for that of her husband Admetus, king of Thessaly. He had been fated to die unless he could find someone to die in his stead. His parents refuse, but his wife agrees. Here is her statement to Admetus, describing her choice to die rather than be deprived of him as husband and father of their children:

Admetus, you see how my situation presents itself.
I want to tell you before I die what I wish.
By giving you higher honour, instead of me
I have arranged it so that you look on the light of life
and I am dying. And this while it was possible for me not to die on your behalf,
for I could have had as husband one of the Thessalians whom I wanted,
and lived in a prosperous house belonging to a ruler.
But I did not want to live, dragged away from you
with orphaned children, and did not spare
my youthful life, although I had those things in which I took delight.
(Euripides, *Alcestis* 280–289)

Alcestis specifies what she wants from Admetus in return for her supreme sacrifice: he must not marry again and bring a stepmother into the house, for it is inevitable that she would be cruel to the children.

Other mythical wives whose actions are destructive are portrayed less sympathetically on the Athenian stage.

In *Agamemnon*, Aeschylus works with elements taken from the Trojan War saga, focusing on the events that took place in Mycenae when King Agamemnon returned from Troy. While the king had taken charge of the Greek troops for ten years at Troy his wife had formed a relationship with his cousin Aegisthus, and the two of them took over the rule of the palace in Argos. When Agamemnon returned, his wife entrapped him in a net and knifed him to death. Aeschylus gives us an unforgettable vignette of her standing triumphantly over the body of her husband, exulting. As his blood gushes forth in spurts she utters words of satisfaction that are redolent of sexual ecstasy.

So I did it; I will not deny it –
that he neither escaped from nor warded off death.
A net around him, inextricable, like one for fish
I cast around him, a deadly wealth of garment.
I struck him twice, and with two cries of agony
he let his limbs go slack. When he had fallen,
I added a third blow, a votive gift
for Zeus of the Underworld, guardian of corpses.
Thus he went down, and gasped out his life.
He spurted out a sharp gushing of blood
and spattered me with a dark rain of gory dew.
I rejoiced no less than does the crop in the god-given moisture
at the time of the bursting forth of the bud.
(Aeschylus, *Agamemnon* 1380–1392)

The *Antigone* is one of three tragedies that Sophocles composed using mythical material connected with the ruling family of King Oedipus of Thebes. After the death of Oedipus, civil war had broken out when his two sons fought for the rule of the city and both died in the conflict. Creon, brother-in-law of Oedipus, took control of Thebes. He declared that Polyneices, the son who declared war on his brother for refusing to relinquish the throne, was a traitor and would not receive funeral rites. (See above, pp. 83–4) Anyone attempting to perform the rituals would be killed. Polyneices' sister Antigone defied the decree of Creon and buried him. When confronted by her uncle she claims his edict is less valid than the eternal laws of the gods that guided her act of piety.

For me it was not Zeus who made that decree.
Nor did that Justice who lives with the gods below
mark out such laws among men.
Nor did I think your proclamations –
being mortal – were so strong as to be able to over-run
the unwritten and unfailing ordinances of the gods.
For not just now or yesterday, you see, but always
do they have life, and no one knows whence they were revealed.
I was not about to pay the penalty among the gods for (disobeying) these,
out of fear of the presumptuous spirit of a single man.
I knew that I would die: how could I not –
even if you had not made the proclamation beforehand. If I die
before my time, I say it is a gain.
One who lives with as many sorrows as I –
how would she not stand to gain by dying?

And as for me, it is in no way painful
to meet with this death. If I had put up with
the son of my own mother dying unburied,
I would have been pained by that. But as for these circumstances, I do not grieve.
If I seem to you just now to be the one doing foolish things,
then I suppose that it is in the eyes of a fool that I incur the charge of foolishness.
(Sophocles, *Antigone* 450–470)

In *Medea*, Euripides follows the story of Jason and Medea, which had begun with Jason's quest to obtain the Golden Fleece. The play is situated in Corinth, where the couple settled after securing the Fleece. Although Medea understood their relationship to be that between husband and wife, Jason decided on a more opportune marriage with the princess of Corinth, a bond that would one day secure for him the rule of the city. The king, Creon, facilitates this by issuing a decree (as did his namesake in Thebes), that Medea would be exiled with her two children. Medea is furious.

The chorus of the play, Corinthian women, are sympathetic to her plight, and sing this song that denounces men for their deceitfulness and a status they do not deserve. The words were revived in the early 20th century by the women fighting for the right to vote. They begin with the announcement that the "natural" order must be reversed.

The streams of the sacred rivers are flowing backwards,
and the entire order of justice is turning in reverse.
It is the designs of *men* that are crooked,
and no longer are pledges secure, taken in the name of the gods.
Common tales shall turn my life around so that it has a positive reputation.
Honour is coming to the race of females. No longer will malicious report attach to
women. (410–420)

When Jason pays a visit to Medea he tells her that she has brought on her own ill fortune – by speaking out against his plan to marry into the royal family – but he offers to make some provision for her and the children in exile. Medea is not impressed.

You, you utterly despicable individual – for this is the worst reproach
with which my tongue can address you, in the face of your unmanliness.
You have come to me – here you are, turned into my worst enemy.
It is not an example of self-confidence or courage
to look your friends in the eye when you have done them wrong;
no, it is the worst of all human diseases:

shamelessness. But you have done well by coming,
for I will speak ill of you and lighten my spirit,
and you will feel pain as you listen. (465–474)

Medea continues with a litany of the sacrifices she had made on Jason's behalf, and the perfidy with which he treated her in return. She plans and executes a vicious revenge, one that includes killing their children.

With treachery I will kill the king's daughter.
For I will send (the children) bearing gifts in their hands –
a finely-woven dress and a golden plaited wreath.
And if she takes the adornments and puts them around her skin
she and all who touch the girl will die horribly.
I will smear the gifts with such poison.
Thereupon, then, I will dismiss this topic.
But I am distressed at the job that must be done next.
For I will kill the children,
my own. There is no one who can rescue them.
And when I have overthrown the whole of Jason's house
I will leave this land, fleeing from the murder of my very dear children,
and I will have dared to do a most unholy deed.
You see, my friends, it is not tolerable to be made a laughing-stock by my enemies.
(Euripides, Medea 783–797)

In Euripides' Hecuba, the story focuses on the former queen of Troy, who had been enslaved by the Greeks along with her daughters when the city was taken. As a mother, her fierceness was familiar to the Greeks through the account of her anger the Homeric Iliad. When Achilles had killed her son Hector and mutilated his body, she told King Priam she wanted to fix her teeth on Achilles' innermost parts and feed on them (Iliad 24.212–213).

In Euripides' play the ghost of Achilles desires Hecuba's beautiful daughter Polyxena to be slain over his tomb, and stills the winds so the Greeks could not sail home. A vote is taken among the Greeks and, persuaded by the smooth-talking Odysseus, they decide collectively to complete the sacrifice. Hecuba addresses Odysseus, outraged at the "barbarism" of the democratic process and his role in it that led to this decision.

Aren't you depraved, by reaching this decision?
And you, who received such treatment from me as you admit you got?
Isn't it the case that you are doing us no good, but as much harm as you can muster?

A thankless brood you are, all of you public speakers
who are after honours from the masses for your speeches. May you not be known
to me!
You who do not think twice about harming your friends
if you can say something to curry favour with the masses.
Now what cleverness did they think it was
to vote for a sentence of death for my daughter?
Or did Necessity induce them to perform a human sacrifice
at the tomb, where it is more appropriate to kill oxen?
(Euripides, *Hecuba* 251–261)

Polyxena is sacrificed, but yet another blow awaits the Trojan queen and mother. Her youngest son had been sent to the king of Thrace for the duration of the war, along with gold treasure. Now he remained her only hope. The king, however, eager for the gold, slew her son, whose body washed ashore by the Greek camp and was brought to Hecuba. She executes her revenge by arranging for the Trojan captive women to blind the king and kill his two young sons.

COMEDY

The real-life background of the Athenian comedies produced in the late 5th century BCE was, ironically, tragic. Of the three plays that featured women protagonists, two were produced in 411, when Athens was in a severely weakened state because of the war with Sparta (*Lysistrata, Women at the Thesmophoria*). The third was performed some twenty years later (*Assemblywomen*), when Athens had been largely stripped of her hegemony over the Greek world after her final defeat in the Peloponnesian War. This had had, of course, a penetrating impact on life in the city, one that could not help but challenge the Athenian way of life, including gender roles and the modes of interaction between men and women. While there are no "femmes fatales" among the comic heroines (unlike the leading women on the tragic stage) comic heroines speak with an authority that could plausibly represent a new and more independent voice emerging from the cracks in the social structure. Male-authored decisions had led to the continuation of a protracted war, one whose cost was felt acutely by women. At the same time, these dramatic heroines who, like their tragic counterparts, were played by men, also gave vent to traditional accusations against the female sex, such as their lack of self-restraint in sex and drink and their devious manipulation of men.

Lysistrata by Aristophanes was performed in 411 BCE, just four years after the disastrous Sicilian expedition of the Athenian fleet, in which their defeat by the combined forces of Sparta and the Sicilian allies had left them decisively weakened, although the final Spartan victory would come several years later. In the play, the lead actor Lysistrata ("Disbander of the Army") marshalls other women from both sides in the war and gets them to swear an oath that they will refuse sex with their men until the latter agree to stop fighting. Although the women struggle as much as the men with their vow of celibacy, the strategy of Lysistrata is ultimately successful, and the play has enjoyed successive performances, most recently as a call for a negotiated settlement to the Iraq War.

At the opening of the play Lysistrata is pacing impatiently on stage as she waits for the women to arrive, detained by their domestic responsibilities. When the Spartan woman, Lampito, arrives, Lysistrata greets her with the traditional Athenian view of the body of a Spartan woman.

[Lys.] Greetings, my dearest Spartan, Lampito!
Honey, how your beauty glows!
How healthy your complexion, how robust your physique!
You could even strangle a bull!
[Lampito] Yes, I think so, by Castor and Pollux.
'Cause I work out, and leap up to kick my buttocks. (78–82)

The assembled women contribute to the ensuing discussion the ways in which war has taken its toll on family life. Lysistrata herself laments the loss of sexual satisfaction from various sources:

Not even the spark of a lover has been left behind;
and ever since the Milesians revolted from us
I haven't laid eyes on an eight-inch dildo,
A little piece of leather that might have been a helpmate. (107–110)

When the women protest against the sex strike on the grounds that men will force them to submit, Lysistrata tries to reason with them.

(In that case) you must give in, but be miserable.
For there is no pleasure in sex for men when they use force.
You must give them grief in other ways, too. Never mind – they will soon give in.
No husband will ever be made happy
if something does not come with his wife's agreement. (162–166)

Lysistrata gets the women to swear over a "blood" sacrifice, in effect a cauldron of undiluted wine, that they will take all measures to avoid games of seduction and will resist a lover or husband, no matter how desperate they become.

When Lysistrata is confronted by an angry magistrate she returns his threats and explains the women's resistance, arising from their experience of the poor decisions made by men.

[Lys.] I used to stay inside, silent.
[Mag.] And if you hadn't kept quiet you would have regretted it!
[Lys.] Well, that's why I kept my mouth shut.
Then I would learn of some wicked deliberation of yours,
and I would ask, "How went these decisions of yours, husband, that you made without a grain of sense?"
And my husband would straightway lower his eyes and say, "You had better go and return to your weaving,
or you will let out a wail from a big smack on your head! War will be the concern of men." (516–520)
(Aristophanes, Lysistrata)

The women, craving sex with their men, begin to defect, and come up with various excuses why they must leave Lysistrata's band of resisters. One feigns pregnancy and an imminent birth, to which Lysistrata replies that she had not been pregnant the day previous. Knocking on the woman's belly, she hears a hollow sound, and unearths a bronze helmet. A husband of one of the women arrives in dire straits begging her to respond to his sexual needs. She protracts his agony by teasing him with seductive moves and a promise to lie with him if he promises to negotiate a peace treaty, but when he is on the point of agreeing she disappears.

A Spartan herald arrives, announcing that Spartan men are suffering as acutely as the Athenians. Ambassadors are summoned from both sides and Lysistrata reminds them of occasions before the current war when they had come to one another's assistance. A female figure emerges from behind stage representing "Reconciliation." The two previously warring sides draw a map on her nude body and redesign the territory that they will now keep under their respective control. We hear no more from Lysistrata, and both sides proceed to celebrate the peace with a banquet.

Aristophanes produced his Women at the Thesmophoria for the City Dionysia in the same year but four months later than Lysistrata (which had been performed at the Lenaia). Unlike the earlier play, this comedy makes virtually no reference to the dire straits in which the Athenians found themselves as a result of their losses in the Peloponnesian War. As with Lysistrata, however, the audience was provoked, often to laughter, by reversals of traditional gender roles and by women's voices of resistance to the ways they were being treated by men. The focal point of this tension is itself a theatrical one, arising from women's anger at the type of tragic heroines (e.g., murderesses and adulteresses) created by the playwright Euripides. This has led directly, the women claim, to increased restraints being placed on wives by their husbands. At the Thesmophoria, the major festival in honour of Demeter and her daughter Kore/Persephone, Athenian matrons gathered (we think) on the site where the Assembly of citizen men was routinely held. All civic business was suspended while wives celebrated their connection to fertility, both agrarian and human. In the play, they hold a session parallel to the Athenian Assembly, voting on a motion to condemn Euripides to death. It becomes clear as the play develops that the women's wish to silence Euripides was motivated by the desire to continue duping their husbands, in ways that conform tidily to traditional accounts of male fantasies and fears about women's secret behaviour.

The play opens with Euripides who, having heard of this motion, solicits with the help of a kinsman the cooperation of a younger tragic poet Agathon, whose effeminacy would make it easy to infiltrate the women's festival. He could thus speak on Euripides' behalf. Agathon refuses to do this, but lends the kinsman clothing and other feminine apparel such as a bra and wig that will serve as a disguise.

As the kinsman arrives at the festival in his garb and takes his seat the female herald is proclaiming a parody of the standard curse against enemies of the state that was issued at the beginning of the regular Assembly. In the play, this is delivered as a curse against enemies of women. Euripides is included with the standard enemies of all Greeks.

If anyone plots harm against
the female citizens, or enters into negotiation
with Euripides or the Medes for the detriment
of women in any way, or has designs on becoming a tyrant
or joins in the installation of a tyrant, or denounces
a woman who has taken another's baby as her own, or is the slave-procuress
for some mistress who whispers (the affair) in the ear of the master,
or someone who, when sent on an errand delivers false messages,
or if someone is a woman's lover and deceives her with lies
or never gives her what he promised,
or is an old hag who gives gifts to a (young) lover,
or a courtesan who receives gifts and then betrays her lover,
or is a bar-man or bar-maid who cheats on the prescribed measure
in a pitcher or a pint:
curse this person and their family, that they perish
wretchedly! (335–350)

When the motion is presented to punish Euripides for criminal activities the women in attendance are invited to speak to it. One comes forward and maligns the poet, describing the consequences for wives of the way he portrays women.

Where has this man not smeared us with wrong-doing?
Where has he not discredited us wherever there are, in short,
spectators and tragic actors and choruses,
for being adultresses, nymphomaniacs when it comes to good-looking men,
wine-guzzlers, betrayers, chatterboxes,
unsound creatures, a great curse to men?
The result of this is that as soon as they come back from the stage
they look at us suspiciously and straightway inspect the house
to see if there is a lover hidden inside.
It isn't possible for us to do anything like we used to do,
for this man has taught our husbands
such terrible things about us. (389–400)

Because of this man, men now put seals and bolts
on the women's quarters to guard them,
and raise Molossian hounds besides,
to frighten away our lovers. (414–417)

The kinsman, still in female disguise, rises to his feet and launches a defence of Euripides.

Why do we accuse that man by leveling these charges,
and bear him such ill will, when he tells of two or three
misdemeanors he knows we commit, when we have actually done thousands?
I myself, to confess first – so that I not mention another woman –
am aware that many awful things can be attributed to me. That one was the worst
then, when I had been a bride of three days
and my husband was asleep beside me. A lover of mine was around,
who had deflowered me when I was seven.
This man came scratching at the door filled with lust for me.
I knew who it was right away. Then I start downstairs stealthily.
My husband asks, "Where are you going?"
"Where, you say? My stomach's churning, and it hurts,
so I am going to the toilet." "Go on, then."
Then he grinds up juniper berries, dill and sage-apples.
But I poured water over the hinges

and slipped out to my lover. Then I got my banging,
leaning forward holding on to the laurel tree by the pillar of Apollo.
These things, you see, Euripides never reported.
Nor does he ever speak about how we get pounded by slaves and mule-drivers,
when there is no one else,
nor whenever we have been getting screwed a lot by someone
during the night how we chew garlic in the morning,
so that our husband won't smell anything when he comes back from the lookout
and suspect that we have been doing something amiss. This, you see,
he has never spoken about. And if he rails against Phaedra,
what is this to us? Nor has he told that story yet,
how the wife showed her husband her robe,
holding it up to see how it looked in the light,
while she sent her lover out of the house all under cover – no, he hasn't told that
one. (473–501)

Aren't these the bad things we do? By Artemis
we certainly do. And then we get mad at Euripides,
though we suffer nothing more than we deserve from what we have done.
(517–519)

The matrons react strongly to this, and threaten to attack him. When another
Athenian effete arrives and delivers the rumour that the festival has been infil-
trated by a spy sent from Euripides they suspect the kinsman and confirm his
sexual identity by undressing him, keeping him under watch as he takes refuge
at the altar in the orchestra of the theatre. The kinsman removes some of the
votive tablets around the altar, scratches a call to rescue and throws them in all
directions, hoping for help from Euripides. Meanwhile, the chorus leader steps
forward on stage and invites the chorus of women to deliver a *parabasis* (direct
address) to the audience, which will consist of a defence of women.

Now is the time for us to step forward and speak positively about ourselves.
This is warranted, for every single man holds forth with many an evil report of the
female sex,
how we are totally bad for the human race and how all evils come from us:
quarrels, strife, painful sedition, grievous suffering, war. But come now,
if we are evil, why do you marry us? If we are truly so bad
why do you forbid us to leave the house or to get caught peeking out –
you want to keep watch on something evil with so much vigilance?
If the little woman goes out and you find her outdoors
you go nuts, when you should toast the gods and rejoice,

if in truth you found the evil thing missing and couldn't lay hands on her inside?
(785–794)

And we claim that we are much better than men.
A woman does not yoke her chariot and go to the city
and take fifty talents from the treasury. At most she would filch
a measure of flour, stealing it from her husband, but gave it back the same day.
But we might reveal many of these men here
to be doing the same things.
And in addition to these offences of ours the men are more likely than we are
to be gluttons, clothes-stealers,
food-snatchers, and slave-dealers.
And what's more, when it comes to their patrimony
they are less inclined than we are to preserve it.
On the other hand, even now,
our loom, our little wool-basket,
our parasol (these are safe).
But when it comes to these husbands of ours,
many of them have lost their spear-shafts
from the house, spear-point and all,
and many others have thrown from their shoulders
in the heat of battle –
their parasols! (810–829)
(Aristophanes, *Women at the Thesmophoria*)

Despite the kinsman's and Euripides' best efforts to obtain the former's release through recitations of rescue scenes from Euripides' plays, the playwright only escapes when the policeman called in to keep watch over him is distracted by a sexy dancing girl. A negotiated settlement is achieved, with Euripides agreeing to slander women no more.

Two decades after the performances of *Lysistrata* and *Women at the Thesmophoria*, Aristophanes' *Assemblywomen* was produced (392 or 391 BCE). Since the earlier performances Athens had suffered through her decisive defeat at the hands of the Spartans. The two decades of social and political upheaval that followed were accompanied by serious reflection and debate about the strengths and weaknesses of the democratic and oligarchic governments that had failed to guide the city successfully. Constitutional arrangements of other states were examined with a view to constructing one that would best suit Athens in the 4th century (Plato's proposals in the *Republic*, in his *Laws* and Aristotle's discussions in his *Politics* were part of this continuing debate. See below, pp. 165–79.) *Assemblywomen* is a comic speculation about the consequences of turning over the rule of Athens to women. This is a utopia that could not have been even imagined without the fall of Athens and her empire and the self-reflection that ensued. In the play, a group of women disguise themselves as men and stack the Assembly, then vote to transfer power to women. Although they continue to keep slaves (who will do all the manual labour), they institute a radical form of communal living, passing decrees to abolish private property and to eliminate marriage. Children will be held in common. In order that the aged not suffer discrimination young men and women must have sex with older men and women before they can go to bed with partners their own age.

In the Prologue, the women gather before dawn, dressed in their husbands' clothing, and try out speeches that might persuade the men of their proposal. Praxagora delivers one that is chosen as the most likely to succeed, arguing for the superiority of women over men.

How (women's) behaviour is better than ours
I will instruct you. First they dye their wool
in hot water following ancient practice,
every last one of them, and you wouldn't see them
trying anything new. But as for the city of the Athenians now,
if something is useful it would not be kept
unless some other new-fangled system were being monkeyed around with.
Women sit down and cook, just like they have done in the past.
They carry things on their heads, just as they did in the past.
They celebrate the Thesmophoria, just like they have done in the past.
They bake cakes just like they have done in the past.
They wear down their husbands, just like they have done in the past.
They keep lovers inside the house, just like they have done in the past.
They buy treats, just like they have done in the past.
They like their wine undiluted, just like they have done in the past.
They love to get screwed, just like they have in the past.
And so, gentlemen, let's hand the city over to the women,
and not just gab about it nor inquire
what they intend to do here, but let's allow them to rule without interference.
Let us consider only this:
first, as mothers they will be eager
to protect the soldiers; next, who would send them food
faster than the one who bore them?
A woman is most resourceful at finding funds,
and she would never be cheated once she held the reins of power,
for women are familiar with the cheating game.

I will leave aside the other arguments. If you trust me in this
you will live out your lives in happiness. (214–240)

The women in disguise are undetected, and their votes ensure that Praxagora's speech is successful. More details of her arguments are reported to her husband Blepyros by Chremes, a man who attended the meeting.

[Chremes] He said that a woman is a thing that is loaded with good-sense
and good at turning a profit. And he said that they never divulge
the secrets from the Thesmophoria,
while you and I always conspire to do this.
[Blep.] By Hermes, he wasn't fibbing about this.
[Chremes] Then he said that they lend their clothes to one another,
their jewelry, their money, their drinking cups,
one-on-one without witnesses,
and always bring all of this back without hanging onto any of it
while most of us, he argued, do this.
[Blep.] By Poseidon, we do it even with witnesses present.
[Chremes] And he praised women in a huge number of other ways.
They don't inform on other people, they don't blackmail
nor overthrow the democracy, but do it lots of good. (441–454)
(Aristophanes, *Assemblywomen*)

The proposals are enacted, with citizens obliged to add their possessions to the common store. Praxagora assures the men that everyone will have an equal share, that there will be no more lawsuits and no more prostitution since women, like the cooking pots, will be available to all. The only restriction will be the requirement that the young and good looking will only be available to those who first have sex with the old and the ugly, provoking some comic competition between the crones and a beautiful young woman that closes the play.

FURTHER READING

Fletcher, J. 2011. *Performing Oaths in Classical Greek Drama*. Cambridge

Foley, H.P. 2001. *Female Acts in Greek Tragedy*. Princeton

Gardner, J.F. 1989. "Aristophanes and Male Anxiety – the Defence of the Oikos," *Greece & Rome* 36, 51–62

Lardinois, A. and L. McClure, L. *Making Silence Speak. Women's Voices in Greek Literature and Society*. Princeton

Loraux, N. 1987. *Tragic Ways of Killing a Woman*. Cambridge/London

Mueller, M. 2001. "The Language of Reciprocity in Euripides' Medea," *American Journal of Philology* 122, 434–504

Ormond, K. 1999. *Exchange and the Maiden. Marriage in Sophoclean Tragedy.* Austin, TX

Powell, A. 1990 ed. *Euripides, Women and Sexuality.* London/New York

Rehm, R. 1994. *Marriage to Death: The Conflation of Wedding and Funeral Rituals in Greek Tragedy.* Princeton

Sommerstein, A.H. 1977. "Aristophanes and the Events of 411," *Journal of Hellenic Studies* 97, 112–126

Stehle, E. 2002. "The Body and its Representations in Aristophanes: Where Does the Costume End?" *American Journal of Philology* 123.3, 369–406

Stroup, S.C. 2004. "Aristophanes' *Lysistrata* and the 'Hetairization' of the Greek Wife," *Arethusa* 37.1, 37–73

Taafe, L. 1994. *Aristophanes and Women.* London/New York

Zeitlin, F. I. 1995. "Travesties of Gender and Genre in Aristophanes' Thesmophoriazousae," in *Playing the Other: Gender and Society in Classical Greek Literature.* Chicago

11

Dorian girls and women

SPARTA

While Athens was populated by a dialectical/cultural group of Greeks known as "Ionian," another group, the "Dorians," lived in the Peloponnese, the southern part of the Greek peninsula, as well as in Crete and many of the colonies in the Greek west. Xenophon (430–356 BCE), who described the ideal Athenian marriage in the view of Ischomachus (see above, pp. 59–65), gives us a far different picture of the situation of women in Sparta. Provided with an estate in the northern Peloponnese by the Spartans where he lived for 20 years, Xenophon composed a *Constitution of the Lacedaemonians* from first-hand experience. He attributes the Spartan legal and social arrangements to the (semi-legendary) lawgiver Lycurgus, whom he credits with the success of the state. Much of what Xenophon observed and recorded about Spartan life is also to be found in the biography of Lycurgus written by Plutarch (late 1st–early 2nd century CE).

The social configuration of Sparta consisted of free citizens, *perioikoi* (dependent subjects without citizenship rights), helots (free Greeks from the surrounding areas who had been defeated and forced into servitude by the Spartans, whom they greatly outnumbered) and slaves.

Birth and childhood

Xenophon starts his record of the Spartan way of life by comparing the treatment of girls to that found elsewhere.

So that I may start at the beginning, I will begin straightway with the begetting of children. With other people, girls who are intending to become mothers and who are respectable girls are raised on a completely modest diet and with the smallest possible number of delicacies. The girls abstain entirely from wine, or their practice is to dilute it with water. Other Greeks think that girls ought to sit alone doing their wool-working, being sedentary like many others who practice a craft. How, then, can they expect that girls raised like this will bear strong children?

But Lycurgus thought that slave women produced clothing that was sufficient, and thinking that producing children was the most important function of free women he first established physical exercise for the female no less than for the male sex. Then he set up competitions in speed and strength just as there were for the men. In this way he also set up contests for females to compete with one another, thinking that the offspring from parents of two fit parents will be stronger.
(Xenophon, *Constitution of the Lacedaemonians* 1.3–4)

Plutarch's description of Lycurgus' reforms highlights the fact that Spartan children were raised to consider themselves as belonging as much to the state as to their families. At birth it was to the tribal elders that the child was brought, where the decision would be taken whether or not to rear it, and eugenics was the primary consideration. (Nothing is mentioned about a different assessment for baby boys than for girls.)

The father who produced the child was not the one to decide whether to rear it, but he took it and carried it to the place called Lesche, where the elders of the tribes were seated and inspected the infant; if it was sturdy and robust they gave orders to rear it, and assigned it a plot from among the 9000 lots. But if it was low-born and misshapen they sent it to the so-called Apothetae, a deep pit at the foot of Mt. Taÿgetus, since it was not better that it live – neither for its own good nor for the city – if even from the outset it was a creature not equipped with health and strength. For this reason the women used to bathe the newborns not with water but with wine, making a test of their strength. For it is said that epileptic and sickly babies lose their senses with undiluted wine, being thrown into convulsions, but the constitution of the healthy ones rather is hardened and strengthened by it. (16.1–2)

The nurses who reared the infants gained a reputation abroad for success in raising children that were contented, strong and courageous.

A particular degree of attention and skill was applied by the nurses such that, rearing the infants without swaddling-bands, they left free movement for their limbs and bodies. They were contented and not fussy over their food, not afraid of the dark nor fearful of being left alone, nor disposed to disagreeable ill-temper and fits of crying. For this reason some foreigners purchase Spartan nurses for their children. (16.3)
(Plutarch, *Life of Lycurgus*)

Plutarch follows this account by mentioning the fact that Alcibiades had the advantage of a Spartan tutor.

We recall from the *partheneia* of Alcman (above, pp. 32–4) and the myth of Helen that female beauty was prized in early Sparta. Herodotus recounts the tale of a nurse who was devoted to her female charge who happened to be uncommonly ugly. Every day she carried the child out of Sparta to the temple of Helen at Therapne.

One day, as she was leaving the temple a woman is said to have appeared to the nurse, and asked her to show her what she carried in her arms. She told her that she was carrying a little child, whereupon (the woman) requested her to show it to her. She refused, for she had been forbidden by the parents to show her to anyone. (The woman) told her in that case to show her immediately. Seeing that the woman was so insistent on seeing it, she then showed her the child. The woman stroked the head of the child, and said that this would be the most beautiful of all Spartan women. From that day her appearance changed.
(Herodotus, *Histories* 6.61)

The stunning beauty of the girl attracted the attention of the Spartan king Ariston, who married eventually her.

Young women

Xenophon's highlights the fact that with the reforms of Lygurgus Spartan girls were, unlike their Athenian counterparts, not married prematurely.

(He) stopped men from taking a wife whenever they chose, and laid it down that marriage would occur when they were in their physical prime, believing that this was an advantage for good breeding.
(Xenophon, *Constitution of the Lacedaemonians.* 1.6)

Plutarch confirms Xenophon's record about the training of Spartan girls before marriage.

(Lycurgus) took pains to attend to the training of women. He saw to the exercising of the bodies of girls through running, wrestling, throwing the discus and javelin, so that the formation of the embryo in those giving birth would, in getting a vigorous beginning in a vigorous body, grow stronger, and the women themselves would withstand childbearing because of their strength and struggle smoothly and easily with the pains of childbirth.

Sparing them softness and a delicate and completely effeminate life, he accustomed girls no less than youths to go naked in processions and at certain festivals to dance and sing where young men were present and watching them. There were times when they would mock and tease in an appropriate way each man whom they caught misbehaving, and again, by performing praises set to music for those who were worthy of these, they instilled in the young men lots of ambition and emulation. For the one who was praised for his courage and became famous among the girls went away exalted by their praises, while the stings of their teasing and mocking was no more blunt than that given with serious admonition, inasmuch as together with the other citizens the kings and the elders were present at the spectacle.

The nudity of the young girls was not at all shameful, for it was accompanied by modesty and there was no wanton behaviour; it produced in them the habit of simplicity and enthusiasm for good health. It instilled in the female sex a taste for thoughts of a noble sort, since they too were shareholders in valour and ambition. Whence it followed for them to speak and think such things as are said of Gorgo the wife of Leonidas. Someone said to her – a foreigner, it seems – "You Spartans are the only women who rule over men," and she replied, "We are the only ones who give birth to men!"
(Plutarch, *Life of Lycurgus* 14.2–4)

The athletic training of young women resulted in a famous victory at Olympia, the four-horse chariot race that was won in the early 4th century (396?) by Cynisca, a woman from the royal house in Sparta. Pausanias comments (500 years later) that this set a precedent.

(The Spartan king) Archidamos had a daughter whose name was Cynisca. She was extremely ambitious to enter the competition at Olympia, and was the first woman to breed horses and the first woman to win an Olympic victory. After Cynisca other women, especially Spartan women, won Olympic victories, but none was so renowned as she. (Pausanias, *Description of Greece* 3.8.1)

The base of the commemorative statue erected by Cynisca has survived at Olympia, inscribed with this epigram commemorating a proud princess:

Kings of Sparta were my fathers and brothers.
   I, Cynisca, victorious in the chariot race with my swift-footed horses,
erected this statue. I assert that I am the only woman
   in all of Greece to have won this crown.
(*IvO* 160 = *AP* 13.16)

At Elis (in the northwestern Peloponnesus) young women ran races at games that were parallel to those at Olympia, using the Olympic stadium.

Every fourth year the Sixteen Women wove a robe for Hera, and these same women hold games called Heraea. The competition is a footrace for young girls. They are not all of the same age: the first to run are the youngest; after them come those who are next in age, and the last to run are those who are the eldest of the girls. They run this way: their hair hangs down loose, a tunic reaches to a little above the knee, and they bare their right shoulder as far as the breast. The Olympic stadium is reserved for these young women for the race, but they shorten the course in the stadium by exactly one-sixth. To the winning girls they present crowns of olive and a portion of the cow sacrificed to Hera. They also set up inscribed statues for them. Those who look after the sixteen are – like the judges of the games – married women. The games of the young women they trace back to ancient times. (Pausanias, *Description of Greece* 5.16.2–4)

We recall the fact that girls' competitive racing was part of the coming-of-age songs composed by the Spartan Alcman (above, pp. 32–4).

Marriage

Plutarch describes the incentives put in place for ensuring that men would choose to marry. Bachelors were prevented from watching young men and women exercise, and in winter were ordered to march around the *agora* in short tunics. In other ways too they suffered public shaming. (*Life of Lycurgus* 15.1)

His description of the marriage ritual and the relationship between bride and groom highlights a dramatic difference from Athenian practices.

(The women) were married by capture, not when they were small nor prematurely for marriage, but when they were at their prime and ripe for it. The so-called "bride's attendant" took charge of the woman who was carried off, cropped her hair close to the scalp, dressed her in the cloak and sandals of a man, and laid her down alone on a pallet in the dark. The bridegroom, not drunken nor unmanned by excess but sober as usual, having dined in the men's hall, came in, untied her belt, lifted her up and carried her to the marriage-bed. After spending some time – not much – with her, he went away discreetly where he had been accustomed to go earlier, to sleep with the young men. And he continued to do this thereafter, spending the days with his contemporaries and sleeping with them at night, but visiting his bride secretly and with caution, embarrassed and fearful lest someone inside the house notice them, while his bride contrived and made arrangements with him so that they might find the right time to escape the notice of the others. This they did not only for a short time, but long enough for some to produce children before they had seen their own wives in daylight. This type of coming together was not only an

exercise in self-control and restraint but drew them together with bodies ready for procreating and always fresh for love-making and ready for sex, not sated or low in energy because of constant intercourse. There was always some lingering spark of desire and delight remaining in both of them.
(Plutarch, *Life of Lycurgus* 15.3–5)

Both Xenophon and Plutarch refer to the Spartan practice of polyandry, whereby wives had sex with other men with a view to producing strong offspring. This could have had an additional advantage for the wives, extending opportunities for them beyond breeding potential.

If it fell out for an old man that he had a young wife, seeing that men of this age are particularly possessive of their wives, (Lycurgus) believed in making arrangements opposite to this. For the older man he made it the case that he would bring into his house a man whose body and mind he admired, for the purpose of bearing children. And if a man did not want to have sex with his wife but desired to have children in whom he could take pride, he put in place a law for him that if he saw a woman who was a good breeder and was of a noble sort he could produce children from her, if he could persuade her husband.

He made allowance for many such arrangements, since the wives wanted to be in charge of two households and the husbands wanted to acquire siblings for their children who had their bloodline and position in common, but did not inherit the property.
(Xenophon, *Constitution of the Lacedaemonians*. 1.7–9)

Whereas Xenophon indicates that these children born outside wedlock would be deprived of an inheritance, Plutarch indicates that the married couple could adopt the offspring of an extramarital union.

It was possible for an older man with a young wife, if he was taken with one of the handsome and noble young men and approved of him, to introduce him to her and adopt the offspring as their own, seeing as it was filled with the seed of nobility. (15.7)

Plutarch recognized that a social order in which wives could have multiple partners and be in charge of more than one household while conducting affairs on their own when their husbands were absent, could result in wives holding the balance of power in the family.

It is not true, as Aristotle says, that in attempting to make the women chaste (Lycurgus) gave up, not being able to control the degree of loose living and power the women had acquired, owing to the many military campaigns of their men. During these (campaigns) the men were compelled to leave their wives in charge, and on account of this (the men) were more deferential than was appropriate, and addressed them as "Mistress." (14.1)

There is considerable evidence for homosexual relationships developing between Spartan boys and men, although different from Athenian practice in that the pairing could be between boys who were age mates and last into adulthood. (Boys left their families at age 7 and lived together with the men for most of their adult lives, a homosocial environment that would foster same-sex bonding.) In one passage, Plutarch refers to this sexual partnering occurring between Spartan women as well, although his account appears to be based on the pederastic model familiar to him from the practice of Athenian men and boys.

With this love (homosexual, between boys) finding approval among them the result was that noble and good women were lovers of young women.
(Plutarch, *Life of Lycurgus* 4.18)

Living in Athens in the early 4th century, Aristotle saw the independence of Spartan women and the fact that they could control property as a display of incontinence and a cause of economic instability, reflecting – as Plutarch noted – the inability of Lycurgus to bring them under control. In his *Politics*, he makes his views clear.

Laxity in regard to women is injurious to the purpose of the state and the happiness of the city. As a husband and wife are part of every household, it is clear that one must consider that the city is about equally divided with regard to the number of men and women. In all constitutions in which there is insufficient regulation of women, one must think that half the population is neglected by law. This is what has happened there. For the lawgiver, wanting to make the state hardy, in the case of men has clearly done such, but in the case of women he has been remiss. For they live with complete licence, with all manner of dissolute living and luxury. The result is that in such a state wealth is honoured, especially if it happens that women are in power, as is the case with other military and warlike societies. (1269b12–26)

In the time when (the Spartans) held political sway many things were managed by women when it came to ruling. Now what difference is there between women ruling and rulers being ruled by women? The result is the same. When it comes to bravery, it is useful for none of the ordinary activities but really in war, and the Spartan women were most harmful in this area. They showed this at the time of the Theban invasion when they were of no use – just like women of other cities – for they supplied more confusion than the enemy! In the beginning it seemed that the freedom awarded to women had come about with good reason for the Spartans, for the men used to be away from home for long periods, warring against the Argives and again against the Arcadians and Messenians. When they were at leisure (the men) turned themselves over to the lawgiver, having been already disposed to obedience because of the military life (there is a good measure of virtue in this); and the women, they say, Lycurgus tried to bring under the laws, but they rebelled and he backed off. So these women are the cause of what happened, in that it is clear that they are responsible for Sparta's failures. But we are not looking at what should or should not be excused, but what is correct or not correct. The situation with respect to women seems to be not one that would earn respect, as was said earlier as well; it not only implies a certain unseemliness in the constitution considered in itself, but also contributes a certain amount to their love of money. After what has been said just now one might blame them for their unequal distribution of wealth. It has happened that some of them have acquired too much property and others extremely little.

On this account the land has come into the hands of a few people. This is also the result of the scant attention to the laws. For although the lawgiver does not commend the purchase or sale of an inheritance, and rightly so, he permits anyone who wishes to give or bequeath it. And it is inevitable that the former and the latter result in the same thing. Nearly two fifths of the whole country is in the hands of women, because of the large number of heiresses and the practice of giving large dowries. It would have been better to have set it in place that there be no dowries or just a small and modest amount. In fact, it is possible to give in marriage an heiress to whomever one wishes, or if a man dies intestate the one whom he leaves as his heir-apparent gives her to whomever he wants. (1269b31–1270a29) (Aristotle, *Politics*)

Spartan heiresses would have increased in number with the deaths of their brothers in war. Lycurgus had in fact outlawed dowries, but they had been reinstated by the time of Aristotle.

Because family ties were subordinated to the needs of the Spartan state, wives and mothers were ready to detach themselves from marital and filial bonds. They became vocal defenders of their warrior culture, as reflected in the pithy *Sayings of Spartan Women* such as the following, recorded by Plutarch as "Sayings of Spartan Women" in his *Moralia*.

[Gorgo, daughter of King Cleomenes] As she was urging on her husband Leonidas when he was setting out for Thermopylae to show himself worthy of Sparta, she asked what she should do. He said, "Marry a good man and bear good children." (240D #6)

[Gyrtias] When a messenger came from Crete announcing the death of Acrotatus she said, "Was he not, when he came to the enemy, intending either to be killed by them or to kill them? It is sweeter to hear that he died, and in a manner worthy of himself and his city and his ancestors, than if he had lived for all time as a coward." (240F #2)

Another woman, when her sons had run away from battle and were standing beside her she said, "Where have you come, shirking your duty, cowardly under-lings? Are you going to go back in here where you made your exit?" And pulling up her garment she exposed herself to them. (241B #4)

Another woman was burying her son when a worthless old woman came up to her and said, "Oh, Woman, what an awful thing!" "No, not by the gods," the woman said, "a good thing, rather, for I bore him so that he would die for Sparta, and this is exactly what happened for me." (241C #8)

A Spartan man, wounded in war and unable to walk, made his way on all fours. He was ashamed at being a laughing-stock, but his mother said, "How much better it is, Son, to rejoice in your bravery rather than to be embarrassed by the laughter of fools!" (241E #15)

Another woman, as she was handing over his shield to her son (going off to war) said, "Child, either (with) this or on this!" (241F #16)

In some of these sayings, the women's wit captures their reputation for self-confidence – even in the face of enslavement.

Another woman, asked by a man whether she would be good if he bought her said, "Yes, and even if you do not buy me!" (242C #29)

Another woman who was being sold as a slave, when the herald asked her what she knew how to do said, "To be free." When the purchaser ordered her to do something not fitting for a free woman she said, "You will be sorry that you begrudged yourself such a possession," and she killed herself. (242D #30)
(Plutarch, *Moralia*)

Lower-class women

Although Xenophon reported that under the arrangements put in place by Lycurgus slave women (*doulai*) would do the wool-working and leave free women able to pursue other activities, it is clear that the presence of a large number of helot servants in the state would have meant that there was no need for a large slave population. Like wives and children, such private property as there was seems to have been available for others to use. This included household slaves, if by *oiketai* in the following passage Xenophon means "slaves" (as in Athens) and not "servants."

(Lycurgus) also made it possible to make use of the household slaves of others, if need arose.
(Xenophon, *Constitution of the Lacedaemonians* 6.3)

Xenophon includes with the *oiketai* hunting hounds, horses and carriages that would be supplied on request. The need for Spartans to purchase slaves increased with the emancipation of a large number of the helots in the first part of the 4th century BCE.

GORTYN

A law code that was carefully inscribed on a circular wall *c.* 450 BCE in the Cretan city of Gortyn was discovered in the 19th century, having remained largely intact for two-and-a-half millennia. It contains valuable information about marriage and family law in this Dorian city, much of which almost certainly had been in place prior to the 5th century. The Code provides valuable documentation that the treatment of women in this city was more liberal than that of Athens.

The social classes of Gortyn consisted of free men and women, *apetairoi* (free men and women who had no civic rights) serfs and slaves. Some of the provisions suggest that the code was evolving from a tradition of marriage and property arrangements that allotted considerable freedom of choice to the women of Gortyn. This is consistent with the statement of Strabo, citing the (4th century) Greek historian Ephorus, that young brides were not immediately taken to the husband's house, but only when they were ready to manage a household. (Strabo 10.482)

Rape and adultery

Unlike Athenian law, the Gortyn law code made no provision for homicide in the case of adultery. Fines were imposed for both rape and seduction/adultery, and the amounts suggest that the distinction between these two offences was less important than the social status of the victim. In the case of the sexual violation of a slave, the slave could testify (without torture) and this evidence had legal force.

If someone rapes a free person (man or woman) he shall pay 100 staters; if (the victim is) an *apetairos* 10; if a slave rapes a free person (man or woman) he shall pay twice as much; if a free man rapes a male or female serf he shall pay 5 drachmas. If a male serf rapes a male or female serf he shall pay 5 staters.

If someone forcibly violates a female slave from the household he shall pay 2 staters. If she has already been violated, 1 obol if during the daytime, 2 obols if at night.

The oath of the female slave is stronger.

If anyone attempts to rape a free woman who is under the care of a relative he shall pay 10 staters if a witness gives evidence.

If someone is caught in adultery with a free woman in her father's house or in her brother's or in her husband's, he shall pay 100 staters. If in another man's house, 50. If it is with the wife of an *apetairos*, 10. If a slave is caught in adultery with a free woman he will pay double. If a slave is caught in adultery with a slave, 5.
(*IC* IV 72 col. II 3–27)

(The value of Greek coinage varied in different locations. The relative value of Athenian staters:obols is 1:12.) Restrictions were in place to discourage someone from using devious means to bring about a charge of adultery:

If anyone should declare that he has been tricked, the captor must swear over 50 staters or more, together with four other people, each one calling down curses upon himself. In the case of an *apetairos* he would be the third (i.e. with two others), and in the case of a serf with his master and one other, swearing that he had captured him while committing adultery, and had not set it up by trickery.
(*IC* IV 72 col. II 36–45)

Divorce

The code assumes that a divorce could be initiated by either husband or wife, and the onus was on the husband to prove that he did not initiate it if the wife accused him of doing so. What property the wife brought into the marriage was inalienable, and should she swear under oath this would determine the judge's assessment of the case.

If a husband and wife divorce, the wife keeps what she had of her own when she came to her husband's house and half the produce, if any remains, and half the fabric, whatever remains of what she has woven in the house. If the husband is the cause of the divorce she is to have 5 staters. If the husband says he is not the cause, the judge decides on oath. If she should carry away anything else belonging to her husband she shall pay 5 staters and what she carries away. What she has stolen she must return. As for what she denies (of the charge) it will be decreed that the wife must swear her denial before the statue of Artemis the Archer in the Amyklaion temple. Whatever someone takes away from her after her oath of denial he shall pay 5 staters and return the thing itself.
(*IC* IV 72 col. II 45–III 12)

Female serfs retained their property in the event of separation, in a way similar to free women.

If a female serf be separated from a male serf while he is alive or if he dies, she keeps her own property. But if she carries away anything else, that is grounds for a trial.
(*IC* IV 72 col. III 40–44)

In the case of women (free or serf) who gave birth after a divorce/separation, the former husband/master had the choice of receiving or refusing the child, but if it was refused, the mother could decide whether to rear it.

If a wife who is separated from her husband should give birth, they are to bring it to the husband under his roof before three witnesses. If he should not receive it, it is up to the mother to rear or expose the child. The relatives and the witnesses shall have the stronger oath, if they brought it. If a female serf who is separated should give birth, they are to bring it to the master of the man who married her, before two witnesses.
(*IC* IV 72 col. III 44–55)

Widows and widowers

If a widow remarried, she retained her property and any gifts from the former husband. If there were children, they inherited the father's portion of property and his share of the profit from this.

If a man dies leaving children, the wife may remarry if she wishes, keeping her own property and whatever her husband gave her that was recorded before three adult free witnesses. But if she should carry away anything else belonging to the children that is grounds for a trial. If he leaves her childless she is to have her own property and half of the weaving that remains and obtain her portion of the profit that is in the house, along with the heirs, and whatever her husband gave her as recorded. But if she should take away anything else, that is grounds for a trial. If a woman should die childless (the husband) is to give her property to her heirs and half of whatever remains of what she has woven and half of the profit that remains, if it is from her own property.
(*IC* IV 72 col. III 17–37)

Heiresses

There are special provisions in the Code for the disposition of property when a father dies leaving a daughter who is the sole offspring and heir of the family. Like her Athenian counterparts, the heiress was obliged to marry the next of kin, but the Gortyn Code takes into account the wishes of the two parties involved.

If the groom-elect is an adult and does not wish to marry the heiress, who is of age and willing to marry him, the relatives of the heiress go to court and the judge orders a marriage within two months. If he does not marry as recorded she holds all the property. If there is another, she marries him. But if there is no groom-elect she marries whomever she wishes of those from the tribe who ask her.
(*IC* IV 72 col. VII 40–52)

Further:

If no one from the tribe should wish to marry her, the relatives of the heiress should call throughout the tribe, "Is there no one who wishes to marry her?" If someone should marry her, it should be within thirty days from this request. If not she should marry someone else, whomever she can.

If a woman becomes an heiress after her father or brother has given her in marriage, if she should not wish to be married to the man to whom they gave her – even if he is willing – if she has had children let her be married to another from the tribe, dividing the property as registered. But if there are no children, she takes all the property and marries the groom-elect.
(*IC* IV 72 col. VIII 13–29)

FURTHER READING

Cartledge, P. 1981. "Spartan Women: Liberation or Licence?" *Classical Quarterly* 31, 84–109

Fantham, E., H.P. Foley, N.B. Kampen, and H.A. Shapiro 1994 (eds). *Women in the Classical World*. "Spartan Women: Women in a Warrior Society," 56–67. Oxford

Kunstler, B. 1987. "Family Dynamics and Female Power in Ancient Sparta," *Helios* 13, 31–48

Pomeroy, S. 2002. *Spartan Women*. Oxford

Redfield, J. 1977/78. "The Women of Sparta," *Classical Journal* 73, 146–161

Willetts, R.F. 1967 ed. *The Law Code of Gortyn*. Berlin

12

Women and the state: Plato and Aristotle

PLATO

In the fifth book of Plato's *Republic*, a dialogue in which he constructs an ideal state that would maximize "just" performance in society, Plato has Socrates describe for Glaucon (Plato's brother) a meritocracy in which women would have the same opportunities as men. The most capable individuals would be permitted the best education, and would become the state's "guardians."

[Soc.] For men, born and educated as we have been discussing, in my opinion there is no other proper acquisition and use of children and women than what we first set in place. We endeavoured in our argument to set them up as guardians of a flock, as it were.
[Gl.] Yes, we did.
[Soc.] Let us continue then by assigning them a birth and upbringing that is analogous, and see if it suits us or not.
[Gl.] In what way?
[Soc.] Like this. Do we think that females among guard dogs should join in guarding whatever the males are guarding, and join with them in hunting and doing other things in common, or do we think they should stay indoors since they are incapable, on account of the bearing and feeding of the pups, while the males work and have the whole job of looking after the flocks?
[Gl.] They work in common, except that we treat the females as weaker and the males as stronger.
[Soc.] "Is it possible," I said, "to use a creature for the same purpose when you do not give it the same rearing and training?"
[Gl.] Not possible.
[Soc.] If, then, we use women for the same purposes as men, the same things must be taught to them.
[Gl.] Yes.
[Soc.] (Training in) music and athletics was what was given to men.
[Gl.] Yes.
[Soc.] Then these two skills, along with warfare must be given to the women, and practised in the same way.

[Gl.] It is likely, from what you say.

[Soc.] Perhaps then, much of what we have been saying might seem ridiculous when contrasted with our present custom, if it were carried out in the way in which it has been discussed.

[Gl.] It certainly would.

[Soc.] What is the most ridiculous of the ideas, in your view? Surely it is the fact that the women would be exercising naked in the gymnasium along with men, not only the young but also the older women, just like old men in gymnasiums when, although wrinkled and not pleasant to see, they nonetheless like to work out?

[Gl.] By Zeus, you're right. It would seem ridiculous, as things stand.

[Soc.] But isn't it the case, since we have set out on this discussion, that we are not to fear teasing from the smart folks – the considerable amount and the sort of things they would say in the face of such a great change brought about, both regarding gymnastics and culture, and not least about the bearing of arms and riding horseback.

[Gl.] You are correct in what you say. (451c–452c)

After a short discussion on the origin and practical nature of exercising in the nude, there is a reaffirmation that despite the physical differences between men and women it was the case that some women were as suited for the role of guardian as some men.

[Soc.] With respect to the male and female sex, if it appears that one sex is suited to one or another skill or practice we will say that this ought to be assigned to each. But if it appears that they differ in just this, the female sex in giving birth and the male in begetting, we shall say that nothing more has been shown yet in our discussion to the effect that the woman differs from the man. But we shall still think that the guardians and their wives should have the same responsibilities.

[Gl.] And rightly so. (454e)

Glaucon agrees with Socrates that intelligence and absorbing instruction are qualities that would make for a good guardian, male or female.

[Soc.] Then, my friend, there is no responsibility for civic governance that belongs to a woman because she is a woman, nor to a man because he is a man, but natural abilities are distributed in like manner to both creatures, and a woman has a share by nature in all responsibilities and men in all, but in everything the woman is weaker than the man.

[Gl.] True.

[Soc.] Shall we assign all (responsibilities) to men, then, and none to women?

[Gl.] And how could we do that?

[Soc.] But we will say, I think, that there is one woman who has the nature of a physician but another not, and one a musical disposition and another is by nature unmusical.

[Gl.] Surely so.

[Soc.] And so is it not the case that one woman is athletic and warlike, while another is not warlike or keen on athletics?

[Gl.] I think you're right.

[Soc.] What then – one is a lover of wisdom and another hates it? And one who is courageous and another lacking in courage?

[Gl.] This too.

[Soc.] Therefore there is also a woman with a guardian nature, and one without it. Or wasn't it such a nature that we looked for in the guardian men?

[Gl.] Certainly.

[Soc.] And the natural ability for being a guardian of the city is the same in a woman as in a man, except that one is weaker by degree and the other stronger.

[Gl.] So it seems.

[Soc.] And women of this sort would be selected to live with men like this and be guardians with them, since they are capable of it and akin to them by nature.

[Gl.] Apparently.

[Soc.] And such (guardian) women are to be chosen to live with such men, and share in the guardianship since they are adequate and akin to the men in nature.

[Gl.] Certainly.

[Soc.] And mustn't the same responsibilities be given to the same natures?

[Gl.] The same.

[Soc.] We have laid down a system that is not impossible nor unrealistic, since we proposed a law that accords with nature. But the system we have in place now when compared to this one is unnatural, it seems.

[Gl.] So it seems. (455d–456c)

After getting Glaucon to agree that the education for future guardians should be the same for women as for men, and that these individuals should be selected from among the best citizens, Socrates suggests a means to accommodate the relative physical weakness of women.

[Soc.] The wives of guardians must strip naked, then, since they will be clothed in excellence instead of cloaks, and they must be partners in fighting and in the other guarding activities for the city, and not do otherwise. But the lighter tasks in these very duties must be given to women rather than to men, on account of the weakness of the female sex. But the man who laughs at undressed women who are exercising because it is better that they do so, is plucking the unripe fruit of the intelligent use of laughter. He knows nothing about the purpose of his laughter, it

seems, nor what he is doing. For this is the finest thing that is spoken, and will be spoken, that the fine is what is helpful, and the harmful is ugly.
[Gl.] Absolutely correct. (457a–b)

Saying once more that for men to jeer at women exercising in the nude is harmful for the state, Socrates continues with a dramatic arrangement for producing and rearing children.

[Soc.] There is a law that follows this and the other things we said previously, I think.
[Gl.] What is it?
[Soc.] That these women shall all be common to all these men, and that no single woman shall co-habit with someone privately. Moreover, the children will be common, and no parent shall know its own offspring nor any child its parent.
[Gl.] This (law) is much more likely to provoke doubt about both its feasibility and its usefulness.
[Soc.] I don't believe that there will be disagreement over its usefulness – no argument against its being the greatest good that women and children be common, if it were possible. But I believe that the question whether it is possible or not – the greatest source of disagreement will arise over this.
[Gl.] It would certainly be argued intensely on both counts. (457c–e)

With the admission that the feasibility of instituting this social arrangement could well be a serious challenge, Socrates continues with the argument that it would still be of great advantage to the state.

[Soc.] Now after this, Glaucon, the rulers will not allow them to have sex in a disorderly manner, nor to do anything else whatever that is not hallowed in a city of the truly happy.
[Gl.] It would not be right.
[Soc.] It is clear that in light of this we will make marriages sacrosanct as far as possible. Those that are sacrosanct would be the most beneficial for the city.
[Gl.] By all means.
[Soc.] How, then, will they be most useful? Tell me this, Glaucon. For I see that in your house you have hunting dogs and a considerable number of fine birds. Have you, by any chance, turned your mind to some feature of the mating and breeding of these?
[Gl.] Like what?
[Soc.] First, that although they are fine creatures, is it not the case that there are some among them who are and become the best?
[Gl.] There are.

[Soc.] And do you breed them all in the same way, from all of them, or are you particularly eager to breed from the best?
[Gl.] From the best. (458d–459a)

Socrates extends the benefit of eugenics to horses and other animals, obtaining agreement from Glaucon, then turns to humans, recognizing that some extraordinary measures might have to be taken to overcome people's resistance.

[Soc.] "From what we have agreed upon," I said, "the best men must cohabit with the best women as often as possible, and the worst with the worst as rarely as possible, and that the offspring of the one must be reared but of the other not, if the flock is to be of the highest order. And how all this happens is to be kept from everyone except the rulers, if the herd of guardians is to be as free from dissension as possible."
[Gl.] Absolutely.
[Soc.] Then some festival days must be legislated in which we would bring brides and bridegrooms together, and hymns must be composed by our poets appropriate for the weddings that occur. But we will leave the total of the marriages in the hands of the rulers, so that as much as possible they may keep the same number of men, taking into consideration wars and diseases and all such things, so that as far as possible our city may not become too great or too small.
[Gl.] Right.
[Soc.] I think some ingenious lottery system must be devised, so that the inferior man will blame his luck when it comes to connecting with a woman, and not the rulers.
[Gl.] Yes indeed.
[Soc.] And for the good ones among the young men, I suppose, those who excel in war or some other pursuit, prizes must be given out, and with more liberality the opportunity to have sex with women, so that at the same time there will be an excuse for having as many children as possible bred from these men.
[Gl.] Right.
[Soc.] And rulers who are appointed for these things take the offspring that are born – rulers who are male or female or both – since, I take it, the offices are open to both women and men.
[Gl.] Yes.
[Soc.] Now, I assume, they will pick up and take the offspring of the good to the nursery, to certain nurses who live apart, in some section of the city. But those of the inferior couples and any of those born to the other set who are defective they will hide away in a secret and undisclosed place as is appropriate.
[Gl.] If indeed it is to be the case that the breed of the guardians will be pure.
[Soc.] These people will also take charge of the rearing of the children, bringing the

mothers to the nursery whenever they are swollen with milk, but devising every means so that no woman will recognize her own, and they will provide others who have milk, if there are not enough mothers. And they will pay attention to these women so that they nurse for a limited time, and the trouble of lack of sleep and the other burdens they will hand over to wet- and regular nurses.

[Gl.] You are talking about a very easy process of child-bearing for the wives of the guardians.

[Soc.] It is right that it should be. But let us continue straight on with what we set out to do. We said that the offspring should come from parents in their prime.

[Gl.] True.

[Soc.] Does it seem to you too that the time for a woman's prime of life is counted as lasting twenty years, but for a man thirty?

[Gl.] How do you calculate this?

[Soc.] In the case of the woman, beginning at her twentieth year until her fortieth she should bear children for the state. For the man, when he has passed his peak in running, he should breed for the state until he has reached the age of fifty-five.

[Gl.] This is the prime of body and mind for both.

[Soc.] Then if someone older than these, or younger, interferes with breeding for the state we shall say that his error is one of impiety and injustice, since it was of someone begetting a child for the state who, if its birth is not detected, will not be born attended by the sacrifices and prayers which the priests and priestesses and the entire city will bless at every marriage, along with the entire city, praying that better offspring will come from good parents and from parents who offer good service will come children that offer better service. But this child will have been born in darkness, out of terrible incontinence.

[Gl.] You're right.

[Soc.] And the same rule applies if some man within the age for begetting lays his hands on a woman of the same age without the support of the rulers. For we will say that he is presenting the state with a bastard, unrecognized and unsanctified.

[Gl.] Absolutely.

[Soc.] But whenever the women and men pass the childbearing age I think that we will leave the men free to bond with whomever they wish, except with a daughter, a mother or the girl-children of their daughters or his mother's female forbears, and likewise for the women, not with a son or father or male kin of these, descendants or forbears. We will have already directed them in all these matters to be particularly careful not to bring to light a single child that was conceived, and if it forces its way, not to feed it, on the grounds that there is no raising a child thus born.

[Gl.] This has been spoken reasonably, but how will the fathers and daughters and all the relations you have mentioned recognize one another?

[Soc.] They won't, but calculating from the day on which he became a bridegroom, of the offspring born in the tenth and the seventh month after this day he will call

the males his sons and the females his daughters, and they will call him father. And he will call their children his grandchildren and they will call these people grandfathers and grandmothers. And those born during that time in which their mothers and fathers gave birth to them will regard each other as brothers and sisters, so that they will not have sexual relations with each other, as we just discussed. But the law will permit brothers and sisters to co-habit, if the lot so falls out and the Delphic oracle approves.
[Gl.] Right you are. (459d–461e)
(Plato, *Republic* 5)

After a failed attempt to persuade a Sicilian tyrant to develop a city-state that would incorporate some of the ideas laid down in his *Republic*, Plato in his later years composed the *Laws*, in which he returned to the question of re-designing civic arrangements for men and women in a state's constitution. The views expressed are somewhat less liberal than in the earlier dialogue.

Socrates is not the primary interlocutor in this dialogue; instead, proposals are offered by an "Athenian stranger" to two older Dorian men – Megillus, a Spartan citizen, and Clinias of Crete. The latter has been charged with designing the laws for a new Cretan colony, and the dialogue takes place on Crete. Permissiveness toward women, the Athenian argues, could lead to public disorder, and control ought to be exercised by the enforcement of public dining.

Clinias and Megillus, the common dining arrangements for men have been put in place splendidly and most admirably, as I said, thanks to some divine necessity. But when it comes to women the arrangement is entirely wrong – no provision whatever, and the custom of public meals for them has not come into the light of day. Instead, the part of the human race that is by nature rather more secretive and cunning – the female sex – owing to its weakness, has been ignored, in disorder because of the flawed permissiveness of the lawgiver. Because of his oversight many points have escaped you, which would have been in much better shape than they are now, if they had been under the control of the laws. For it is not only, as it might seem, a case of its being only half our responsibility – i.e., the lack of attentiveness to regulation when it comes to women – but to the degree that it is in the nature of the female sex to be inferior to males when it comes to excellence, it affects more than half (the human race). It is better, then, for the prosperity of the state, to revise and correct and arrange all provisions for women and men alike. But now the human race is so far from arriving at this fortunate position that a person of intelligence doesn't mention the topic in places and states where public meals have received no civic recognition. How then in fact will someone attempt, without being scorned, to force on women the consumption of food and drink in full view of everyone? There would be nothing more difficult for this female sex to endure, being accustomed to living a life of retirement and obscurity. If brought into the light using all measure of resistance they will certainly get the upper hand over the lawmaker. As I said elsewhere, they would not put up with mention of the proper policy without all manner of loud protest, but perhaps in this colony they will. (Plato, *Laws* 6.780e–781d)

The Athenian visitor gives Megillus and Clinias some concrete suggestions about how to arrange athletics and education in the new state, and once again Plato is proposing a similar regime for men and women, to take full advantage of women's abilities.

[Ath.] My law would prescribe that everything would apply to females to the same degree as for men, and that one should train the women in the same way. Without any hesitation I would take this position about horseback riding or athletics: as they would be suitable for men they would be no less suitable for women. Hearing the old tales I have been convinced, and I now know, that there are pretty well countess myriads of women – those around Pontus whom they call Sauromatians, to whom is assigned the joint responsibility for handling bows and other weapons and who practise it equally. In addition to the foregoing I maintain some such reasoning as this: I claim that if these arrangements are capable of being achieved in this way, what goes on in our quarters is the height of folly, the fact that all men are not of one accord in rendering the same services with the women with all their strength. In nearly every case only half a state instead of double this develops in this way, and comes about from the same taxation and effort. And wouldn't it be an astonishing mistake for a lawgiver, this very arrangement!
[Clinias] So it would seem, at any rate. However, stranger, a great number of those things proposed just now are contrary to our customary political arrangements. (Plato, *Laws* 7.804d–805b)

The Athenian argues again for the feasibility of this arrangement on the basis of its having been tried successfully in other places, and raises the question of what kind of separate arrangement would otherwise have to be put in place for women.

Then which of the systems currently in front of us would we legislate instead of this common way of life which we are prescribing for the women? Shall it be the one which the Thracians practise, and many other peoples, who use their women for working the land and herding the oxen and pasturing the sheep and doing service no differently from slaves? Or that which we (Athenians) employ and all those around (the Athenian) district? For now this is how it has been worked out with

regard to these arrangements among us: into a single dwelling we "collect all our goods," as the saying goes, handing them over to the women to manage, together with the control of the shuttles and all kinds of wool-working. Or, Megillus, shall we make a compromise between these arrangements, adopting the Spartan way? Here girls must live sharing in athletics and music together, with the women abstaining from wool-working but weaving for themselves a type of laborious life – one in no way insignificant nor useless – and thus arrive at a sort of mid-point of domestic service and management and, what's more, child-rearing, but taking no part in warfare – with the result that, not even if there should occur some crisis obliging them to fight on behalf of their city and their children, would they be able to join in wielding the bow, like the Amazons, nor any other weapon with skill. Nor could they stand up valiantly against the wasting of their fatherland, taking spear and shield and imitating the goddess, nor could they strike terror in the enemy, if nothing more by being seen in some kind of battle-array. They would not by any means dare to mimic the Sauromatian women, adopting the way of life where their women would seem – unlike women – to be men. Whoever wants to register approval, let him commend your Spartan lawgivers when it comes to this; my position is that it not be pronounced otherwise. The lawgiver ought to go the whole way and not stop half-way, leaving the female sex to indulge in luxury and expense, conducting a disorderly way of life, while regulating that of males. In the end he is bequeathing to the city only half of a life of prosperity instead of twice this much.
(Plato, *Laws* 7.805d–806c)

The lawgiver also prescribes appropriate arrangements for the regulation of sexual activity, confining this to heterosexual marital sex.

[Ath.] We know, I take it, that at present most men, however lawless they are, are prevented effectively and strictly from having sexual relations with beautiful people, and this not against their will but they are, as far as possible, utterly willing to comply.
[Megillus] When do you say this happens?
[Ath.] Whenever someone has a brother or sister who is beautiful. Also in the case of a son or daughter the same law, although unwritten, prevents men most effectively from sleeping with them either openly or secretly or from being eager to touch them in any other way. On the contrary, there is no desire whatsoever for this kind of intermingling in most men.
[Megillus] You are correct.
[Ath.] Isn't it the case that a brief pronouncement stifles all such desires?
[Megillus] What sort of thing you talking about?
[Ath.] The pronouncement that "these activities are by no means sanctioned, but

hated by the gods and are the basest of abominations." And isn't the reason this, that no one speaks of them otherwise, but each one of us right from birth hears them saying this over and over everywhere, repeated not only in comedies but in all serious tragedy, many times – as whenever they bring on Thyestes or an Oedipus or a Macareus having sex secretly with a sister? They are seen promptly bringing death upon themselves, as punishment for their sin.

[Megillus] You are most correct in saying this much, that the factor of public opinion obtains some surprising influence, when no one ever tries to breathe a word otherwise, contravening the law.

[Ath.] Isn't it true, what was spoken just now, that a lawgiver who wants to tame one of those passions, particularly those that especially enslave men, easily learns the method that would subdue them, namely by making this proclamation sanctified in the view of everyone – slaves and free men and children and women and the whole state alike – and thus he will have constructed the firmest foundation for this law.

[Meg.] Certainly so. But how will it be possible for everyone to be willing to say that such a proclamation holds?

[Ath.] You have responded with a good question. For what I said was this, that in reference to this law I would have recourse to a device for employing intercourse only for the production of children, in compliance with nature: staying away from homosexual intercourse and not killing off the human population deliberately nor sowing seeds on rocks and stones where it will never take root and leave behind offspring – the natural legacy from itself – and also by keeping one's distance from all female fields in which you would not want the seed to develop. Now this law – when it is permanently in place and continues to prevail – just as now it is effective against having sex with one's parents if it is also the rule in other cases has countless advantages. For in the first place it follows the course of nature, and serves to prevent men from sexual frenzy and madness and all kinds of illicit sex, together with excesses of all manner of drink and food, and makes husbands faithful and affectionate to their wives. If one were able to implement this law there would arise other countless blessings.

(Plato, *Laws* 8.838a–839b)

It is perhaps worth noting that Diogenes Laertius (3rd century CE) quotes Dicaearchus as saying there were two female pupils of Plato's, Lasthenia of Mantinea (the Arcadian home of Diotima, the wise woman who instructs Socrates on the nature and purpose of love in Plato's *Symposium*) and Axiothea of Phlius, who left the Peloponnese to come to Athens and study with Plato after reading the *Republic* (Themistius, *Orations* 23.295c). Dicaearchus (late 4th century BCE) comments on Axiothea's cross-dressing when she joined the Academy.

There were many others (pupils of Plato), among whom were two women, Lasthenia of Mantinea and Axiothea of Phlius, who dressed as a man, as Dicaearchus says. (Diogenes Laertius, *Lives of Famous Philosophers* 3.46 = Dicaearchus, fr. 44Wehrli)

ARISTOTLE

Aristotle, who has left us such an extensive legacy when it comes to attempting to define what is "natural," had this to say in his *Politics* about the biological and social place of men and women in Greece and elsewhere.

It is the case, then, as we say, that it is possible first to observe in a living creature the rule of both despot and statesman. For the soul rules the body with a despot's control, while the intellect rules the appetites with a constitutional and kingly type of control. In these examples it is clear that the rule over the body by the soul is natural and expedient and (likewise) for the emotional part to be governed by the intellect and the part possessing reason; but for the two pairs to be on equal footing or in inverse relationship is harmful in all respects. Again, it is the same for all living creatures as it is for humans. Domestic animals are superior by nature to wild ones, and for all of the former it is better that they be ruled by humans, since in this way it turns out that they are preserved.

Furthermore, when it comes to males – comparing them to females –the one is by nature superior in strength and the other weaker, so the one is the ruler and the other the one ruled. The same principle is of necessity applicable to all humankind. Therefore, as many men as there are differ as widely as the soul does from the body, and as a human does from a beast (i.e., the situation of those whose job involves the use of the body and this is the best to expect from them) – these are by nature slaves, and it is better for them to be governed by this authority. (1254b2–21)

The discussion of slaves continues: a slave can recognize the rational principle, but does not possess it, hence must serve.

The usefulness (of slaves) differs little (from that of domestic animals). For bodily service for the necessities of life comes from both, from slaves and domestic animals alike. (1254b24–26)

These limitations of the composition of the slave makes it natural that the free should govern the servile population. But there is a third component in the social configuration of a household.

Since it was established that there are three divisions to household management – one the rule of master to slave, about which we spoke earlier, one between fathers and sons, and the third between husband and wife – for we speak of the rule over wives and children (as over free persons in both cases but not the same type of rule, for over the wife it is a constitutional rule but over the children the rule of a monarch). For the male is by nature more capable of being in charge than the female (unless I suppose it has been arranged in a way that is contrary to nature), and the older and more mature person over the younger and the less mature. (1259a37–1259b4)

A household was made up of individuals with varying degrees of rational capabilities and moral virtue, with women and slaves lower in the hierarchy.

So there are by nature many categories of rulers and ruled, for in different ways the free rules the slave, the male the female and the man the child. The parts of the soul are present in all of them, but present in different degrees. The slave does not possess the deliberative faculty at all; the female has it but without authority; the child possesses it but in an undeveloped form. Hence the ruler must possess the intellectual virtue in its completeness (for his task is absolutely that of the master craftsman and it is reasoning that is the master craftsman), but each of the other groups has as much as belongs to them. We must assume that it is necessarily similar in the case of the moral virtues: all must possess them, but not in the same way, but to each as much as is appropriate for its own function. The result of this is that it is clear that there is a moral virtue peculiar to all previously named groups. There is not the same self-restraint in a woman and a man, nor the same courage nor justice – as Socrates thought – but for the one it is the courage of commanding, in the other that of being subordinate, and the same holds true of the other virtues. (1260a8–24)

The qualities and behaviour of those in a household were measured against those of the master.

Hence we must be of the view, as the poet said of women, "Silence brings credit to a woman." This is not the case with a man, however. Since the child is not fully developed it is clear that its virtue is not to be taken with reference to himself, but as relative to the completely mature individual and the one having authority over him. Similarly, the virtue of a slave is to be understood with reference to its master. (1260a28–33)

Aristotle then assesses the constitutional arrangements proposed by Plato in his *Republic* and argues that the proposal that the citizen men should have their wives in common is unworkable. He argues instead that a successful state preserves essential class distinctions as well as private property. As we saw earlier (pp. 157–8), in discussing the Spartan constitution he argues that allowing freedom to women risks anarchy and lawlessness.

And again, laxity when it comes to women is harmful to the principles of the constitution and the prosperity of the state. For just as a man and wife are part of a household, it is clear that the state must be considered as more or less divided in two, into the population of males and females, with the result that in all constitutions in which the arrangements regarding women are slack one must regard half the state as being lawless. This is what has happened in Sparta. The lawmaker, wishing the whole state to be robust, is clear about this intention when in comes to men, but when it comes to women has been inattentive. For they live wantonly, with all kinds of licence, and in luxury. The result of this is that in a state such as this it is inevitable that wealth is prized, especially if the people happen to be dominated by their women, as most of the military and warlike peoples are, except for the Celts and a few others – if they openly approve of sex between males. For it seems that the first one to tell the story was not without reason in joining Ares with Aphrodite. All such warlike people seem driven toward love either with men or with women. So this was characteristic of Spartans, and under their political hegemony many things were managed by the women. Yet what difference does it make if women rule or the rulers rule under the sway of women? You get the same result. Courage is of no use for any of the everyday activities, but if it is needed it is called for in war; in this regard the Spartan women caused the most harm. They demonstrated this during the Theban invasion, for they were useful in no way, just like women in other cities, and caused more uproar than the enemy. The slack regulation of the Spartans when it came to their women seems from the beginning to have come about with good reason, for the men were living away from home on their military expeditions for lengthy periods of time, making war against the Argives and again against the Arcadians and Messenians. When they were at peace they put themselves into the hands of the lawmaker, having already been made familiar (with obedience) through living the military life (for this has many virtuous aspects). But as for the women, they claim that Lycurgus attempted to bring them under the laws, but when they resisted he backed off again. So these women are responsible for what happened, and are clearly so for this error. But we are not scrutinizing the situation for someone who should be pardoned or blamed, but for what is right or wrong about it. And as was said before, the way things are regarding women seems to be unbecoming, not only in producing a certain impropriety in the constitution as it is constructed but also in contributing somewhat to their love of money. (1269b13–1270a15)

The discussion turns to the qualities of a good ruler and a good citizen who sometimes rules and sometimes is ruled. These qualities can differ in degree and kind in an individual, depending on the role being played, as it will if one is a woman.

It is clear that the virtues of a good man – for example his justice – will not be of one and the same kind when he is being ruled and when he is free, but will take different forms when he will rule and when he will be ruled. Just so, moderation and courage are different for a man and a woman, for a man would seem to be cowardly if he were only as brave as a brave woman, and a woman would be considered a chatterbox if she were only as restrained in her conversation as a good man. Wherefore household management is also different for a man and a woman – his task is the acquisition and hers the preservation. (1277b18–25)

In reviewing the different ways of governing a state, Aristotle argues that tyranny can be produced by an autocratic ruler, or by an extreme form of democracy that awards too much freedom to women and slaves.

The things that occur in connection with the final form of democracy all dispose it toward tyranny – the power exercised by women in their homes so that they become public informers on their husbands, and the laxness shown to the slaves, for the same reason. For slaves and women do not conspire against tyrants, and when they prosper they must feel well disposed towards both tyrannies and democracies. (1313b32–38)

On the question of families and the production of children, Aristotle argues that the lawgiver should regulate the age at which women should become mothers, for several reasons.

For since the time for producing children is confined to – speaking generally – the outer limit of the age of seventy for men and fifty for women, the beginning of their mating should fall within these years in respect of their age. The mating of the young is inadequate for the production of children, for in all living creatures the offspring of the young are not fully formed and more likely to produce female children and those small in size – so it must be the case that this same thing happens for humans also. Proof of this is found in the fact that in those states where it is the custom for young men and young women to mate the people are poorly formed and small of body. And furthermore, young mothers labour more in childbirth and are more apt to die. Some say that this is the reason why the oracle ("cut not a new furrow") was given to the people of Troezen, since many of them were dying because of the marrying of their young women, and it did not refer

to the gathering of the harvest. And still more, it contributes to chastity to give women in marriage when they are older, for they seem to be more wanton when they have had sex as young women. (1335a8–24)
(Aristotle, *Politics*)

FURTHER READING

Bar On, Bat-Ami. 1994. *Engendering Origins: Critical Feminist Readings in Plato and Aristotle.* Albany, NY

Clark, S. 1982. "Aristotle's Woman," *History of Political Thought* 3, 177–191

Fortenbaugh, W.W. 1975. "On Plato's Feminism in Republic V," *Apeiron* 9, 1–4

Pomeroy, S. 1974. "Feminism in Book V of Plato's Republic," *Apeiron* 8, 32–35

Smith, N. 1983. "Plato and Aristotle on the Nature of Women," *Journal of the History of Philosophy* 21, 467–478

Staufer, D.J. 2008. "Aristotle's Account of the Subjection of Women," *Journal of Politics* 70, 929–941

Tuana, N. 1994 ed. *Feminist Interpretations of Plato.* University Park, PA

Wender, D. 1973. "Plato: Misogynist, Paedophile and Feminist," *Arethusa* 6, 75–90

13

Warrior women

AMAZONS

The Amazons, a mythical band of fearless female warriors, were believed by the Greeks to have descended from the Wargod Ares, and lived in the Black Sea area during the heroic age. Their character may have been based on reports of historical women belonging to Scythian or Sauromatian tribes who fought on horseback with bows and arrows.

In the 2nd century BCE Apollodorus collected a wide range of Greek myths and recorded them. In his *Epitome* he described the defeat of the Amazon Penthesilea by the Greek hero Achilles, after she had killed the physician attending the Greeks at Troy, and (unwittingly) her own queen.

Penthesilea, daughter of Otrere and Ares, accidentally killed Hippolyte and was purified by Priam. She killed many when battle occurred, among whom was Machaon. Then later she died at the hand of Achilles, who fell in love with the Amazon after her death.
(Apollodorus, *Epitome* 5.1)

Fascination, erotic attraction, fear and eventual defeat of the Amazons characterize Greek accounts of the Amazons. In the Archaic period the myth of Heracles' ninth labour, in which he wrests the girdle belt from the queen of the Amazons, became popular and was frequently depicted in vase paintings. In the 5th century the hero's quest was celebrated by the chorus in Euripides' *Heracles* (*c.* 417 BCE).

(Heracles) set off for the mounted troop of Amazons around Maiotis of the many rivers through the surging waves of the Black Sea, gathering a group of friends. Who was there left in Greece? He went sailing off after the garment of the daughter of Ares in a deadly hunt for the warrior-belt belonging to the gold-bedecked garment of the daughter of Ares. Greece obtained the famous prize from the foreign girl and keeps it safe in Mycenae.
(Euripides *Heracles* 408–417)

The 5th-century historian Herodotus described an attempt by Greeks to intermarry with some Amazons in Scythian territory. After some Greek youths managed to have sex with the Amazons they invited the women to return with them to live as their wives among the Greeks. The Amazons declined the offer.

To this (invitation) the women replied: "We would not be able to live with your women, for we and they do not have the same customs. We shoot with the bow and throw the javelin and ride horses, but have not learned the crafts of women. And your women do none of these things we have told you about, but remain in their wagons and work at women's tasks, nor do they go out on a hunt or for any other activity. Therefore, we would never be able to agree with them. But if you wish to have us as wives and to be thought of as men who have the reputation of being most fair, go to your parents and get your share of their possessions and then let us go and dwell by ourselves." (Herodotus, *Histories* 4.114)

The Greek geographer Strabo, who lived in the Roman period (2nd century CE) passed on information about the Amazons that had been written in the 2nd and 1st centuries BCE by the historians Metrodorus and Hypsicrates, who lived in areas of the Greek-speaking East near the supposed traditional habitat of the Amazons. According to these historians, this tribe of women lived in the foothills of the Caucasus, and received their name from the removal of the right breast (*mazon*) soon after birth.

Metrodorus of Scepsis and Hypsicrates who are not themselves unfamiliar with the region, say that they live on the borders of the Gargarians in the foothills on the north side of the Caucasus mountains, those called Ceraunian. (They say that) they spend part of their time working on their own at several individual tasks, including plowing, cultivating, and activities related to pasturing, but especially those involving horses. The bravest of them excel in hunting on horseback and train in military exercises. They all sear off the right breast of the infant females, so that they easily wield their (right) arm for every purpose, most importantly for throwing the javelin. They also use the bow and the *sagaris*-blade and the light shield; they make the skins of wild beasts serve as helmets and clothing and belts. They have two chosen months in the spring, in which they go up a nearby mountain that separates them from the Gargarians. And the Gargarians too climb up, according to some long-held custom, to sacrifice with them and to have sex with the women for the purpose of begetting children. They do this out of sight and in the dark, any man with whichever woman he comes across. After making them pregnant they send them away. The Amazons themselves keep the females to whom they give birth, but they bring the males to the men to be reared. Each man claims as his own whatever one is brought to him, regarding him as his son, not knowing otherwise. (Strabo, *Geography* 11.5.1)

The Sicilian Diodorus composed a work purporting to encompass all of Greek history until his time (1st century BCE). Consulting the work of Dionysius Skytobrachion, who composed fanciful utopian tales in the Egyptian city of Alexandria in the mid-2nd century BCE, Diodorus describes a tribe of Amazons who, with other races of warlike women such as the Gorgons, lived in Libya, in North Africa. He describes their way of life, following the same Greek tradition as reported by Strabo that accounts for their name.

It was the custom among these women to work hard at war, and for a fixed period it was obligatory to serve in the army, preserving their virginity. When the years of their military service were over, they went to their men for the production of children, but they continued to manage the ruling offices and all the public affairs of state. The men, just like married women among us, carried out their life inside the house, submitting to the orders laid down by the women with whom they lived. They took no part in military campaigns nor political office, nor in any kind of free speech that was part of public affairs, as a consequence of which they might become presumptuous and attack the women. After the birth of their children the babies were handed over to the men, who brought them up on milk and certain other mashed foods suitable for the age of the infants. If it happened that a girl was born, its breasts were cauterized, so that they might not take their shape at puberty. For they thought that breasts projecting out from the body would be more than an incidental impediment on military campaigns. Because they are deprived of these (breasts) they are called "Amazons" by the Greeks.
(Diodorus Siculus, *Historical Library* 3.53.1–3)

Amazons became a useful rhetorical tool for Athenians, particularly in the early 5th century BCE as they celebrated their defeat of an invader also from the East, the Persians. Public funeral orations eulogizing the warrior dead were occasions on which attention was drawn to Athenian history and glory. The following is taken from one such address that may have been given by the orator Lysias. It describes the Amazons as a worthy foe who were weakened when faced with Athenians, then were justly defeated.

Now first I will recount the perils of old endured by our ancestors, drawing my memorial tribute from the reputation they established. For it is worthwhile for every person to recall them, celebrating them in songs and talking about them in the records of the men of worth, honouring them on occasions such as this and instructing the living through the deeds of the dead.

There were the Amazons of ancient times, daughters of Ares, living beside the River Thermodon. They alone of those living near them were armed with iron, and they

were the first of all to mount horses, with which – because of the inexperience of their enemies – they caught some by surprise as they fled or outstripped those who pursued them. Because of their courage they used to be thought of as men rather than, because of their physical features, women. They seemed to surpass men in their spirits, rather than be inferior to them in their appearance. They ruled over many tribes, and in fact enslaved many of those around them. Hearing by report of the great reputation of this land, they mustered the most warlike nations and marched against this city, for the sake of earning great glory and because of their high ambition. But encountering courageous men they acquired spirits akin to those belonging to their sex. Acquiring a reputation that was the reverse of their former one, they appeared to be women, more as a result of the ordeals they faced than because of their bodies. For them alone it did not fall out that they learned from their mistakes and made better plans for the future. Not going home, they did not report their own misfortune and the valiant performance of our ancestors, for they died right here and paid the penalty for their foolishness. They made the memory of our city imperishable because of its bravery, and rendered their own city nameless because of their disaster in this place. These women, because of their unjust greed for the property of others, justly destroyed their own.
("Lysias" *Funeral Oration* 3–6)

FEMALE LEADERS IN WAR

Telesilla

The city of Argos in the Peloponnese was known by Greeks of the Classical period for its vigorous cultural life. It was home to an important school of sculpture, and Herodotus mentions that in the late 6th century the Argives had earned the name of being the best musicians (3.131). One of these famous Argive musician-poets was a woman, Telesilla, whose work was still circulating in the 2nd century CE. Most of it is lost now, however, apart from one fragment that describes the attempts of the nymph Arethusa to escape the advances of the river god Alpheus.

Telesilla was connected with an important military event in Argos *c.* 494 BCE. Pausanias (2nd century CE) gives us the story behind a statue that had been erected at a temple of Aphrodite in Argos. The poet was depicted with her songs scattered at her feet, holding a helmet that she was about to put on her head. Here is Pausanias' account, which may be derived from a Hellenistic Argive historian.

Telesilla was especially distinguished among the women, particularly for her poetry. As the story goes, it happened that there had been a terrible disaster for the Argives at the hands of Cleomenes, the son of Anaxandrides, and the Spartans. Some had

fallen in the battle, and all those who had fled to the grove of Argos, even these perished. At first they left the sanctuary in accordance with an agreement, then, when they realized that they had been deceived, the rest were burnt to death in the grove. So when Cleomenes led the Spartans to Argos it was bereft of men. But Telesilla mounted on the wall the household slaves and as many as were unable to bear arms because of their youth or old age. She herself, collecting as many weapons as had been left in the houses, and those from the sanctuaries, armed those women who were in the prime of life and, arming them, she positioned them in the place where she knew the enemy would attack. When the Spartans came up close the women were not terrified by their war-cry and took them on, fighting aggressively. Thereupon the Spartans realized that to destroy women would obtain an odious success for them, and should they be defeated they would become the butt of reproaches. They gave way before the women.
(Pausanias, *Description of Greece* 2.20.8–9)

Plutarch adds the detail that in his own time (600 years later) the Argives still celebrated a festival each year on the day of Telesilla's victory, when men and women cross-dressed. (*Moralia* 245c)

Artemisia and the Persians at Salamis

In 480 BCE the Persians invaded Greece for the second time in a decade. After they ravaged the Acropolis in Athens King Xerxes and the Persians with their supporters met the Greeks for a showdown in a sea battle, in the narrow straits between the island of Salamis and the western coast of mainland Greece. The Persians were ultimately defeated because of their tactical disadvantage at being unable to manoeuvre their ships in such a confined space. King Xerxes was warned of this weakness in advance of the battle by Queen Artemisia of Caria. After the death of her husband, Artemisia had taken over the rule of this region, earlier settled by Greeks on the west coast of Asia Minor. The Carians were important subject allies of the Persians, and Xerxes was disposed to take Artemisia's strategic advice at Salamis but was dissuaded by one of his chief generals, Mardonius – sealing the Persian fate. The story is told by the Greek historian Herodotus in his *Histories*.

When they had sat down in order, Xerxes asked Mardonius to test each (leader) over whether they should engage in a sea-battle.

Mardonius went about questioning them, beginning with the Sidonian (commander). The others replied with one and the same opinion, bidding them to go to battle at sea, but Artemisia said the following: "Tell the king for me, Mardonius, that I say this, not speaking as the weakest one in the sea-battles off Euboea nor having displayed the least courage. Master, it is fair that I bring forward my view as I see it, the one I happen to think is the best for your situation. I am telling you this – spare your ships and make no battle at sea! For their men are as much stronger than yours at sea as men are stronger than women. Why should you put yourself at risk on all fronts in a naval battle? Don't you have control of Athens, for the sake of which you set out on this campaign? And don't you control the rest of Greece? No one stands in your way. Those who opposed you suffered the reverses that were called for. Just how I think the enemy's actions will play out I will tell you. If you do not press on to engage in a sea-battle but keep your ships here, remaining close to land or even going on to the Peloponnese, then, Master, you will easily make way for what you had in mind when you came here. The Greeks are not able to hold out against you for a long time, but you will scatter them and each will flee to his own city. There is no food for them on this island, as I have ascertained, nor is it likely, if you drive your infantry into the Peloponnese, that those who have come from there will remain unaffected. They won't be inclined to fight a sea-battle on the side of the Athenians. But if you press forward immediately to fight at sea I fear lest your fleet suffer some mishap and bring ruin upon your army as well."

When she said these things to Mardonius, all those who were well-disposed to Artemisia considered that disaster attended her words, inasmuch as she would suffer some ill-doing from the king because she did not lean towards engaging in battle at sea. But those who were jealous of her and mean-spirited towards her, inasmuch as she had been foremost in the honour in which she was held by all the allies, took pleasure in her answer, considering that she would be destroyed as a result. But when her opinions were reported to Xerxes he took great pleasure in the counsel of Artemisia. Even previously he had thought of her as worthy of attention but now he held her in even greater esteem. (8.67.11–69.10)

Xerxes was nonetheless persuaded to follow the recommendation of the majority and the sea battle began. In a short time most of the vessels of the Persians and their allies were shattered. Artemisia, however, by a clever tactic outran an Athenian vessel in eager pursuit of her.

When a great deal of confusion was descending upon the king's side, the ship of Artemesia at this moment was being pursued by a vessel from Attica. Not having a way to escape, for other friendly ships were in her way, it happened that she was the one nearest to the enemy. She resolved to do the following, which when she did it turned to her advantage. Pursued by the Attic ship she charged a friendly ship of Calyndian men and the king of the Calyndians himself who was sailing with them, Damasithymus. (8.87.4–12)

Herodotus wonders whether there may have been some personal grudge at stake here, but continues:

When she had attacked and sunk the ship, experiencing good fortune she worked a double advantage for herself. For when the captain of the Attic trireme saw her attacking a ship of foreigners he supposed that the ship of Artemisia was either Greek or one deserting from the foreigners who was fighting on the Greek side, so he turned away and went in the direction of others. (8.87.16–88.1)

This earned her even greater esteem in the eyes of Xerxes, when it was confirmed for him that it was indeed Artemisia who had sunk a ship. (None of the observers reporting this to the king had noticed that the vessel was one fighting on the Persian side, and there were no survivors to accuse her.) Xerxes' praise was unreserved.

It is said that Xerxes replied to the report with "My men have become women, and the women men!" (8.88.14–15)
(Herodotus, *Histories*)

After the rout of the Persians and their allies at Salamis, Mardonius was determined to launch a further attack on the Greeks, this time on land, in the Peloponnese. Xerxes called for Artemisia to offer advice and consulted with her privately, acknowledging that her earlier assessment of their situation had proved to be accurate. The queen advised him to leave Mardonius to fight on land if he wished, but that he should return with his retinue to Persia. Should Mardonius be successful, she said, the honours would ultimately be enjoyed by the king. If he failed, Xerxes and his household would still survive and continue to enjoy the report of their sack of Athens; the only loss would be that of his servant. Xerxes thanked her, followed her advice and entrusted his sons to her, to take with her to Ephesus. (Herodotus 8.101–103)

FURTHER READING

duBois, P. 1982. *Centaurs and Amazons. Women and the Pre-History of the Great Chain of Being*. Ann Arbor, MI
Munson, R.V. 1988. "Artemisia in Herodotus," *Classical Antiquity* 7, 91–106
Tyrrell, W.B. 1984. *Amazons. A Study in Athenian Mythmaking*. Ann Arbor, MI
Wilde, L.W. 2000. *On the Trail of the Women Warriors. The Amazons in Myth and History*. New York

14

The female body

THE HIPPOCRATIC WRITERS

Although we have good reason to believe that there was a Greek medical practitioner and teacher named Hippocrates born on the island of Cos during the 5th century BCE, we cannot assume that he composed the surviving medical writings that were ascribed to him, consisting of various accounts of symptoms, diagnoses and reflections on the human body. This "Hippocratic Corpus" dates from the 5th and 4th centuries BCE, and at least one quarter of these works describe the symptoms and treatment of women's diseases. From these treatises we can gain much understanding of what was generally assumed to be the nature and function of the female body. Because dissection of human bodies was not permitted, medical practitioners made assumptions based on clinical observations (including wounds), evidence from animals and the patients' descriptions of their own experiences. In their observations the most significant difference between the female and male body was in their reproductive systems, which can help to explain the Hippocratic focus on the uterus as the centre of female pathology.

The so-called women's diseases. The uterus is the cause of all such diseases. For the uterus, when it is displaced from its normal position, whether forward or back, causes diseases. Whenever the uterus has been moved away and does not bring its mouth towards or touch the lips of the vagina, the illness is minor. But if the uterus moves to the front and brings its mouth against the lip, first of all it causes pain, and then because the uterus is blocked and closed off by its contact with the lips of the vagina, the so-called "menstrual flow" does not happen. This flow if held back causes swelling and pain. If the uterus moves downward and is turned aside so that it makes contact with the groin, it causes pain. If it retreats upward and is diverted and blocked off, it causes illness through its porousness. Whenever the uterus is diseased because of this problem, it causes pain in the hips and the head. When the uterus is distended and swollen, nothing flows and it becomes filled up. When it is filled, it touches the hip-joints. Whenever the uterus is filled, distended with moisture, it does not move; it touches the hip-joints, causing pain in both the hip-joints and the groin; something like balls roll through the stomach, and cause

pain in the head, sometimes in one part, and other times in all of it, according to how the disease develops.
(*Places in Man* 47 = 6.344 Littré)

The following Hippocratic writer also reflects the general assumption – one that was long lived – that the uterus was not fixed but moved around the woman's body in search of moisture. In a properly functioning body, women's excess moisture, accumulated from food and drink, was assumed to be released through menstruation. The basic constitution of the female body was identified as softer and more moist than that of a man.

I say that a woman's flesh is more porous and softer than a man's: since this is so, the woman's body draws moisture both with more speed and in greater quantity from the belly than does the body of a man.

Given that the woman is soft-fleshed, when her body is full of blood and the blood does not get evacuated, with her flesh full and heated, pain occurs. For a woman has warmer blood and for this reason she is warmer than a man. But if the surplus of blood that is generated is evacuated, no pain or heat would be produced by the blood. A man, being more solid in flesh than a woman, is not so overfilled with blood that pain occurs if a certain amount of his blood does not exit each month. He draws whatever quantity of blood is needed for the nourishment of his body; since his body is not soft it does not become overstrained nor is it overheated by fullness, as in the case of a woman. What contributes greatly to this in the case of a man is the fact that he works harder than a woman, for hard work draws off some of the fluid.
(*Diseases of Women* 1.1 = 8.12–14 Littré)

The "equilibrium" established in women by the periodic release of excess moisture through menstruation was seen as crucial to their health. Various (acute) illnesses were ascribed to the blockage of this outflow. The solution was twofold: intercourse for young women soon after puberty, then childbirth. After mentioning that many people suffer from delusional visions of demons etc. this writer claims that nubile virgins will suffer from these most acutely.

As a result of such visions, many people have hanged themselves, more women than men, for the constitution of women is less courageous and feebler. And if virgins remain unmarried at the appropriate time for marriage they experience this more frequently, especially at the time of their first monthly period, although previously they had no terrible experiences such as these. Later the blood collects in the uterus so that it may flow out, but when the mouth of the exit is not opened up, and blood flows into the uterus more abundantly on account of both food and the growth of the body size, then the blood which has no outlet leaps up to the heart and to the diaphragm because of its quantity. When these are filled with blood, the heart becomes sluggish and then, because of its sluggishness, numb, and then, because of the numbness, delirium takes hold. Just as when one has been sitting for a long time the blood that has been pressed away from the hips and the thighs collects in the calves and feet, it brings numbness, and as a result of the numbness, one's feet are useless for walking until the blood goes back where it belongs. It returns most quickly when one stands in cold water and wets the tops of one's ankles. This numbness is easily remedied, since the blood flows back quickly because of the straightness of the blood vessels, and this place in the body is not critical. But blood flows back slowly from the heart and from the diaphragm. There the blood vessels are on an angle, and it is a critical site for delirium and one suited to madness.

When these parts are filled with blood, shivering also sets in, with fever. They call these "erratic fevers." When this is the case, a girl goes crazy because of the violent inflammation, and she becomes murderous because of the putrefaction, and is afraid and fearful of the dark. Because of the constriction around their hearts girls try to strangle themselves; their spirit, distraught and anguished because of the bad condition of the blood, brings trouble upon itself. An afflicted girl could say dreadful things: and (her delusions) order her to leap up and throw herself into wells and drown, as if this were better for her and advantageous in all kinds of ways. Whenever she is without delusions, (she senses) a certain pleasure from desiring death as if it were a form of good. With the return of reason to the individuals, the women consecrate to Artemis many objects, but especially the most valuable of their female robes, at the behest of seers, but they are deceived. The cure for this happens when nothing impedes the outflow of blood. I recommend that virgins, whenever they have such an experience, cohabit with men as quickly as possible. If they become pregnant, they will be healthy. If they don't do this, either right at puberty or a little later they will be seized by this, if not by another sickness. Among married women, those who are sterile suffer more from this.
(On Virgins 1 = 8.466–70 Littré)

The following Hippocratic writer speculates on the connection between intercourse and conception and the degree to which women contribute generative material to the embryo. He claims that women, like men, contribute "semen" (a seed), and that the sex of the child is determined by the "strength" of the seed. His account reflects some familiarity with the woman's experience during intercourse.

In women, I say that during intercourse when the vagina is rubbed and the uterus is moved, a tickling, as it were, comes upon them which produces pleasure and warmth in the rest of the body. A woman also releases something from her body, sometimes into the uterus, which then becomes moist, and sometimes externally as well, if the uterus opens wider than it should. She feels pleasure, once intercourse begins, during the whole time until the man ejaculates in her. If the woman is eager for intercourse she ejaculates before the man, and for the remainder of the time she does not feel the same pleasure; but if she is not in a passionate state, then her pleasure terminates with the man's. It is like this: if someone pours cold water into water that is boiling, the water stops boiling. In the same way, the man's seed dropping into the uterus extinguishes both the warmth and the pleasure of the woman. Both the pleasure and the heat reach their peak simultaneously with the arrival of the sperm in the uterus, and then it ceases. Just so, if someone were to pour wine on a flame at first it happens that the flame flares up and increases briefly with the pouring of the wine, then it dies. In the same way the woman's heat flares up in response to the man's sperm, and then dies away. The woman feels much less pleasure than the man during intercourse but it lasts for a longer time. The reason that the man feels more pleasure is that the secretion from the bodily fluid for him occurs suddenly, and is the result of a more intense shuddering than in the woman's case.

There is also this point about women: if they have intercourse with men they are more likely to be healthy, and less healthy if they do not. First, the uterus becomes moist in intercourse and not dry; when the uterus is drier than it should be it contracts more strongly than it should, and this contracting causes severe trouble in the entire body. Second, as soon as there is intercourse the blood is heated and becomes more fluid, and makes an easier passage for the menstrual fluid; if the menstrual fluid does not flow, women's bodies become prone to disease. (4)

When a woman has had intercourse, if she is not going to conceive, the seed from both partners generally falls out, whenever the woman wishes it. But if she is going to conceive, the seed does not fall out but remains in her uterus. For when the uterus has received it, it closes up and keeps it inside itself, because the opening contracts in response to the moisture. And what is mixed together is what comes from the man and the woman in like measure. If the woman is experienced in childbirth, and notices when the seed does not come out but is retained, she will know the day on which she has conceived. (5)

Now there is also this fact. Sometimes what the woman emits is stronger, and sometimes weaker; and it is the same case for the man. In a man is both female and male semen, and likewise in a woman. The male sex is stronger than the female, so it follows that it comes from stronger semen. If the stronger type of semen comes from both parents a male is produced. If it is the weaker type, a female. Whichever type exceeds in quantity, that produces the result. For if the weak semen is much more plentiful than the strong it prevails over the strong, and having been mixed with the weak it turns out to be a female. But if the strong semen is more plentiful than the weak, the weaker is overcome, and it evolves into a male. It is just as though one were to mix together beeswax with fat, using a larger quantity of fat, and then one were to melt them together over a fire. While the mixture is still fluid, the prevailing type is not apparent. But when it solidifies then it is clear that the fat prevails over the wax because of its quantity. And it is just the same with the male and female seed. (6)

It produces the conclusion that in both the woman and the man is a seed, and that they each have both male and female seed is obvious. For many women have already borne daughters to their husbands and then, going and having sex with other men, have produced sons. And those same men to whom their wives bore daughters, by going and having intercourse with other women, have produced male offspring; and for those men to whom male offspring were born, when they had intercourse with other women they produced female offspring. Now this analysis will attest to the fact that both the man and the woman have male and female seed. For in those couples to whom a daughter was born the stronger (seed) was overwhelmed by the larger quantity of the weaker and produced a female, while for the couples to whom a son was born the stronger prevailed and produced a male. From the same man a strong seed does not always come forth, nor a weak one on every occasion, but it varies on different occasions. And it is the same case with women. So one is not to be surprised that the same women and the same men produce male and female offspring. It holds true also for animals, concerning their male and female offspring. (7)
(*On Generation* 4–7 = 7.474–80 Littré)

For the medical writers, menstruation was an important indication of women's general health or illness, and a reflection of the state of the uterus. Blockage of the menses or a dry uterus was to be avoided.

The following is about women's diseases. I say that a woman who has never given birth is more seriously affected and more readily from menstruation than a woman who has given birth to a child. For whenever a woman does give birth, her small blood vessels become more smooth-flowing for menstruation. The passage of the lochia and the stretching open of the body make the menses more smooth-flowing ... (1)

Whenever in a woman who has never given birth the menses are suppressed and cannot find a way out, illness results. This happens if the mouth of the uterus is

closed or bent back, or if some part of her vagina is contracted. For if one of these things is the case, the menses will not be able to find a way out until the uterus returns to a healthy state. This disease occurs especially in women who have a uterus narrow at the mouth or who have a cervix that lies further into the vagina. For if either of these is the case and if the woman does not have intercourse with a man, and if her belly is emptied more than is right because of some suffering, the uterus is displaced. The uterus is not damp of its own accord, since the woman is not having intercourse, and there is space for the uterus inasmuch as the belly is emptier, so that the uterus is displaced, by reason of its being drier and lighter than is right. (2)
(*Diseases of Women* 1.1, 1.2 = 8.10, 14 Littré)

A healthy menstrual flow, apart from being a sign of general health in a woman, boded well for her ability to give birth to a healthy child. A heavy flow could leave her weak and imperil the foetus, and a feeble flow could indicate that she was less womanly.

The blood flows like that from a sacrificial victim, and it quickly coagulates if the woman is healthy. Women in whom the cleansing takes place as a rule for more than four days, and the menstrual fluid pours out really heavily – these women become thin. Their embryos are thin and weak. But in those women in whom the cleansing is less than three days or is slight, these women are robust; they have good colour and a manly appearance. They are not keen on producing children nor do they become pregnant.
(*Diseases of Women* 1.6 = 8.30 Littré)

The belief that the uterus was not firmly attached inside the woman's body led to the assumption that it would move in search of moisture and cause various pathologies including "suffocation" (the respiratory system was only vaguely understood).

If suffocation occurs suddenly. This happens especially to women who do not have sex with men and in women who are older, rather than to young ones, for their uteruses are lighter. It happens mainly because of the following: when a woman is empty and works harder than she normally does, her uterus, becoming heated from the hard work, turns because it is empty and light. There is empty space for it to turn in because the abdomen is empty. When the uterus turns, it strikes the liver and together with it strikes against the abdomen. For it rushes and goes upward towards the moisture because it has been dried out more than usual by her working harder. The liver is, after all, moist. But when the uterus strikes the liver, it produces sudden suffocation by taking up the breathing space around the belly.

Sometimes, at the same time as the uterus begins to make for the liver, phlegm also flows down from the head to the abdomen; as one might expect she experiences suffocation. There is the case where, at the same time as there is a flow of phlegm, the uterus leaves the liver, returning to its place and the suffocation ceases. The uterus goes back, then, when it has absorbed moisture and has become heavy. There is a gurgling sound from it when it returns to its customary place. When it has returned, it can happen that the stomach becomes more moist than previously, for the head releases phlegm into the stomach. When the uterus goes toward the liver and the abdomen and suffocates the woman, the whites of her eyes roll back and she becomes cold. In some cases they turn livid. Her teeth chatter and saliva pours into her mouth. (Such) women resemble those who suffer from epileptic seizures. (*Diseases of Women* 1.7 = 8.32 Littré)

Hippocratic writers often explain the apparent movement of symptoms in diseases between different parts of the body by internal fluxes through vessels or along other supposed channels. In many female disorders, sweet- or foul-smelling substances were applied to the nose and/or genitalia, suggesting that there was a belief in an internal connection between the head and the uterus. Fumigation was one of the most common therapies, based on the assumption that the uterus was thought of as somehow sentient, with a life of its own.

The following remedies should be prepared: if the uterus has only moved forward and it is possible to smear on ointment, use any foul-smelling ointment you wish, either cedar or myssotos (a garlic infusion), or some other strong and bad-smelling substance, and fumigate. But do not administer a vapour-bath, and do not give food or a diuretic drink during this time, nor wash her in warm water. If the uterus has turned back up but is not diverted, use sweet-smelling applications that warm her at the same time. These include myrrh or perfumed oil, or some other aromatic and warming substance. Use these applications and from below fumigate with wine vapour and wash with warm water, and use diuretics. This is a clear indication: if the uterus has turned upwards and is not turned aside, the flow occurs.

But if the uterus is diverted then there is no so-called menstrual flow. This malady must be treated first with the following vapour-bath: putting wild figs into wine, heat this with a gourd placed around the mouth of the vessel in which the mixture is heated as follows: cutting the gourd through the middle hollow it out, and cutting off a bit of its top, cap this over the skin vessel, so that the fumes travelling through the narrow chamber will reach the uterus. Bathe with warm water, then you should apply applications of drugs with thermal properties. Thermal medications are those of the foregoing that bring on menstruation, namely this sort: cow

dung, bull's bile, myrrh, alum, galbanum, and anything similar, using as much of these as possible. Evacuate from below by laxative drugs in the amount that does not cause vomiting. Then dilute it, so that it does not become a violent purgative by being too strong.
(*Places in Man* 47 = 6.344–6 Littré)

Because of a belief in a channel connecting the head and the genitalia, this aromatherapy was applied to both the vaginal area and the upper orifices.

When a woman's uterus moves against her liver, she will suddenly lose her voice, clench her teeth and take on a dark colouring. This condition happens suddenly, even if she is in good health. The problem particularly affects unmarried girls, old women and widows – or if they are young and widowed after having borne children. When this condition occurs, thrust your hand down, push the uterus down and away from the liver and bind it with a band under the abdomen. Opening her mouth, pour in some very fragrant wine. Hold foul-smelling vapours under her nostrils and below her uterus sweet-scented fumes.
(*On the Nature of Women* 3 = 7.314 Littré)

Our word "hysteria" comes from a belief in the mental effects of a uterine disease. Here is an account of some symptoms of hysteria and treatments for it.

If her uterus affixes itself up against the abdomen, she suffocates as if she had taken hellebore; her breathing is tight and she has severe pains in her heart. Some women vomit up acid saliva, their mouths are full of fluid, and their legs become cold. Women such as these, if the uterus does not leave the upper abdomen directly, lose their voices, and their head and tongue are numb. If you find such women unable to speak and with their teeth clenched, insert wool as a suppository, thrusting it in as far in as possible, having wound it around a feather. Dip it either in white Egyptian perfume or perfume of myrtle or bacchar (hazelwort) or marjoram. Into her nostrils, taking a spatula, stuff some black medicine (used for the head). If this is not available, smear the inside of her nostrils with silphium juice or dip a feather in vinegar and insert it, or induce sneezing. When her mouth is closed tight and she is unable to speak, give her some castoreum in wine to drink. Dip your finger in seal oil and smear it on her nostrils. Leave the wool suppository in place until the uterus returns. When the symptoms cease you must remove it. But if, when you take the suppository out, the uterus moves back again insert the suppository in the same way, and fumigate beneath her nostrils with scrapings of the black horn of a goat or stag, sprinkling over it hot ashes, so that it is smoking as much as possible. Have her inhale the odour through her nostrils as far as she can. But the best for

fumigation is seal oil. Placing coals on a piece of pottery, cover the patient but let her hold her head out so that the scent is taken in as much as possible. Drip some animal fat over it and let her inhale the odour. She must keep her mouth closed. If (the uterus) falls upward this is what you must do.
(*Diseases of Women* 2.126 = 8.270–272 Littré)

The following seems to be addressing the condition of a prolapsed uterus. Once again, fumigation is advised, along with some invasive treatments and a special diet that included cantharid beetles.

If her uterus rushes out towards her hips, her menses stop coming and pain develops in her lower abdomen and in her flank on that side. If you palpitate with your finger, you will discover the mouth of the uterus next to her hip-joint. When this occurs, bathe the woman with warm water, give her garlic to eat, as much as she can. Let her drink undiluted sheep's milk after she has eaten. Then, after putting her in a vapour bath, give her a purgative medication. When she has been cleaned out, once more fumigate the uterus, mixing fennel and absinthe. Right after the vapour bath, draw up the mouth of the uterus with your finger. Then insert a suppository made with squill (a bulbous onion-like plant); after this, waiting for a while, insert a suppository of narcissus. If you think that she has been cleansed, have her apply oil of bitter almonds, and on the next day, rose perfume. She should stop this application on the day before her period, and start again the day after it stops.

At the time of the menstrual flow, if the blood flows well, fine. If there is no flow, let her drink a mixture of four cantharid beetles with their legs cut off, along with their wings and heads, five black peony seeds, cuttlefish eggs, and a little celery seed in wine. If she has a pain and discomfort with urination, let her sit in warm water and drink honey mixed with water. If she is not cured by the first procedure, let her drink again until her menstrual flow returns. When it happens, let her abstain from food and have intercourse with her husband. During her period she should eat mercury plant and boiled octopus, and consume soft foods. If she becomes pregnant she will be cured of this disease.
(*On the Nature of Women* 8 = 7.322–8.324 Littré)

Not all women wanted to become pregnant. Here is an unusual recipe for a contraceptive.

If a woman does not want to become pregnant, dissolve copper ore to the amount of a bean in water, make her drink it, and she will not become pregnant for a year.
(*On the Nature of Women* 98 = 7.414 Littré)

It was sometimes in the interests of others that a woman not become pregnant.

I will relate how I saw a seed that was six days old. There was a very valuable girl, a musical performer belonging to a female kinswoman of mine, one who was having relations with men but whom she needed to keep from getting pregnant lest she lose her value. Now this singing girl had heard the sort of thing women say to each other – that when a woman is going to conceive, the seed remains inside her and does not fall out. When she heard this she took notice, and was always on guard; when she perceived that the seed had not come out she told her mistress, and the story came to me. When I heard it, I told her to jump up and strike her buttocks. After she had done this seven times, the seed fell out on the ground and there was a noise. The girl saw it and examined it in wonder. I will tell you what it looked like: it was as if someone had removed the shell from a raw egg, and the fluid inside was visible through the interior membrane. In short, its appearance was something like this, I would say: it was red and roundish, and inside there were broad white fibres enclosed by a thick red fluid, and around the membrane on the outside there was bloody material. In the middle of the membrane something slender projected: it seemed to me to be an umbilical cord, and that it was through this that the embryo first breathed in and out. The entire membrane stretched out from this, enclosing the seed. Such then was the six-day-old seed that I saw.
(*On the Nature of the Child* 13 = 7.490–492 Littré)

Miscarriages were attributed to several factors.

There are also many other dangers by which embryos are destroyed; if, for example, a pregnant woman is sick and weak, and if she lifts up a burden with effort, or if she is struck, or leaps up, or goes without food, or suffers from fainting, or takes too much or too little nourishment, or has had a fright and is scared, or screams or loses control. Food is a cause of miscarriage, as is an excess of blood. Uteruses by themselves also have natural features through which miscarriage can occur – those that are flatulent, compact or loose, oversized or undersized, and other similar types.

If a pregnant woman suffers in her belly or in her lower back, one must be concerned lest the embryo be miscarried, because the membranes that surround it have been ruptured.

There are also women who lose their children if they eat or drink something pungent or bitter, contrary to their usual habits – if the foetus is still in its early stage.
(*Diseases of Women* 25 = 8.66–8 Littré)

From tomb inscriptions we know that many women and infants died in childbirth. Here is some advice for dealing with a difficult birth.

If for a pregnant woman the time for birth is already past and labour pains seize
her, and if for a long time the woman is not delivered of the child or relieved of
her condition, generally the child is coming out sideways or feet first– whereas it
should come out head first. This is how the disorder comes about: it is just as if
someone dropped an olive pit into an oil flask with a small mouth; the pit naturally
can't be taken out when it is turned on its side. In the same way the presentation of
the embryo when it is sideways is difficult for the woman, for it doesn't come out.
Difficult also is the situation where it is leaving feet first; oftentimes the women die,
or the children, or even both. This too is a major cause of the child's not coming
out easily – if it is dead, or paralyzed, or if there are two of them.
(*Diseases of Women* 33 = 8.78 Littré)

How did women relate to the male medical practitioners? For many ailments
associated with pregnancy and childbirth they would doubtless first have
consulted female kin and midwives. The following advice to other physicians
indicates that at least some spoke directly to an attending male doctor about
their symptoms, and that their information should be taken seriously. (The
calculation of the length of pregnancy is based on the lunar month of 29½
days.)

You must not refuse to believe women on the subject of childbearing. For they
always say the same thing, and say what they know; they would not be persuaded
either by act or argument of anything that is contrary to what they know about
what is happening in their own bodies. It is possible for those who wish, to say
something different, but women who form a judgement and argue convincingly
will always say and claim that they give birth to seven- and eight- and nine- and
ten-month babies, and of these the eight-month ones do not survive. And they
claim that the majority of miscarriages occur in the first 40 days.
(*On the Eight Months' Child* 4 = 7.440–442 Littré)

This Hippocratic writer acknowledges that both the woman and the physician
must be aware of the particular ailments affecting women; otherwise, the
woman can be at serious risk.

There are times when women themselves do not know what sickness they have,
until they have experienced the diseases which come from menses and they
become older. Then both necessity and time teach them the cause of their illnesses.
Sometimes for those women who do not know why they become ill the diseases end

up becoming incurable before the doctor has been correctly instructed by the sick woman what has made her sick. For they are embarrassed to tell, even when they know, and it seems shameful to them because of their inexperience and their lack of knowledge. At the same time the doctors also make mistakes, by not learning the cause of the illness from accurate information, but treating it like they would men's diseases. Indeed, I have already seen many women die from this kind of treatment. But one must ask accurate questions immediately about the cause. For the healing of the diseases of women differs greatly from the healing of men's diseases. (*Diseases of Women* 62 = 8.126 Littré)

AESCHYLUS, *THE EUMENIDES*

The question of the degree to which women participated in the generation of life was raised in places other than in medical writings. In 458 BCE three tragedies were performed on the Athenian stage that the playwright Aeschylus had developed from the myth of Agamemnon's return from Troy. Arriving home in Mycenae the king was murdered by his wife, Clytemnestra. She was then killed by her son, Orestes, who was taking revenge for the murder of his father. Pursued by the Furies (divinities who seek retribution for kin murder) Orestes took refuge in Athens, where the goddess Athena presided over a trial where jurists would vote for Orestes' condemnation or exoneration.

The god Apollo, who had given Orestes ritual purification for his homicide, justified his support for the son's act by an appeal to his view of embryology, one that is contrary to that of the last Hippocratic writer we heard from.

I will tell you this, and take in the fact that I will be speaking accurately. It is not the so-called "mother" who is the parent of the child, but she is a just a nurse of the newly-planted embryo. The parent is the one who does the mounting, but she, being unrelated, preserves the seed for one who is unrelated to her – unless a god injures their seed. (Aeschylus, *Eumenides* 657–661)

Apollo supports his contention by pointing to Athena, patron goddess of Athens, born not from a woman but from the head of Zeus.

PLATO

In one of his dialogues Plato has Timaeus, a Pythagorean philosopher, speculate on the nature of male and female reproductive organs and sexual desire, as these were created by the gods. The penis is described as having an independent will and acting like an animal filled with uncontrollable desires. Likewise, the uterus in women is an independent self-willed organ driven to satisfy its own passion for intercourse – an activity that resembles plowing and sowing.

Wherefore, on the subject of the nature of the genital organs in men, it is ungovernable and (behaves like) an independent creature, like a living being heedless of reasoning, trying to control everything because of its raging lusts. And just so in women, where the so-called "cervix" and "uterus" consist of a creature living inside them, possessed of the desire to beget children. Whenever it goes without bearing fruit for a long time beyond its proper season, it becomes angry and irritable, and strays everywhere throughout the body. It stops up the passages for the breath and prevents respiration; it casts the body into extreme helplessness and brings on all sorts of other diseases until the desire and passion bring both partners together. As if they were picking fruit from trees, they sow into the field that is the uterus living beings that are invisible because too small to be seen and formless. These again they separate out, nourishing to a large size within the uterus, and after that bring them to the light and so complete the generation of living creatures. Thus women and the whole female race have been born.
(Plato, *Timaeus* 91b–d)

ARISTOTLE

Aristotle gives an account of intercourse and human conception that is consistent with the image of plowing a field. He awards to the man alone the power of generating new life; the woman provides the matrix, akin to soil for a seed. The inability to contribute directly to the life of an embryo is in fact what defines the female, in Aristotle's view as he expresses it in his *On the Generation of Animals*.

In accordance with what we said, one might above all set down as the first principles of generation the female and the male component, with the male possessing the principle of movement and generation, but the female contributing the matter. One would most readily believe this by looking at how the seed comes to be, and from where. (716a5–7)

So it is clear that the menstrual fluid is a residue, and as the semen is in males, so is the menstrual fluid in females analogous. The corresponding signs show that this statement is correct. At the same time of life that semen begins to appear in males and is emitted, in females the menstrual discharge bursts forth; their voices change and their breasts begin to be noticeable; and in the declining phase of life the power to generate ceases in males and the menstrual discharge ceases in females. (727a2–10)

Furthermore, their blood-vessels are not similar; in women they are smoother and more delicate than men's, because the collection of the residue which goes to these (the blood-vessels) is discharged in the menstrual fluid. One must suppose that this same thing is the reason why the body mass in females who give birth to live offspring is smaller than in males. For in these females alone the discharge of the menstrual fluid is external, and (among such animals) most obvious among females are the humans, for a woman discharges the most secretion of living creatures. On this account it is always very noticeable that she is pale, and her blood vessels are not prominent; in comparison with men she has an obvious deficiency in her physique. Since this is what happens in females, corresponding to the seed in males, it is not possible for there to be two seminal secretions at the same time. It is clear that the female does not contribute a seed to generation, for if there were semen, there would not be any menstrual fluid; but since this happens there is no semen. (727a16–30)

Some think that the female contributes semen in intercourse because sometimes a woman derives pleasure from it comparable to that of men, and produces a fluid secretion at the same time. This fluid, however, is not seed-bearing; it is peculiar to the part from which it comes in each woman. There is a discharge from their uterus, which happens in some women but not in others. For it happens in fair-skinned women and those who are feminine in appearance for the most part, but it does not happen in dark-skinned women and those who are masculine-looking. (727b34–728a4)

Further, a boy actually resembles a woman in physique and a woman is, so to speak, a sterile male; the female, in fact, is female on account of an incapacity of sorts, by being unable to concoct semen from the final stage of the nutriment. (728a17–21)

Hence, it is clear that it is reasonable to hold that generation takes place from this process; for the menstrual fluid is semen, not indeed pure, but needing still to be worked upon. (728a25–27)
(Aristotle, On the Generation of Animals)

FURTHER READING

Carson, A. 1990. "Putting Her in Her Place. Women, Dirt and Desire," in D. Halperin, J.J. Winkler, and F. Zeitlin (eds) Before Sexuality. The Construction of the Erotic Experience in the Ancient Greek World, 135–170. Princeton

Dean-Jones, L. 1994. *Women's Bodies in Classical Greek Science*. Oxford/New York

Hanson, A.E. 1990. "The Medical Writers' Woman," in D. Halperin, J.J. Winkler, and F. Zeitlin (eds) *Before Sexuality. The Construction of the Erotic Experience in the Ancient Greek World*, 309–337. Princeton

King, H. 1998. *Hippocrates' Woman. Reading the Female Body in Ancient Greece*. London/New York

MacLachlan, B. 2006. "Voices from the Underworld: The Female Body Discussed in Two Dialogues," *Classical World* 99.5, 423–33

Porter, J. 1999. *Constructions of the Classical Body*. Ann Arbor, MI

Wyke, M. 1998. ed. *Parchments of Gender. Deciphering the Body in Antiquity*. Oxford

PART 3

THE POST-CLASSICAL PERIOD

15

Women in the Hellenistic era

After the defeat of Athens in the Peloponnesian War Greek power gradually shifted north from Athens to Macedon, with the military expansion first of King Philip II and then of his son, Alexander the Great. With the death of the latter in 323 BCE three kingdoms were established in the Mediterranean world ruled by Macedonian dynasties – in Macedon itself, in Syria and in Egypt. Greeks from across the mainland and the islands emigrated to the kingdoms to the East. They constituted the governing and middle class, but in many centres they became open to adapting their traditional customs in light of their proximity to other (vibrant) cultures such as that of the Egyptians who were ruled by the (Greek) Ptolemies. We have much more direct information about the daily lives of women during this time than was available for the Archaic and Classical periods, and most of it suggests that Greek women now conducted themselves with greater agency and confidence.

We are fortunate in our investigation that papyri have been recovered from the sands of Egypt, which record domestic arrangements such as marriage contracts. These, although differing in the degree to which women could act independently, reflect considerably more gender parity than what we know of husbands and wives in an Athenian marriage during the Classical period.

The following document comes from Elephantine, a city up the Nile that housed a Greek garrison. It is dated to 311/310 BCE and was drawn up for a Greek couple who had emigrated from the island of Cos. It is worth noting that both the mother and father of the bride give her to the groom, although the father and son-in-law will decide on the residence of the couple.

Contract of marriage of Heraclides of Temnos and Demetria. Heraclides takes as his lawful wife Demetria of Cos from her father Leptines of Cos and her mother Philotis, a free man, she a free woman bringing with her to the marriage clothing and jewelry valued at 1000 drachmas. Heraclides shall supply to Demetria all that is suitable for a freeborn wife and we shall live together wherever it seems best to Leptines and Heraclides, determining this together.

If Demetria is caught in fraudulent behaviour to the dishonour of her husband Heraclides she shall forfeit everything that she has brought with her, but Heraclides

shall prove whatever he brings as a charge against Demetria before three men whom they both agree upon. It shall not be lawful for Heraclides to bring home another woman for himself in such a way as to insult Demetria, nor to beget children by another woman, nor to engage in fraudulent machinations against Demetria on any pretext. If Heraclides is caught doing any of these things, and Demetria proves it before three men whom they both agree upon, let Heraclides return to Demetria the dowry of 1000 drachmas which she brought, and also forfeit 1000 drachmas of the silver coinage of Alexander. There will be in place the right to action for Demetria and those representing Demetria as if seeking justice through the law, to exact payment from Heraclides and from his property on both land and sea. ... Heraclides and Demetria shall have the right to keep the contracts themselves, keeping custody of their own copies and to produce them against each other.
(*P. Eleph.* 1 = *Select Papyri* 1.1)

The contract was signed in the presence of named witnesses, and specified that a copy would be kept by both parties to the agreement to be presented if required, and would be valid in any location.

The following contract, part of the collection from Tebtunis, was drawn up in 92 BCE on papyrus that was ultimately used for wrapping a mummified crocodile. Unlike the arrangements in the earlier contract the brother of the bride acted as her *kyrios* in this transaction, reflecting the fact that Greek families in Egypt could elect to comply with (the more restrictive) Greek or (the less restrictive) Egyptian practice.

Philiscus son of Apollonius, a Persian of the Epigoni (*descendants of Alexander's successors*) acknowledges to Apollonia, also called Kellaluthis, daughter of Heraclides, Persian, with Apollonius her brother as guardian, that he has received from her in copper money two talents and 4000 drachmas, the amount agreed upon with him for the dowry for Apollonia. Let Apollonia stay with Philiscus, obeying him as is suitable for a wife with her husband, being in charge with him of the property they hold in common. Let Philiscus furnish to Apollonia all necessities, both clothing and whatever else is required for a wedded wife, whether he is home or abroad, in keeping with the resources available to them. It is not lawful for Philiscus to introduce any other wife but Apollonia, nor to keep a concubine nor a boy-lover, nor to produce children from another wife while Apollonia is alive, nor to inhabit another house over which Apollonia is not in charge, nor to throw her out or insult her or treat her badly, nor to alienate any of their property to the disadvantage of Apollonia. If he is shown to be doing any of these things or does not supply her with the necessities or clothing or the other things in accordance with what has been written, let Philiscus immediately pay back to Apollonia the dowry of two talents and 4000 drachmas of copper.

In the same manner it is not lawful for Apollonia to be absent from the house of Philiscus for a night or day without the agreement of Philiscus, nor to have sex with another man, nor to ruin the common household nor to bring shame upon Philiscus in anything that brings shame to a husband.

If Apollonia wishes of her own free will to separate from Philiscus let Philiscus return to her the dowry intact within 10 days from the day that she requests for it to be returned. But if he does not repay it as has been written let him forfeit to her immediately the dowry that he received, plus one-half.
(P. Tebt. 1.104)

Four witnesses are named, and the contract ends by recording the fact that Dionysius (guardian of the contract) also wrote it, since Philiscus was illiterate.

In addition to contracts, papyri record letters that give us an inside view of domestic life in Hellenistic Egypt. One such letter, fragmentary in form but probably addressed to a family member in a position of authority, appeals to this person to act as the agent to annul his marriage. This follows his taking an oath to return his wife's dowry. The letter is dated 156 BCE.

[T]hirty-six drachmas of silver ... and four quarters of gold ..., on condition that (she?) annuls with me our contract of cohabitation.
Good-bye. The twentieth year, Tubi 21.
I swear by King Ptolemy and Queen Cleopatra his sister and their ancestors that I will act in accordance with this.
(P. Tebt. 3.1.809).

The following letter (in Greek) was sent by an Egyptian woman to a local official, appealing to him to intercede and forbid her husband to mortgage/sell their house which, according to Egyptian law, was to be surety for her upkeep. The letter is dated to the early 2nd century BCE.

To Ptolemaus, magistrate, from Senesis daughter of Menelaus, inhabitant of Oxyrhyncha in the division of Polemon. I am living with Didymus son of Peteimouthes, an inhabitant of this village, in accordance with the terms of an Egyptian alimentary contract of silver ... gold pieces in keeping with the laws of the country. For this sum and for my upkeep all his available property, among which was the house in the above-mentioned village (was pledged). The accused, wishing to deprive me of this, approached each and everyone of this same village, for he wanted to alienate it. But since these people did not submit to him because I did not consent, after this he worked at giving it to the treasury as surety for Heraclides the tax-farmer, and in this way thinks that he will exclude me from my rights.

I therefore, as a defenceless woman, am making a claim and begging you not to overlook me, deprived of what was pledged for my dowry because of the fraudulent behaviour of the accused but, if it seems right, to order a letter to be written to Ptolemaeus the financial officer, forbidding him to accept in surety the house of the said Didymus. If this happens, I will succeed in gaining your assistance. Farewell. (P. Tebt. 3.1.1776)

From the Roman period (13 BCE) we have evidence provided by the following letter that divorce could be mutually arranged by husband and wife, a practice that may not have differed from earlier, at least the late Hellenistic, period.

To Protarchus (the head of a local tribunal) from Zois, daughter of Heraclides, with her *kyrios*, her brother Irenaus son of Heraclides, and from Antipater son of Zenon. Zois and Antipater agree that they have separated from each other, from their agreement to live together in accordance with the agreement made before the same tribunal in Hathur in the current 17th year of Caesar. Zois gives her word that (she possesses) from the hand of Antipater, from his house, what he held as dowry, clothes valuing 120 drachmas and a pair of gold earrings. Henceforth the agreement of marriage shall be void, and neither Zois nor anyone else acting on her behalf shall take action against Antipater for restitution of the dowry, nor shall either take action against the other about living together nor about any other matter whatsoever up to the present day. From this time it shall be lawful for Zois to join together with another man, and for Antipater with another woman, with neither being liable to the other. In addition to this agreement being valid, moreover, the one who transgresses it shall be liable to the damages and to the prescribed penalty.
(BGU 4.1103 = Select Papyri 1.6)

In the following contract, dated to 284/3 BCE a concubine or hetaera has undertaken a legal contract with a man who was supporting her, buying herself out of the agreement.

Elaphion of Syria, with Pantarces as her guardian, paid Antipatrus of Arcadia a fee of 300 silver coins for her upkeep. May it not be lawful for Antipatrus to bring charges against her, claiming that he is supporting her, or to reduce her to slavery on any pretext, nor lawful for anyone acting on behalf of Antipatrus. Otherwise, may the suit be invalid where they are concerned, and may Antipatrus be subject to a fine of 3000 drachmas paid to Elaphion or to the man currently maintaining her. Let this contract be valid under all circumstances from the time when Elaphion or someone acting on her behalf serves it on Antipatrus, as it is written on behalf of Elaphion.
(P. Eleph. 4)

In addition to her guardian Pantarces, six men from various Greek centres are listed as witnesses.

For a description of life among the urban proletariat in Hellenistic Alexandria we have the "*mimiambi*" of Herodas (also called Herondas). Unlike contracts and letters this is literary, rather than documentary, evidence. It combines the performance genre of "mimes" – humorous, spirited, often improvised dialogues about the life of ordinary people that are first attested in Sicily in the late 5th century – with "*iambi*" – poems that circulated in the Archaic period, frequently characterized by abuse and ridicule (recall Archilochus, Semonides and Hipponax).

The following consists of a conversation between two wives about the virtues of a dildo – and the irritating behaviour of slaves and husbands. Metro has arrived for a visit with Koritto, who is in possession of an impressive dildo.

[Kor.] Metro, sit down. (to her slave) Get up and place the stool for the lady.
I have to order you to do everything –
you wouldn't do anything on your own, you wretch.
Lord, you're a stone, not a slave,
sitting in the house. But if I am measuring out your ration of barley
you count the crumbs, and if ever so little should drop
you mumble and grumble for the whole day,
until the walls can't bear the weight of you seething.
Oh, now you are polishing (the stool) and making it shiny,
just now when we need it – you thief. You should give thanks
to this woman, since if she weren't here you would get a taste of my hands.
[Metro] Dear Koritto, you are worn down by the same yoke as I.
I too snap day and night,
barking like a bitch at these unmentionable creatures.
But the reason I came to you –
[Kor.] Get the hell out of here,
you sharp ones, all ears and tongues,
but idle louts the rest of the time.
[Metro] Please, dear Koritto,
don't lie to me, who in the world was it who stitched together
the scarlet pacifier for you? (1–19)

(The conversation that follows indicates that the dildo has been eagerly passed around among other women before Koritto had a chance to use it.)

[Kor.] Oh, for goodness sake, why are you pleading with me?
Kerdon made it.
[Metro] Who is he, pray tell, Kerdon? (47–48)

The details of the dildo-maker emerge:

[Kor.] He comes – I don't know – either from Chios or Erythrae,
bald-headed, a little man. (58–59)
[Kor.] He works at his home, dodging the market,
for every door now quivers because of the tax-collectors.
But his workmanship, truly Coan! You would think
they were the hands of Athena, not Kerdon's.
I – he came bringing two of them, Metro –
as soon as I saw them my eyes swelled out of their sockets.
Men don't produce pricks like this,
(now that we are alone) – erect! And not only this,
but it's as soothing as sleep, and its little straps
are like wool not thongs. If you went looking
you wouldn't find a friendlier piece of leather.
[Metro] Why did you let the other one go?
[Kor.] What didn't I do, Metro?
What form of persuasion didn't I bring to bear against him?
I snuggled up to him, I stroked his bald head,
poured out a sweet drink for him, I called him "Daddy."
Only my body did I not grant him for his pleasure.
[Metro] Well, if it seemed like a good idea you should have given it to him.
[Kor.] Yes, I suppose I should have. But it is not appropriate to act out of turn.
(63–80)
(Herodas, *Mimiambus* 6)

Theocritus is thought to have been Sicilian by birth but he lived in Alexandria,
the Egyptian capital, during the reign of Ptolemy Philadelphus (283–246 BCE).
Following an Egyptian pattern the king was married to his sister Arsinöe II,
a queen with a reputation of exerting strong influence in the social, political
and cultural life of Egypt. Theocritus' poetic *Idylls* bear many of the features of
mimes, describing the life of ordinary people.

In *Idyll* 15, he gives us a conversation between Gorgo and Praxinoa, two
Sicilian women who are living in Alexandria, as they set off to attend a lavish
festival for Adonis mounted by Arsinoë.

[Gorgo] Is Praxinoa in?
[Prax.] Gorgo dear, how long it's been! I'm in.
A wonder that you have come now. (to her slave) Eunoa, see to getting a stool for her,
and put a cushion on it.

[Gorgo] It's fine as it is.

[Prax.] Do sit down.

[Gorgo] What a helpless soul I am! I hardly got here in one piece,
Praxinoa, with that great crowd and all those four-horse chariots.
Men's boots everywhere, and everywhere men in cloaks.
And the road is endless; you live further and further away.

[Prax.] This is the doing of that senseless lout of mine. Going to the ends of the earth
he gets us a hut, not a house, so that we won't be neighbours
of each other, out of spite, envious brute – he never changes.

[Gorgo] Don't say such things of your husband Dinon, my dear,
when the little one is nearby. See how he's looking at you, woman. (to the child)
Never mind, Zopyrion, sweet child, she's not talking about your daddy.

[Prax.] Pray, the child understands.

[Gorgo] Handsome daddy!

[Prax.] Still that daddy, just lately –just the other day I said to him,
"Papa, go and get baking soda and rouge at the booth,"
and he came back bringing me salt, that great hulk of a man.

[Gorgo] Mine's just the same. Diocleidas is a disaster when it comes to spending
money. Yesterday for seven drachmas he bought bits of dog's hair, pluckings of old
wallets –
five fleeces, all of it dirt, work without end.
But come on, get your robe and your shawl.
Let's go and see the Adonia in the palace of the rich king Ptolemy.
I hear that the queen has done up a fine show.

[Prax.] Everything's grand when it comes to grand people.

[Gorgo] (Yes, but) things you've seen you could speak of when you've seen them
but another person hasn't.
It would be time to move along.

[Prax.] It's always leisure time for those who don't work.
Eunoa, pick up the spinning and move it here, you cocky thing.
Put it back in place: weasels like to sleep where it is soft.
Move! Bring me some water, on the double. I need water first,
and she brings me soap. Never mind, give it to me. Not so much, thief!
Pour the water. Fool, why are you pouring it on my undergarment?
Enough now. It looks like I have cleaned up enough for the gods.
Where is the key of the big clothing-chest? Bring it here. (1–33)

The women, accompanied by Eunoa, work their way through crowds of people
and horses. Unlike in Athens, the Adonia in Alexandria is open to men, and
the women are reprimanded by one of the men for their chattering. A female

singer performs, praising the beauty of Aphrodite and Arsinoë and the lush abundance that accompanies Adonis, who will die and return again, with more cakes for his votaries. Then Gorgo initiates their departure.

[Gorgo] Praxinoa, the young woman is a marvel of the highest order.
Blessed she is, knowing so much, and totally blessed with a voice so sweet.
But we have to head home. Diocleidas hasn't had lunch.
The man is a complete sour-puss, and don't go near him when he's hungry.
Farewell, beloved Adonis, and may you come back again to happy folks. (145–149)
(Theocritus, *Idyll* 15)

The use of magic (particularly to enhance erotic power) was associated with women in the Hellenistic period, when they often enlisted the help of the goddess Hecate. In *Idyll* 2, Theocritus presents us with Simaitha, who has been abandoned by her lover Delphis. She attempts to win him back through the use of magic and with the help of her maid Thestylis, who acts as her assistant and go-between. Simaitha's chanting accompanies the spinning of a wheel (the *iunx*), which she turns in magical imitation of drawing Delphis to her side.

Where are my bay-leaves? Bring them, Thestylis. And where are my magic love-charms? Garland the bowl with the choicest crimson wool,
so that I may bind a spell upon my lover,
who is being hard on me. The beast hasn't come near me for eleven days now,
and he doesn't know whether I am dead or alive.
He hasn't even knocked on my door, the cruel man.
Now for sure Eros has gone off along with Aphrodite, taking his fickle heart elsewhere. Tomorrow I will go to Timagetus' wrestling-ring
so that I can see him, and I will scold him for treating me so.
But now I will bind him with fiery spells. Now then, shine bright, O Moon.
For I will chant to you softly, goddess,
and to Hecate of the Underworld, before whom the dogs also tremble,
as she comes up from the graves of the dead and their dark blood.
"Hail, dread Hecate, and attend me to the end,
making these drugs in no way inferior to those of Circe
or Medea or Perimede of the golden hair."
Magic wheel, draw that man to my house.

First, barley melts on the fire. Now sprinkle them on,
Thestylis. Fool! whither have your wits taken flight?
Have I become loathsome to you, then, and some sort of laughing-stock?

Sprinkle them on and say this at the same time, "I sprinkle the bones of Delphis."
Magic wheel, draw that man to my house.

Delphis has distressed me. I burn this bay for Delphis.
As it catches fire and crackles loudly
and catches all of a sudden, and we see not so much as the ashes from it,
so too may the flesh of Delphis be consumed in the flame.
Magic wheel, draw that man to my house.

Now I will burn the bran. You, Artemis, could move
even the adamant in Hades and anything else, however fixed.
Thestylis, the dogs are howling throughout the town;
the goddess is at the crossroads. Sound the bronze, as quickly as possible!
Magic wheel, draw that man to my house.

See there! The sea is still, and still are the breezes.
But the anguish in my breast is not still.
I am all ablaze for him who made me a sorry wretch
instead of a wife – a disgrace and no virgin.
Magic wheel, draw that man to my house.

As I melt the wax with the help of the goddess,
so straightway may Delphis of Myndus melt away with love.
And as the bronze rhombus spins with Aphrodite's power
so may he spin in front of my door.
Magic wheel, draw that man to my house.

Three times do I pour libation, and three times, O Lady, do I cry aloud –
whether it be a woman or a man who lies beside him –
may he forget them, as once they say Theseus forgot
fair-tressed Ariadne on Dia.
Magic wheel, draw that man to my house.

Coltsfoot is a herb that grows in Arcadia, and for it
all the colts and the swift mares run mad through the mountains.
So may I see Delphis, and just like one maddened
may he come to this house from the bright wrestling ring.
Magic wheel, draw that man to my house.

Delphis lost this fringe from his cloak,
which I now shred and throw in the wild flames.

Ah, torturing Eros, why have you been clutching me,
clinging and drinking the black blood from my skin like some of the marsh leeches?
Magic wheel, draw that man to my house.

I will grind up a lizard, and bring him an evil potion tomorrow.
But now, Thestylis, take these herbs and knead them
over his doorway while it is still night,
and say in a whisper, "I knead the bones of Delphis."
Magic wheel, draw that man to my house.
(Theocritus *Idyll* 2.1–62)

Simaitha eventually sends Thestylis to summon Delphis directly. He complies and the couple make love. He proves unfaithful once again, however, and Samaitha resumes her love magic, vowing to keep poisonous drugs on hand to give him the ultimate punishment.

Simaetha referred to Medea and Circe, mythical women who used magical powers to concoct potent drugs. Medea's magic is described in the Hellenistic epic of Apollonius of Rhodes, the librarian in charge of the great library in Alexandria in the mid-3rd century BCE. His poem, *Argonautica*, was based on the myth of Jason's quest for the Golden Fleece.

In Book 3, the gods prevail on Aphrodite to ensure that Medea (daughter of the king in Colchis who is in possession of the fleece) will fall in love with the hero. Medea uses her magical powers, inherited from her grandfather Helios the Sungod, to protect Jason during the physical trials imposed on him by her father. In the following passage Medea is preparing the magical ointment.

She called to her handmaids, all twelve of them,
who lodged in the forecourt of her fragrant bedchamber –
age-mates who did not yet share a bed with husbands.
She called them to yoke mules swiftly to the cart,
so that they would take her to the very beautiful temple of Hecate.
Her handmaids then set about equipping the mule-cart.
She, meanwhile, drew from a hollow chest
a drug that they call "Promethean."
If a man were to appease with nocturnal sacrifices
Daira (*a cult name for Hecate*), who was singly born, and were to anoint his body with it,
he would not be pierced by blows from bronze weapons,
nor would he yield to blazing fire, but on that day
he would surpass others in daring and power – in equal measure.
The plant first grew and sprang up when the flesh-eating eagle

let drop to the ground on the peaks of the Caucasus
the bloody ichor from tormented Prometheus.
Its flower came up a cubit high above the ground,
in colour like the Corycian crocus,
supported on twin stems. Its root in the ground
looked like flesh newly-cut.
Its juice, dark like that from a mountain beech tree,
she drew off in a Caspian shell to make the ointment.
She bathed seven times in ever-flowing water,
and seven times called on Brimo, protectress of children.
Brimo, who travels by night, from the Underworld, queen of the dead –
travelling in the murky night wearing black garments.
And the dark earth shook, bellowing from below
when the root of the Titan was cut. He himself groaned too,
the son of Iapetus, wounded in his heart.
Medea took the drug and put it underneath the fragrant band
that she wore beneath her ambrosial breasts.
(Apollonius Rhodius, *Argonautica* 3.838–68)

From the Hellenistic period there is documentary evidence in the form of curse tablets, inscribed for ordinary Greek women in everyday situations who turned to magic as an informal means of seeking justice in their lives. These curses were written on thin pieces of lead and buried in graves or sanctuaries of Underworld gods or left in springs. Not infrequently the women sought redress through the agency of Hecate, Demeter or Persephone, or the Furies.

In Attica, a lead tablet was found dating to the 3rd or 2nd century BCE, containing a curse from a woman named Bitto against Sosiclea, another woman who appears to have enjoyed a higher degree of success.

I shall bind Sosiclea and her possessions and her great reputation and her success and her mind. May she become hateful to her friends. I will bind her under murky Tartarus with harsh bonds, and with the help of Hecate of the Underworld.

Sosiclea, Bitto (*inscribed upside-down*). and with/to the Furies who distract the mind.
(Kaibel 1136)

The following curse tablet (somewhat fragmentary) was inscribed on bronze. It came from a Greek settlement in South Italy, and was composed sometime before the 3rd century BCE. Here a woman named Kollyra is attempting to get back a cloak and three gold coins, stolen by an unnamed man and a woman named Melita. Kollyra enlists the help of a goddess, likely Persephone, along with her temple attendants, transferring custody of the missing items to divinity so as to invite punishment from this source. The magical powers conferred by the tablet are felt to be contagious.

Kollyra consecrates to the attendants of the goddess ... her cloak, the dark-coloured one, that someone took and is not giving back, and ... uses it and knows where it is. Let this person dedicate to the goddess twelve times its worth with half a medimnus of incense, as the city requires. May the one who has my cloak not breathe freely until he makes the dedication to the goddess.

Kollyra consecrates to the attendants of the goddess the three gold coins which Melita took and is not giving back. Let her dedicate to the goddess twelve times their worth with a medimnus of incense, as the city requires. May she not breathe freely until she has made the dedication to the goddess. If she should drink with me or eat with me and I not know it, or go under the same roof as I, may I be unharmed. (DT 212)

Some poetry composed by women in the Hellenistic period has survived. One of these poets was Nossis, who lived near the location where the above tablet was found, in the West Greek colony of Locri. She wrote short epigrams, and considered herself a successor to Sappho. The following poem addresses someone sailing to Lesbos.

Stranger, if you sail towards Mytilene of the beautiful dances
　　that set Sappho alight, blossom of the Graces,
tell them that the Locrian land bore someone dear to the Muses,
　　equal to her, and that my name is Nossis. Go!
(Nossis, AP 7.718)

Nossis' devotion to the poetic celebration of love is reflected in the following poem:

"Nothing is sweeter than love. Among blessings all take second place.
　　I spat even honey away from my mouth."
Nossis says this. Whomever Cypris has not treated kindly
　　will not know what sort of blossoms her roses are.
(Nossis, AP 5.170)

Another female Hellenistic poet was Anyte, who lived in the rustic mountainous interior of the Peloponnese about the same time as Nossis, and like her composed a number of dedicatory epigrams. The following two commemorate the deaths of young girls.

These last words Erato spoke to her dear father,
    throwing her arms around him while drenched with fresh tears:
"Oh Father, I am yours no longer. Murky Death
    covers my eyes in blackness, as I am already fading away."
(Anyte, AP 7.646)

Oftentimes on this, her daughter's tomb, did Cleina
    call out to her dear short-lived child in lamentation,
summoning the soul of Philaenis who, before her wedding,
    crossed over the pale stream of the River Acheron.
(Anyte, AP 7.486)

Anyte also composed funerary epigrams for young men.

The soil of Lydia holds Amyntor, son of Philip,
    who grappled hand-to-hand with iron-hard war on many occasions.
It was not painful disease that took him of to the House of Night
    but he perished holding his round shield over his comrade.
(Anyte, AP 7.232)

Some of the poems ascribed to Anyte are poignant funerary epigrams for other creatures.

For her grasshopper, nightingale of the field,
    and for her cicada, a creature that frequents the oak tree, Myro has made a common tomb,
a young girl shedding maidenly tears; for twice the inexorable one came
    and took away her playthings – Hades.
(Anyte, AP 7.190)

Also contemporary with Nossis and Anyte was Moero, who is thought to have lived in Byzantium. This epigram of Moero's may have accompanied a man's dedication of statues to some water nymphs, or may simply be a formal wish for good health for the dedicator.

Water nymphs, daughters of the river Anigrias,
    you ambrosial beings who always tread the depths with rosy feet,
greetings, and preserve Cleonymus, who set up these fair images

for you under the pines, goddess.
(Moero, AP 6.189)

Details about the poet Erinna are not secure. All that remains of her work to date are three epigrams, and fragments from some poems in the epic metre (hexameters). Likely writing in the latter half of the 4th century BCE, Erinna was highly praised in antiquity as the equal of Homer, Sappho and Callimachus. The importance of her work was linked by some to the belief that she died young. The following (anonymous) poem attests to this way of remembering Erinna.

Just as you were giving birth to the springtime of honey-filled hymns,
    and just as you were uttering verses with the voice of a swan,
Fate, mistress of the thread-spinning distaff,
    drove you to Acheron, over the wide waves for the dead.
But the beautiful labour of your verses, Erinna, cries out that
    you have not died, but intermingled with them you have taken your place in the
dances of the Pierian Muses.
(Erinna, AP 7.12)

Two of Erinna's poems are funerary epigrams for her childhood companion Baucis, who apparently died as she was about to be married. In the following poem Erinna gives voice to Baucis from her tomb.

Columns (of the tomb marker) and my Sirens, and you, mournful urn,
    who hold the little heap of ashes for Hades,
say "Greetings!" to those passing by my tomb,
    whether they are local citizens or from another town.
And say this, too, that the tomb holds me as a bride,
    and say that my father called me Baucis and that my lineage
is from Tenos, so they may know. And say too that my companion
    Erinna engraved these letters on my tomb.
(Erinna, AP 7.710)

The loss of Baucis was clearly at the heart of Erinna's long hexameter poem, widely known as "The Distaff," sadly quite fragmentary (54 broken lines remain). In it, she recalls the games the two girls played as children, their dolls and the shapeshifting monster Mormo whom they feared. Although difficult to reconstruct, the text suggests that Erinna was not able to participate in the death rituals for her friend, and the poem may have served as her personal funerary lament.

Mormo trailed fear ... she roamed on foot ... changing her face ... (25–27)
for my feet would not enter the house ... (32)
nor see ... nor cry the lament (33)
with uncovered hair ... (34)
nineteen ... Erinna ... the distaff. (37–39)
(Erinna, *Supp. Hell.* 401)

The poignancy of a young woman's death is also reflected in this fragmentary
inscription from a young woman's tomb in Egypt, engraved in the 2nd or 1st
century BCE.

Dosithea, daughter of ... Stranger, looking at these letters on the polished rock,
weep. The son of Thallo, Chaeremon, married me in his house ... I die with the
bitterest pain; escaping the pangs of childbirth I met with the fate of my kinsman,
leaving behind the breath of life when I was 25 years old. (Dying) from a disease that
he died of before, I too succumbed. I lie here in Schedia, getting this for my tomb. As
you pass by, wayfarers, all of you, say, "Fine Dosithea, be well, even among the dead."
(Peek 1233)

Egypt's reputation for the serious practice of medicine was acknowledged as
early as the second millennium BCE. With the arrival of the Greeks, particularly
after the foundation of Alexandria by Alexander the Great and the ensuing
concentration of scholars working in the great Library, this city became the
centre for major advances in scientific medicine. Herophilus (335–280 BCE)
was a Greek physician from Chalcedon who moved to Alexandria. Inheriting
Hippocratic and Aristotelian views about the structure of the human body, he
made dramatic advances in human anatomy by taking advantage of dissection,
an option that had not been available to his forbears. He was particularly
interested in obstetrics and gynecology, and wrote a treatise on midwifery.
Unlike earlier writers he began with the assumption that the woman's body was
not fundamentally different from the man's. The female reproductive organs,
according to Herophilus, had particular functions but were made of the same
elements as the rest of the human body, and were subject to similar disorders.
He made a substantial contribution with his discovery of the fixed position of
the uterus and of the Fallopian tubes. His view that the ovaries were analogous
to the testicles and the Fallopian tubes to the spermatic ducts unfortunately
directed him away from understanding the full nature of conception, however.

The following excerpt from his treatise on anatomy was preserved by the
Greek physician Galen (2nd–3rd century CE), who practised in Rome. Galen
acknowledged the advances made by Herophilus while regretting the fact that
he believed that the female "seed" was discharged through the bladder.

Herophilus, however, says that the seed of females is somehow (I don't know how) discharged to the outside, even though he wrote accurately about the testicles (*ovaries*) in females in Book 3 of his *Anatomy*, saying this at the beginning:

"In females the two testicles are attached to each shoulder of the uterus, the one on the right and the other on the left, not both in one scrotum but each one separate, enveloped in a thin membranous skin. They are small and somewhat flat, like glands, sinewy around the covering that encircles them but easily injured in the fleshy part, just like those (testicles) of males. In mares they are also of impressive size. They are attached with a number of membranes to the uterus, with a vein and an artery implanted into them from the uterus. (1–15)

"The spermatic duct from each one is not too easily seen, but is attached to the uterus from the outside, the one on the right and the other on the left. It is coiled throughout its front part in a way similar to that of the male (seminal duct), and it is varicose (*enlarged*) almost the entire length to the end. From each testicle – as with the male – it is attached to the fleshy part of the neck of the bladder, being thin and curved in the forward part where it touches the bones of the hips." (18–25)
(Herophilus 61 Von Staden = Galen *De Semine* 2.1)

There was a surge in philosophical movements in the Greek world during the Hellenistic period, and there is evidence that women were active in some of them. One of these "schools" was that of the Cynics, whose founder Diogenes promoted a lifestyle that rejected material possessions and comfort in favour of personal freedom and self-sufficiency. This independence, it seems, included the rejection of traditional gender roles and monogamy.

A striking example of this comes from ancient testimony about the life of Hipparchia, whose betrothal to the Cynic Crates ran dramatically counter to the normal practice in Athens, where they lived.

(Hipparchia) fell in love with the speeches and the life-style of Crates, and was not influenced by any of her suitors – their wealth, their good breeding or their good looks. But Crates was everything to her. She even threatened her parents that she would kill herself if she were not given in marriage to him. Crates, therefore, was entreated by her parents to dissuade their daughter. He did everything, and in the end when he did not persuade her he stood up and, taking off his clothes in front of her he said, "This is your bridegroom, here are his possessions, this is what you are choosing. For you will be no joint partner unless you apply yourself to the same practices."
(Diogenes Laertius, *Lives of Famous Philosophers* 6.96)

Details of the life chosen by Hipparchia are described in an epigram by Antipater of Sidon, a poet of the 2nd century BCE.

I, Hipparchia, did not choose the tasks of full-robed women,
   but the strong-bodied lifestyle of the Cynics.
Not for me are fine robes fastened with brooches, nor a thick-soled
   slipper, nor a glistening hair-net.
A pouch, fellow-traveller to a walking-staff, and in keeping with this
   a double-folded cloak, and a coverlet on the ground for a bed.
I say: my reputation will exceed that of Arcadian Atalanta
   by the degree to which wisdom is greater than running over mountains.
(Antipater of Sidon, AP 7.413)

Women were also active in the Pythagorean philosophical movement, which was active in the Greek West in the 6th century BCE. From the Hellenistic period, during a revival of this movement known as "Neopythagoreanism," we have letters/pamphlets purportedly written by women to other women, discussing ideas and offering advice on how to live. The reputation and the writing attributed to these women indicate that they had achieved a considerable degree of education.

The following letter illustrates the seriousness with which they approached the material they studied. A woman called Theano (by the ancients referred to as wife or student of Pythagoras) is struggling with the meaning of a work of Plato – one that is considered extremely difficult even by today's readers. She writes to another woman in the Pythagorean circle, Rhodope, who has asked for the Platonic text. Theano specifies what makes for a good man, then likens the overwhelming brightness but impenetrability of this work of Plato to looking directly at the sun.

Theano to Rhodope, a philosopher. So you're upset? I am upset too. Are you cross because I have not yet sent you the book of Plato's, which he entitled "The Forms" or "Parmenides"? But as for me, I am particularly distressed because no one has yet met with me to talk about Cleon. For I would not send off the book before someone came to explain (the work of) such a man. This is because I love the soul of that man, in one respect because he is a philosopher, in another because he is someone determined to do good works, and in another as someone who stands in awe of the underworld gods. And don't understand what has been said otherwise, for I am semi-mortal and as for the star shining in daytime, I can't bear to look on the sun.
(Hercher p. 607, no. 10)

In the following letter, Theano advises Eurydice to put up with the fact that her husband is sleeping with a courtesan. The text seems at the same time to be praising Eurydice by comparison with the other woman, as someone more complex and richly gifted – something that her (morally inferior) husband is not able to absorb. Theano uses as an analogy the effect of listening to a harmonically rich musical performance.

Theano to magnificent Eurydice. What grief has gripped your soul? Are you distressed by nothing else than the fact that the man with whom you live comes to a courtesan and takes his bodily pleasure with her? But you shouldn't, marvelous woman that you are (and I am exceedingly impressed with you) feel this way. For don't you see that listening, when it is filled with the pleasure of hearing and is filled with musical melody – when satisfaction is reached with this – (makes) one love the aulos and listen with pleasure to the reed-pipe? And further, what sort of bonding isn't there, with the aulos and the musical notes and the wondrous sound of the instrument of honey-sweet quality? Just so, when it comes to something like you and the courtesan with whom your husband is consorting, your husband will reflect upon your quality and your nature and your reasoning, but then when the time comes that he has taken his satisfaction he will easily head down the path to the courtesan. (Reflect that) for those in whom a destructive taste is stored up there is a passion for nourishment by things that are not good.
(Hercher p. 606, no. 7)

FURTHER READING

Barnard, S. 1978. "Hellenistic Women Poets," *Classical Journal* 73, 208–210

Bowman, L. 1998. "Nossis, Sappho and Hellenistic Poetry", *Ramus* 27.1, 9–59

Burton, J. 1995. *Theocritus's Urban Mimes: Mobility, Gender, and Patronage*, Berkeley, CA

Dean-Jones, L. 1994. *Women's Bodies in Classical Greek Science*. Oxford/New York

Faraone, C. and D. Obbink. 1991 (eds) *Magika Hiera. Ancient Greek Magic and Religion.* Oxford/New York

Griffiths, F.T. 1981. "Home Before Lunch: The Emancipated Woman in Theocritus", in *Reflections of Women in Antiquity*, ed. H. Foley, 247–73. New York

Lambropoulou, V. 1995. "Some Pythagorean Female Virtues," in R. Hawley and B. Levick (eds), Women in Antiquity: New Assessments, 122–134. London

Pomeroy, S.B. 1990. *Women in Hellenistic Egypt from Alexander to Cleopatra*. Detroit, MI

Rowlandson, J. *Women and Society in Greek and Roman Egypt: A Sourcebook*. Cambridge

Snyder, J. 1989. "Women Poets of Hellenistic Greece" and "Women Philosophers of the Hellenistic and Roman Worlds," in *The Woman and the Lyre. Women Writers in Classical Greece and Rome*, 64–113. Carbondale/Edwardsville, IL

Waithe, M.E. 1987 ed. *A History of Women Philosophers*, vol. 1. Hingham, MA

Whitehorne, J. 1995. "Women's Work in Theocritus, Idyll 15," *Hermes* 123.1, 63–75

General Bibliography

Blundell, S. 1995. *Women in Ancient Greece.* Cambridge MA

Cameron, A. and A. Kuhrt 1983 (eds) *Images of Women in Antiquity.* Detroit

Cantarella, E. 1987. *Pandora's Daughters. The Role and Status of Women in Greek and Roman Antiquity.* (transl. M.B. Fant) Baltimore/London

Cohen, D. *Law, Sexuality and Society. The Enforcement of Morals in Classical Athens.* Cambridge

DeForest, M. 1993 ed. *Woman's Power, Man's Game. Essays on Classical Antiquity in Honor of Joy K. King.* Wauconda IL

Dillon, M. 2002. *Girls and Women in Classical Greek Religion.* London

Fantham, E., Foley, H.P., Kampen, N.B., Pomeroy, S. and Shapiro, H.A. 1994. *Women in the Classical World. Image and Text.* New York/Oxford

Foley, H. 1981. *Reflections of Women in Antiquity.* New York

Foxhall, L. 1989. "Household, Gender and Property in Classical Athens," *Classical Quarterly* 39, 22–44

Hawley, R. and Levick, B. 1995 (eds) *Women in Antiquity. New Assessments.* London/New York

Humphreys, S. 1983. *The Family, Women and Death. Comparative Studies.* London/Boston

Just, R. 1989. *Women in Athenian Law and Life.* London/New York

Lefkowitz, M.R. 1981. *Heroines and Hysterics.* New York

Lefkowitz, M.R. 1986. *Women in Greek Myth.* Baltimore

Lefkowitz, M.R. and Fant, M.B. 1982, 1992. *Women's Life in Greece and Rome.* Baltimore

Oakley, J.H. and R. H. Sinos 1993. *The Wedding in Ancient Athens.* Madison WI

Peradotto, J. 1978 ed. *Women in the Classical World.* Special edition of *Arethusa.* Buffalo NY

Pomeroy, S.B. 1975. *Goddesses, Whores, Wives and Slaves: Women in Classical Antiquity.* New York

Pomeroy, S.B. 1991. *Women's History & Ancient History.* Chapel Hill NC/London

Schaps, D. 1977. "The Women Least Mentioned: Etiquette and Women's Names," *Classical Quarterly* 27, 323–330

Sealey, R. 1990. *Women and Law in Classical Greece.* Chapel Hill NC/London

Skinner, M. 1987 ed. *Rescuing Creusa: New Methodological Approaches to Women in Antiquity.* Special edition of *Helios.* Lubbock TX

Snyder, J. 1989. *The Woman and the Lyre. Women Writers in Classical Greece and Rome.* Carbondale/Edwardsville

Sorkin Rabinowitz and Richlin, A. 1993 (eds) *Feminist Theory and the Classics.* New York/London

Sullivan, J.P. 1973 ed. *Women in Antiquity.* Special edition of *Arethusa.* Buffalo NY

Index of ancient authors and texts

General Index